Published by
Profile Books Ltd
3 Holford Yard
Bevin Way
London WC1X 9HD

Published under exclusive licence from
The Economist by Profile Books, 2016

Material researched by

drea Burgess, Lisa Davies, Mark Doyle, Ian Emery, Conrad Hein
Carol Howard, David McKelvey, Guy Scriven, Roxana Willis,
Christopher Wilson

greatest care has been taken in compiling this book. Howeve
responsibility can be accepted by the publishers or compilers
for the accuracy of the information presented.

Typeset in Officina by MacGuru Ltd

Printed and bound in Italy by L.E.G.O. Spa

A CIP catalogue record for this book is available
from the British Library

ISBN 978 1 78125 607 7

The Economist

POCKE
WORL
FIGUR

2017 Edition

Contents

7   Introduction
8   Notes

---

11 **Part I   World rankings**

Geography and demographics

12 Countries: *natural facts*
     Countries: the largest   Largest exclusive economic zones
     Mountains: the highest   Rivers: the longest
     Deserts: the largest non-polar   Lakes: the largest

14 Population: *size and growth*
     Largest populations, 2014   Largest populations, 2025
     Fastest-growing populations   Slowest-growing populations

16 Population: *matters of breeding and sex*
     Highest and lowest crude birth rates   Teenage births
     Highest and lowest fertility rates   Highest and lowest sex ratios

18 Population: *age*
     Highest and lowest median age
     Oldest and youngest populations

19 City living
     Biggest cities   Fastest- and slowest-growing cities
     Highest and lowest urban growth   Biggest urban populations
     Biggest rural populations   City liveability index   Tallest buildings

22 Migrants, refugees and asylum seekers
     Biggest migrant populations   Refugees as % of migrant population
     Refugees by country of origin
     Countries with largest refugee populations
     Origin of asylum applications to industrialised countries
     Asylum applications in industrialised countries

Economics

24 The world economy
     Biggest economies   Biggest economies by purchasing power
     Regional GDP   Regional purchasing power
     Regional population   Regional international trade

26 Living standards
     Highest and lowest GDP per person
     Highest and lowest purchasing power

28 The quality of life
     Highest and lowest human development index
     Inequality-adjusted human development index
     Highest and lowest Gini coefficient

30 Economic growth
     Highest economic growth   Lowest economic growth
     Highest services growth   Lowest services growth

CONTENTS

32 **Trading places**
Biggest exporters   Most and least trade-dependent
Biggest traders of goods   Biggest earners from services and income

34 **Balance of payments:** *current account*
Largest surpluses   Largest deficits
Largest surpluses as % of GDP   Largest deficits as % of GDP
Official reserves   Official gold reserves   Workers' remittances

37 **Exchange rates**
The Economist's Big Mac index

38 **Inflation**
Highest and lowest consumer-price inflation
Commodity prices: change   House prices: change

40 **Debt**
Highest foreign debt   Highest foreign debt burden
Highest debt and debt service ratios   Household debt

42 **Aid**
Largest recipients   Largest donors   Biggest changes to aid

44 **Industry and services**
Largest industrial output
Highest and lowest growth in industrial output
Largest manufacturing output   Largest services output

46 **Agriculture and fisheries**
Largest agricultural output   Most and least economically dependent
Biggest producers: cereals, meat, fruit, vegetables, roots and tubers
Fisheries and aquaculture production

48 **Commodities**
Leading producers and consumers of: wheat, rice, sugar, coarse
grains, tea, coffee, cocoa, orange juice, copper, lead, zinc, tin, nickel,
aluminium, precious metals, rubber, cotton, major oil seeds and
vegetable oils, oil, natural gas, coal   Top proved oil reserves

54 **Energy**
Largest producers   Largest consumers
Most and least energy-efficient
Highest and lowest net energy importers
Largest consumption per person   Sources of electricity

56 **Labour markets**
Highest and lowest labour-force participation
Most male and female workforces   Highest rate of unemployment
Highest rate of youth unemployment   Minimum wage
Average hours worked   Poverty pay

Business

59 **Business costs and foreign direct investment**
Office rents   Foreign direct investment

60 **Business creativity and research**
Entrepreneurial activity   Brain drains
R&D expenditure   Innovation index

62 **Businesses and banks**
Largest non-financial companies   Largest banks
Largest sovereign-wealth funds

64 **Stockmarkets**
Largest market capitalisation
Largest gains and losses in global stockmarkets
Largest value traded   Number of listed companies

Politics and society

66 **Public finance**
Government debt   Government spending   Tax revenue

67 **Democracy**
Most and least democratic   Most and fewest parliamentary seats
Women in parliament

68 **Education**
Highest and lowest primary enrolment
Highest secondary enrolment   Highest tertiary enrolment
Least literate   Highest and lowest education spending

70 **Marriage and divorce**
Highest marriage rates   Lowest marriage rates
Highest divorce rates   Lowest divorce rates
Youngest and oldest mean age of women at first marriage

72 **Households, living costs and giving**
Biggest number of households   Average household size
Highest and lowest cost of living   World Giving Index

74 **Transport:** *roads and cars*
Longest road networks   Densest road networks
Most crowded road networks   Most road deaths
Highest car ownership   Lowest car ownership   Car production
Cars sold

78 **Transport:** *planes and trains*
Most air travel   Busiest airports   Longest railway networks
Most rail passengers   Most rail freight

80 **Transport:** *shipping*
Largest merchant fleets   Most shipbuilding deliveries
Busiest ports

81 **Crime and punishment**
Murders   Robberies   Prisoners

82 **War and peace**
Defence spending   Armed forces   Arms traders
Global Peace Index

84 **Space**
Space missions   Orbital launches

85 **Environment**
Biggest emitters of carbon dioxide
Largest amount of carbon dioxide emitted per person
Most polluted capital cities   Lowest access to an improved water source
Lowest access to electricity   Largest forests   Most forest

Deforestation   Number of species under threat
Biggest nationally protected land and marine areas
Environmental Performance Index   Worst natural catastrophes

Health and welfare

90 Life expectancy
Highest life expectancy   Highest male life expectancy
Highest female life expectancy   Lowest life expectancy
Lowest male life expectancy   Lowest female life expectancy

92 Death rates and infant mortality
Highest death rates   Highest infant mortality
Lowest death rates   Lowest infant mortality

94 Death and disease
Diabetes   Cardiovascular disease   Cancer   Tuberculosis   Ebola
Measles and DPT immunisation   HIV/AIDS prevalence and deaths

96 Health
Highest health spending   Lowest health spending
Highest and lowest population per doctor   Obesity
Highest and lowest food deficits

Culture and entertainment

98 Telephones and the internet
Mobile telephones   Digital adoption index   Internet users
Broadband

100 Arts and entertainment
Music sales   Book publishing
Cinema attendances   Top Oscar winners

102 The press
Daily newspapers   Press freedom

103 Nobel prize winners
Peace   Medicine   Literature   Economics   Physics   Chemistry

104 Sports champions and cheats
World Cup winners and finalists: men's and women's football, cricket,
rugby   Olympic games: Summer and winter
Anti-doping rule violations

106 Vices
Beer drinkers   Smokers   Gambling losses

107 Tourism
Most tourist arrivals   Biggest tourist spenders
Largest tourist receipts

109 Part II Country profiles

242 WORLD RANKINGS QUIZ
248 Glossary
250 List of countries
254 Sources

Introduction

This 2017 edition of *The Economist Pocket World in Figures* presents and analyses data about the world in two sections:

The **world rankings** consider and rank the performance of 184 countries against a range of indicators in six sections: geography and demographics, economics, business, politics and society, health and welfare, and culture and entertainment. The countries included are those which had (in 2014) a population of at least 1m or a GDP of at least $3bn; they are listed on pages 250–53. New rankings this year include topics as diverse as fisheries and aquaculture production, age at first marriage, natural disasters, Ebola, digital adoption and anti-doping rule violations. And in this edition some of the rankings data are shown as charts and graphs.

The **country profiles** look in detail at 64 major countries, listed on page 109, plus profiles of the euro area and the world.

Test your *Pocket World in Figures* knowledge with our new **World Rankings Quiz** on pages 242–7. Answers can be found in the corresponding world rankings section.

Notes

The extent and quality of the statistics available vary from country to country. Every care has been taken to specify the broad definitions on which the data are based and to indicate cases where data quality or technical difficulties are such that interpretation of the figures is likely to be seriously affected. Nevertheless, figures from individual countries may differ from standard international statistical definitions. The term "country" can also refer to territories or economic entities.

Definitions of the statistics shown are given on the relevant page or in the glossary on pages 248–9. Figures may not add exactly to totals, or percentages to 100, because of rounding or, in the case of GDP, statistical adjustment. Sums of money have generally been converted to US dollars at the official exchange rate ruling at the time to which the figures refer.

Some country definitions

Macedonia is officially known as the Former Yugoslav Republic of Macedonia. Data for Cyprus normally refer to Greek Cyprus only. Data for China do not include Hong Kong or Macau. Data for Sudan are largely for the country before it became two countries, Sudan and South Sudan, in July 2011. For countries such as Morocco they exclude disputed areas. Congo-Kinshasa refers to the Democratic Republic of Congo, formerly known as Zaire. Congo-Brazzaville refers to the other Congo. Curaçao qualifies for inclusion but there are few data as yet. Euro area data normally refer to the 19 members that had adopted the euro as at December 31 2015: Austria, Belgium, Cyprus, Estonia, France, Finland, Germany, Greece, Ireland, Italy, Latvia, Lithuania, Luxembourg, Malta, Netherlands, Portugal, Slovakia, Slovenia and Spain. Euro area (18) excludes Lithuania, which adopted the euro on January 1 2015. Euro area (15) refers to the 15 countries in the euro area that are members of the OECD. Data referring to the European Union include the UK, which in June 2016 voted in a referendum to leave the EU. Negotiations over the country's departure will take some time. For more information about the EU, euro area and OECD see the glossary on pages 248–9.

Statistical basis

The all-important factor in a book of this kind is to be able to make reliable comparisons between countries. Although this is never quite possible for the reasons stated above, the best route, which this book takes, is to compare data for the same year or period and to use actual, not estimated, figures wherever possible. In some cases, only OECD members are considered. Where a country's data are excessively out of date, they are excluded. The research for this edition was carried out in 2016 using the latest available sources that present data on an internationally comparable basis.

Data in the country profiles, unless otherwise indicated, refer to the year ending December 31 2014. Life expectancy, crude birth, death and fertility rates are based on 2015–20 estimated averages; energy data for 2013 and religion for 2010; marriage and divorce, employment, health and education, consumer goods and services data refer to the latest year for which figures are available.

Other definitions

Data shown in country profiles may not always be consistent with those shown in the world rankings because the definitions or years covered can differ.

Statistics for principal exports and principal imports are normally based on customs statistics. These are generally compiled on different definitions to the visible exports and imports figures shown in the balance of payments section.

Energy-consumption data are not always reliable, particularly for the major oil-producing countries; consumption per person data may therefore be higher than in reality. Energy exports can exceed production and imports can exceed consumption if transit operations distort trade data or oil is imported for refining and re-exported.

Abbreviations and conventions
(see also glossary on pages 248–9)

bn	billion (one thousand million)	km	kilometre
EU	European Union	m	million
GDP	gross domestic product	PPP	purchasing power parity
GNI	gross national income	TOE	tonnes of oil equivalent
ha	hectare	trn	trillion (one thousand billion)
kg	kilogram	...	not available

World rankings

Countries: natural facts

Countries: *the largest*[a]

'000 sq km

1	Russia	17,098	32	Venezuela	912
2	Canada	9,985	33	Namibia	824
3	United States	9,834	34	Mozambique	799
4	China	9,597	35	Pakistan	796
5	Brazil	8,515	36	Turkey	784
6	Australia	7,692	37	Chile	756
7	India	3,287	38	Zambia	753
8	Argentina	2,780	39	Myanmar	677
9	Kazakhstan	2,725	40	South Sudan	659
10	Algeria	2,382	41	Afghanistan	653
11	Congo-Kinshasa	2,345	42	Somalia	638
12	Saudi Arabia	2,207	43	Central African Rep.	623
13	Mexico	1,964	44	Ukraine	604
14	Indonesia	1,911	45	Kenya	592
15	Sudan	1,879	46	Madagascar	587
16	Libya	1,676	47	Botswana	582
17	Iran	1,629	48	France	552
18	Mongolia	1,564	49	Yemen	528
19	Peru	1,285	50	Thailand	513
20	Chad	1,284	51	Spain	506
21	Niger	1,267	52	Turkmenistan	488
22	Angola	1,247	53	Cameroon	476
23	Mali	1,240	54	Papua New Guinea	463
24	South Africa	1,221	55	Sweden	450
25	Colombia	1,142	56	Morocco	447
26	Ethiopia	1,104		Uzbekistan	447
27	Bolivia	1,099	58	Iraq	435
28	Mauritania	1,031	59	Paraguay	407
29	Egypt	1,002	60	Zimbabwe	391
30	Tanzania	947	61	Japan	378
31	Nigeria	924	62	Germany	357

Largest exclusive economic zones[b]

Million sq km ● Marine territories ● Land area

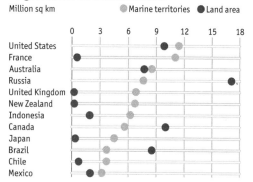

a Includes freshwater.   b Extending 200 nautical miles (370km) from the coast.

Mountains: *the highest[a]*

Name	Location	Height (m)
1 Everest	China–Nepal	8,848
2 K2 (Godwin Austen)	China–Pakistan	8,611
3 Kangchenjunga	India–Nepal	8,586
4 Lhotse	China–Nepal	8,516
5 Makalu	China–Nepal	8,463
6 Cho Oyu	China–Nepal	8,201
7 Dhaulagiri	Nepal	8,167
8 Manaslu	Nepal	8,163
9 Nanga Parbat	Pakistan	8,126
10 Annapurna I	Nepal	8,091

Rivers: *the longest*

Name	Location	Length (km)
1 Nile	Africa	6,695
2 Amazon	South America	6,516
3 Yangtze (Chang Jiang)	Asia	6,380
4 Mississippi–Missouri system	North America	5,959
5 Ob'–Irtysh	Asia	5,568
6 Yenisey–Angara–Selanga	Asia	5,550
7 Yellow (Huang He)	Asia	5,464
8 Congo	Africa	4,667

Deserts: *the largest non-polar*

Name	Location	Area ('000 sq km)
1 Sahara	Northern Africa	8,600
2 Arabian	South-western Asia	2,300
3 Gobi	Mongolia/China	1,300
4 Patagonian	Argentina	673
5 Syrian	Middle East	520
6 Great Basin	South-western United States	490
7 Great Victoria	Western and Southern Australia	422
8 Great Sandy	Western Australia	395

Lakes: *the largest*

Name	Location	Area ('000 sq km)
1 Caspian Sea	Central Asia	371
2 Superior	Canada/United States	82
3 Victoria	East Africa	69
4 Huron	Canada/United States	60
5 Michigan	United States	58
6 Tanganyika	East Africa	33
7 Baikal	Russia	31
Great Bear	Canada	31

a Includes separate peaks which are part of the same massif.
Notes: Estimates of the lengths of rivers vary widely depending on eg, the path to take through a delta. The definition of a desert is normally a mean annual precipitation value equal to 250ml or less. Australia is defined as a continent rather than an island.

Population: size and growth

Largest populations
Million, 2014

1	China	1,393.8	37	Canada	35.5
2	India	1,267.4	38	Iraq	34.8
3	United States	322.6	39	Morocco	33.5
4	Indonesia	252.8	40	Afghanistan	31.3
5	Brazil	202.0	41	Venezuela	30.9
6	Pakistan	185.1	42	Peru	30.8
7	Nigeria	178.5	43	Malaysia	30.2
8	Bangladesh	158.5	44	Saudi Arabia	29.4
9	Russia	142.5	45	Uzbekistan	29.3
10	Japan	127.0	46	Nepal	28.1
11	Mexico	123.8	47	Mozambique	26.5
12	Philippines	100.1	48	Ghana	26.4
13	Ethiopia	96.5	49	North Korea	25.0
14	Vietnam	92.5		Yemen	25.0
15	Egypt	83.4	51	Australia	23.6
16	Germany	82.7		Madagascar	23.6
17	Iran	78.5	53	Taiwan	23.4
18	Turkey	75.8	54	Cameroon	22.8
19	Congo-Kinshasa	69.4	55	Angola	22.1
20	Thailand	67.2	56	Syria	22.0
21	France	64.6	57	Romania	21.6
22	United Kingdom	63.5	58	Sri Lanka	21.4
23	Italy	61.1	59	Ivory Coast	20.8
24	Myanmar	53.7	60	Niger	18.5
25	South Africa	53.1	61	Chile	17.8
26	Tanzania	50.8	62	Burkina Faso	17.4
27	South Korea	49.5	63	Malawi	16.8
28	Colombia	48.9		Netherlands	16.8
29	Spain	47.1	65	Kazakhstan	16.6
30	Kenya	45.5	66	Ecuador	16.0
31	Ukraine	44.9	67	Guatemala	15.9
32	Argentina	41.8	68	Mali	15.8
33	Algeria	39.9	69	Cambodia	15.4
34	Sudan	38.8	70	Zambia	15.0
	Uganda	38.8	71	Zimbabwe	14.6
36	Poland	38.2	72	Senegal	14.5

Largest populations
Million, 2025

1	India	1,461.6	11	Ethiopia	125.1
2	China	1,414.9	12	Japan	122.8
3	United States	345.1	13	Philippines	116.2
4	Indonesia	284.5	14	Egypt	108.9
5	Nigeria	233.6	15	Congo-Kinshasa	104.5
6	Pakistan	227.2	16	Vietnam	102.1
7	Brazil	223.0	17	Iran	86.5
8	Bangladesh	179.1	18	Turkey	84.9
9	Mexico	141.9	19	Germany	80.0
10	Russia	141.2	20	Tanzania	72.1

Note: Populations include migrant workers.

Fastest-growing populations
Average annual % change, 2015–20

1	Niger	4.0	24	Liberia	2.5
2	Burundi	3.2		Nigeria	2.5
	Chad	3.2		Syria	2.5
	Uganda	3.2		Togo	2.5
5	Angola	3.1	28	Cameroon	2.4
	Congo-Kinshasa	3.1		Eritrea	2.4
	Gambia, The	3.1		Ethiopia	2.4
	Tanzania	3.1		Ivory Coast	2.4
	Zambia	3.1		Sudan	2.4
10	Malawi	3.0	33	Afghanistan	2.3
	Mali	3.0		Guinea-Bissau	2.3
12	Senegal	2.9		Mauritania	2.3
13	Burkina Faso	2.8		Rwanda	2.3
	Equatorial Guinea	2.8		Yemen	2.3
	Iraq	2.8		Zimbabwe	2.3
	Somalia	2.8	39	Ghana	2.2
17	Madagascar	2.7	40	Gabon	2.1
	Mozambique	2.7		Kuwait	2.1
	South Sudan	2.7		Namibia	2.1
	West Bank & Gaza	2.7		Sierra Leone	2.1
21	Benin	2.6		Tajikistan	2.1
	Congo-Brazzaville	2.6		Timor-Leste	2.1
	Guinea	2.6			

Slowest-growing populations
Average annual % change, 2015–20

1	Bulgaria	-0.8		Italy	0.0
2	Romania	-0.7		Montenegro	0.0
3	Lithuania	-0.6		Slovakia	0.0
4	Latvia	-0.5		Spain	0.0
	Ukraine	-0.5	30	Armenia	0.1
6	Bermuda	-0.4		Chile	0.1
	Croatia	-0.4		Czech Republic	0.1
	Hungary	-0.4		Lebanon	0.1
	Portugal	-0.4		Macedonia	0.1
	Serbia	-0.4		Slovenia	0.1
11	Andorra	-0.3		Turkey	0.1
	Belarus	-0.3		Virgin Islands (US)	0.1
	Bosnia & Herz.	-0.3	38	Barbados	0.2
	Estonia	-0.3		Malta	0.2
15	Albania	-0.2		Taiwan	0.2
	Greece	-0.2		Thailand	0.2
	Japan	-0.2	42	Austria	0.3
	Moldova	-0.2		Bahamas	0.3
19	Georgia	-0.1		El Salvador	0.3
	Germany	-0.1		Finland	0.3
	Martinique	-0.1		Jamaica	0.3
	Poland	-0.1		Mauritius	0.3
	Puerto Rico	-0.1		Netherlands	0.3
	Russia	-0.1		Trinidad & Tobago	0.3
25	Cuba	0.0			

Population: matters of breeding and sex

Crude birth rates
Births per 1,000 population, 2015–20

Highest			Lowest		
1	Niger	49	1	Monaco	6
2	Angola	44	2	Bosnia & Herz.	8
	Chad	44		Greece	8
4	Somalia	43		Italy	8
5	Burundi	42		Japan	8
6	Mali	41		Portugal	8
	Uganda	41		Taiwan	8
8	Congo-Kinshasa	40	8	Andorra	9
	Gambia, The	40		Channel Islands	9
10	Zambia	39		Croatia	9
11	Burkina Faso	38		Germany	9
	Malawi	38		Hungary	9
	Mozambique	38		Malta	9
	Nigeria	38		Romania	9
15	Tanzania	37		Singapore	9
16	Ivory Coast	36		South Korea	9
	Senegal	36		Spain	9
	South Sudan	36	18	Austria	10
19	Cameroon	35		Bulgaria	10
	Guinea	35		Cuba	10
	Guinea-Bissau	35		Hong Kong	10
				Poland	10

Teenage births
Women aged 15–19, 2010–15

Total, '000			Per 1,000 women aged 15–19		
1	India	8,762	1	Niger	208.5
2	Nigeria	5,021	2	Mali	178.8
3	Bangladesh	3,321	3	Angola	175.9
4	Brazil	2,878	4	Mozambique	153.7
5	Indonesia	2,788	5	Chad	152.0
6	Congo-Kinshasa	2,349	6	Guinea	145.9
7	Mexico	1,899	7	Malawi	140.2
8	Pakistan	1,877	8	Ivory Coast	135.1
9	Ethiopia	1,794	9	Uganda	126.6
10	China	1,645	10	Congo	125.5
11	Tanzania	1,595	11	Sierra Leone	125.3
12	United States	1,551	12	Congo-Kinshasa	124.3
13	Philippines	1,382	13	Madagascar	122.8
14	Uganda	1,263	14	Tanzania	122.7
15	Mozambique	1,088	15	Liberia	117.4
16	Angola	1,084	16	Nigeria	117.0
17	Egypt	1,064	17	Cameroon	115.8
18	Kenya	1,060		Gambia, The	115.8
19	Niger	954	19	Burkina Faso	115.4
20	Sudan	844	20	Equatorial Guinea	114.3
21	Ivory Coast	781	21	Zimbabwe	113.3
22	Madagascar	770	22	Gabon	111.2
23	Mali	755	23	Somalia	110.4

Fertility rates
Average number of children per woman, 2015–20

Highest			Lowest		
1	Niger	7.5	1	Taiwan	1.1
2	Somalia	6.1	2	Bosnia & Herz.	1.2
3	Mali	5.9		Moldova	1.2
4	Angola	5.8	4	Andorra	1.3
	Chad	5.8		Greece	1.3
6	Burundi	5.7		Hong Kong	1.3
	Congo-Kinshasa	5.7		Macau	1.3
8	Gambia, The	5.5		Poland	1.3
	Uganda	5.5		Portugal	1.3
10	Nigeria	5.4		Singapore	1.3
11	Timor-Leste	5.3		South Korea	1.3
12	Burkina Faso	5.2	12	Cyprus	1.4
	Mozambique	5.1		Germany	1.4
14	Zambia	5.1		Hungary	1.4
15	Malawi	4.9		Mauritius	1.4
	Tanzania	4.9		Slovakia	1.4
17	Ivory Coast	4.8		Spain	1.4
	Senegal	4.8	18	Armenia	1.5
19	Guinea	4.7		Austria	1.5
	South Sudan	4.7		Channel Islands	1.5
21	Congo-Brazzaville	4.6		Croatia	1.5
	Guinea-Bissau	4.6		Czech Republic	1.5
23	Benin	4.5		Italy	1.5
	Cameroon	4.5		Japan	1.5
	Equatorial Guinea	4.5		Malta	1.5
	Liberia	4.5		Monaco	1.5
				Romania	1.5
				Thailand	1.5

Sex ratios
Males per 100 females, 2015

Highest			Lowest		
1	United Arab Emirates	274.0	1	Martinique	84.5
2	Qatar	265.5	2	Latvia	84.8
3	Oman	197.0	3	Lithuania	85.3
4	Bahrain	163.0	4	Guadeloupe	86.0
5	Saudi Arabia	130.1	5	Ukraine	86.3
6	Kuwait	128.2	6	Armenia	86.5
7	India	107.6	7	Belarus	86.8
8	Afghanistan	106.5		Russia	86.8
9	Brunei	106.3	9	Estonia	88.0
	China	106.3	10	El Salvador	88.4
11	Pakistan	105.6	11	Hong Kong	88.5
12	Equatorial Guinea	105.1	12	Portugal	89.9
13	Jordan	105.0	13	Hungary	90.8
14	French Polynesia	104.2	14	Virgin Islands (US)	91.0
15	Cyprus	104.1	15	Georgia	91.2
	Papua New Guinea	104.1	16	Rwanda	91.9
17	Nigeria	103.8	17	Barbados	92.0

Population: age

Median age[a]

Highest, 2015			Lowest, 2015		
1	Monaco	51.1	1	Niger	14.8
2	Japan	46.5	2	Uganda	15.9
3	Germany	46.2	3	Chad	16.0
4	Martinique	46.1	4	Angola	16.1
5	Italy	45.9	5	Mali	16.2
6	Portugal	44.0	6	Somalia	16.5
7	Greece	43.6	7	Gambia, The	16.8
8	Bulgaria	43.5	8	Congo-Kinshasa	16.9
9	Austria	43.2		Zambia	16.9
	Hong Kong	43.2	10	Burkina Faso	17.0
	Spain	43.2	11	Mozambique	17.1
12	Lithuania	43.1	12	Malawi	17.2
	Slovenia	43.1	13	Tanzania	17.3
14	Latvia	42.9	14	Afghanistan	17.5
15	Croatia	42.8	15	Burundi	17.6
16	Netherlands	42.7	16	Nigeria	17.9
17	Channel Islands	42.6	17	Senegal	18.0
18	Finland	42.5	18	Ivory Coast	18.4
19	Switzerland	42.3	19	Cameroon	18.5
20	Romania	42.1		Guinea	18.5
21	Liechtenstein	42.0		Sierra Leone	18.5
22	Estonia	41.7		Timor-Leste	18.5

Most old people

% of population aged 65 or over, 2015

1	Monaco	30.4
2	Japan	26.3
3	Italy	22.4
4	Greece	21.4
5	Germany	21.2
6	Portugal	20.8
7	Finland	20.5
8	Bulgaria	20.0
9	Sweden	19.9
10	Latvia	19.4
11	Malta	19.2
12	France	19.1
	Martinique	19.1
14	Denmark	19.0
15	Croatia	18.9
16	Austria	18.8
	Estonia	18.8
	Lithuania	18.8
	Spain	18.8
20	Belgium	18.2
	Netherlands	18.2
22	Czech Republic	18.1
23	Slovenia	18.0
	Switzerland	18.0

Most young people

% of population aged 0–19, 2015

1	Niger	60.7
2	Uganda	59.2
3	Chad	58.8
4	Angola	58.4
5	Mali	58.1
6	Somalia	57.8
7	Gambia, The	56.8
	Zambia	56.8
9	Congo-Kinshasa	56.6
10	Burkina Faso	56.4
11	Mozambique	56.3
12	Malawi	56.2
13	Afghanistan	55.8
14	Tanzania	55.6
15	Burundi	54.7
16	Nigeria	54.3
17	Senegal	54.2
18	Ivory Coast	53.5
19	Cameroon	53.3
	Ethiopia	53.3
21	Guinea	53.2
	Sierra Leone	53.2
23	South Sudan	53.1
	Timor-Leste	53.1

a Age at which there is an equal number of people above and below.

City living

Biggest cities[a]
Population, m, 2020

1	Tokyo, Japan	38.3
2	Delhi, India	29.3
3	Shanghai, China	27.1
4	Beijing, China	24.2
5	Mumbai, India	22.8
6	São Paulo, Brazil	22.1
7	Mexico City, Mexico	21.8
8	Dhaka, Bangladesh	21.0
9	Cairo, Egypt	20.6
10	Osaka, Japan	20.5
11	Karachi, Pakistan	19.2
12	New York, US	18.8
13	Lagos, Nigeria	16.2
14	Buenos Aires, Argentina	15.9
15	Kolkata, India	15.7
16	Chongqing, China	15.2
	Guangzhou, China	15.2
18	Istanbul, Turkey	15.1
19	Kinshasa, Congo-Kinshasa	14.1
20	Manila, Philippines	13.9
21	Rio de Janeiro, Brazil	13.3
22	Tianjin, China	12.8
23	Los Angeles, US	12.5
	Moscow, Russia	12.5
25	Bangalore, India	11.8
26	Jakarta, Indonesia	11.3
	Paris, France	11.3
	Shenzhen, China	11.3
29	Chennai, India	11.2
30	Lima, Peru	10.8
	London, UK	10.8
32	Bogotá, Colombia	10.7
33	Johannesburg, South Africa	10.4
34	Hyderabad, India	10.3
35	Bangkok, Thailand	10.1
36	Lahore, Pakistan	10.0
37	Seoul, South Korea	9.8
38	Nagoya, Japan	9.5
39	Chicago, US	8.9
	Tehran, Iran	8.9
41	Chengdu, China	8.8
42	Ahmedabad, India	8.5
	Nanjing, China	8.5
44	Wuhan, China	8.4
45	Ho Chi Minh City, Vietnam	8.3
46	Kuala Lumpur, Malaysia	7.8
47	Dongguan, China	7.7
48	Hangzhou, China	7.6

City growth
Average annual % change, 2015–20

Fastest

1	Miluo, China	7.3
2	Hosur, India	7.2
3	Samut Prakan, Thailand	6.9
4	Lokoja, Nigeria	6.6
	The Woodlands, US	6.6
6	Choloma, Honduras	6.5
7	Roorkee, India	6.3
8	Batam, Indonesia	6.2
	Begusarai, India	6.2
10	Ouagadougou, Burkina Faso	6.0
11	Bujumbura, Burundi	5.9
12	Al-Hasakah, Syria	5.7
	Mbouda, Cameroon	5.7
	Mwanza, Tanzania	5.7
	Nnewi, Nigeria	5.7
16	Al-Raqqa, Syria	5.6
	Bunia, Congo-Kinshasa	5.6
	Zinder, Niger	5.6

Slowest

1	Riga, Latvia	-1.4
2	Makiivka, Ukraine	-1.3
	Nizhny Tagil, Russia	-1.3
4	Dnipropetrovsk, Ukraine	-1.0
	Ivanovo, Russia	-1.0
6	Nizhny Novgorod, Russia	-0.9
	Oryol, Russia	-0.9
	Saratov, Russia	-0.9
9	Bryansk, Russia	-0.8
	Kurgan, Russia	-0.8
	Lugansk, Ukraine	-0.8
	Ulyanovsk, Russia	-0.8
	Yaroslavl, Russia	-0.8
14	Donetsk, Ukraine	-0.7
	Kaluga, Russia	-0.7
	Magnitogorsk, Russia	-0.7
	Mariupol, Ukraine	-0.7
	Sendai, Japan	-0.7

a Urban agglomerations. Data may change from year to year based on reassessments of agglomeration boundaries.

Urban growth
Average annual % change, 2015–20

Highest			Lowest		
1	Rwanda	5.6	1	Trinidad & Tobago	-0.8
2	Burundi	5.5	2	Latvia	-0.6
	Niger	5.5		Lebanon	-0.6
4	Burkina Faso	5.3	4	Bulgaria	-0.4
	Uganda	5.3		Estonia	-0.4
6	Mali	5.0		Moldova	-0.4
	Tanzania	5.0		Ukraine	-0.4
8	Eritrea	4.7	8	Lithuania	-0.3
9	Angola	4.6		Serbia	-0.3
	Ethiopia	4.6	10	Russia	-0.2
11	Madagascar	4.5	11	Armenia	-0.1
12	Zambia	4.4		Georgia	-0.1
13	Nigeria	4.3		Slovakia	-0.1
14	Kenya	4.2			

Biggest urban populations
m, 2020

1	China	874.4	15	United Kingdom	54.9
2	India	470.7	16	France	53.7
3	United States	278.8	17	Philippines	48.9
4	Brazil	183.3	18	Italy	42.9
5	Indonesia	154.2	19	South Korea	42.2
6	Japan	119.4	20	Colombia	40.7
7	Nigeria	108.7	21	Argentina	40.5
8	Mexico	106.3	22	Egypt	39.9
9	Russia	104.4	23	Spain	38.6
10	Pakistan	83.7	24	Thailand	37.9
11	Bangladesh	64.5	25	South Africa	37.0
12	Iran	63.7	26	Congo-Kinshasa	36.7
13	Germany	62.5	27	Vietnam	35.7
14	Turkey	60.8	28	Algeria	32.2

Biggest rural populations
m, 2020

1	India	882.6	16	Russia	35.6
2	China	558.4	17	Myanmar	35.4
3	Pakistan	119.6	18	Thailand	30.0
4	Indonesia	115.3	19	Sudan	28.9
5	Bangladesh	105.1	20	Brazil	27.8
6	Nigeria	101.5	21	Mexico	25.7
7	Ethiopia	87.2	22	Afghanistan	25.4
8	Philippines	61.5	23	Nepal	23.8
9	Vietnam	61.3	24	Iran	20.4
10	United States	59.2	25	Mozambique	20.2
11	Egypt	51.2	26	Uzbekistan	19.8
12	Congo-Kinshasa	44.6	27	Turkey	19.5
13	Tanzania	39.2	28	Germany	19.4
14	Uganda	38.7	29	Niger	18.7
15	Kenya	38.2	30	Italy	18.5

City liveability[a]

100 = ideal, 0 = intolerable, 2015

Best			Worst		
1	Melbourne, Australia	97.5	1	Damascus, Syria	30.2
2	Vienna, Austria	97.4	2	Lagos, Nigeria	36.0
3	Vancouver, Canada	97.3	3	Dhaka, Bangladesh	38.7
4	Toronto, Canada	97.2	4	Port Moresby, Papua New Guinea	38.9
5	Adelaide, Australia	96.6	5	Tripoli, Libya	40.0
	Calgary, Canada	96.6	6	Algiers, Algeria	40.9
7	Sydney, Australia	96.1		Karachi, Pakistan	40.9
8	Perth, Australia	95.9	8	Harare, Zimbabwe	42.6
9	Auckland, New Zealand	95.7	9	Douala, Cameroon	44.0
10	Helsinki, Finland	95.6	10	Kiev, Ukraine	44.1
	Zurich, Switzerland	95.6	11	Tehran, Iran	47.2
12	Geneva, Switzerland	95.2	12	Dakar, Senegal	48.3
13	Hamburg, Germany	95.0	13	Colombo, Sri Lanka	49.6
14	Montreal, Canada	94.8	14	Abidjan, Ivory Coast	49.7
15	Frankfurt, Germany	94.7	15	Phnom Penh, Cambodia	50.7
	Tokyo, Japan	94.7	16	Kathmandu, Nepal	51.0
17	Osaka, Japan	94.5		Lusaka, Zambia	51.0
18	Brisbane, Australia	94.2	18	Caracas, Venezuela	51.3
19	Honolulu, US	94.1	19	Ho Chi Minh City, Vietnam	52.7
20	Berlin, Germany	94.0			

Tallest buildings

Completed, height, metres

a EIU liveability index, based on a range of factors including stability, health care, culture, education, infrastructure.

Migrants, refugees and asylum seekers

Biggest migrant populations[a]

m, 2015

1	United States	46.6
2	Germany	12.0
3	Russia	11.6
4	Saudi Arabia	10.1
5	United Kingdom	8.5
6	United Arab Emirates	8.1
7	Canada	7.8
8	France	7.7
9	Australia	6.8
10	Spain	5.9
11	Italy	5.8
12	India	5.2
13	Ukraine	4.8
14	Thailand	3.9
15	Pakistan	3.6
16	Kazakhstan	3.5
17	Jordan	3.1
	South Africa	3.1
19	Turkey	3.0
20	Kuwait	2.9
21	Hong Kong	2.8
22	Iran	2.7
23	Malaysia	2.5
	Singapore	2.5
25	Switzerland	2.4
26	Ivory Coast	2.2
27	Argentina	2.1
28	Israel	2.0
	Japan	2.0
	Lebanon	2.0
	Netherlands	2.0

As % of population, 2015

1	United Arab Emirates	88.4
2	Qatar	75.5
3	Kuwait	73.6
4	Liechtenstein	62.6
5	Andorra	59.7
6	Macau	58.3
7	Monaco	55.8
8	Virgin Islands (US)	53.4
9	Bahrain	51.1
10	Channel Islands	50.3
11	Singapore	45.4
12	Guam	44.8
13	Luxembourg	44.0
14	Oman	41.1
15	Jordan	41.0
16	French Guiana	39.5
17	Hong Kong	38.9
18	Lebanon	34.1
19	Saudi Arabia	32.3
20	Bermuda	30.8
21	Switzerland	29.4
22	Australia	28.2
23	Israel	24.9
24	New Caledonia	24.4
25	Brunei	24.3
26	New Zealand	23.0
27	Canada	21.8
28	Guadeloupe	21.0
29	Kazakhstan	20.1
30	Austria	17.5

Refugees as % of migrant population[b]

2015

1	Jordan	88.4
2	Chad	88.0
3	Syria	81.5
4	Lebanon	80.9
5	Afghanistan	78.6
6	Iraq	76.6
7	Yemen	70.1
8	Cameroon	69.1
9	Ethiopia	61.5
10	Mauritania	57.9
11	Turkey	53.5
12	Egypt	53.2
13	Kenya	50.8
14	Uganda	47.8

15	Pakistan	44.4
16	Sudan	40.8
17	Guinea-Bissau	38.9
18	Algeria	38.8
19	Iran	36.0
20	Tanzania	34.7
21	Liberia	33.6
22	Niger	32.3
23	Ecuador	31.5
24	China	30.8
25	South Sudan	29.2
26	Malta	23.9
27	Congo-Kinshasa	21.9
28	Bosnia & Herz.	19.8

a People living in a country that is not their place of birth.
b Excludes West Bank & Gaza.

Refugees[a] by country of origin
'000, 2014

1	Syria	3,887.5	11	Colombia	360.3
2	Afghanistan	2,596.3	12	Pakistan	336.0
3	Somalia	1,106.4	13	Vietnam	313.4
4	Sudan	666.0	14	Ukraine	237.6
5	South Sudan	616.2	15	China	210.8
6	Congo-Kinshasa	516.7	16	Mali	139.3
7	Myanmar	479.0	17	Sri Lanka	122.0
8	Central African Rep.	412.0	18	West Bank & Gaza	97.2
9	Iraq	370.0	19	Nigeria	90.9
10	Eritrea	363.1	20	Ethiopia	86.9

Countries with largest refugee[a] populations
'000, 2014

1	Turkey	1,587.4	11	Afghanistan	300.4
2	Pakistan	1,505.5	12	Sudan	277.8
3	Lebanon	1,154.0	13	Iraq	271.1
4	Iran	982.0	14	United States	267.2
5	Ethiopia	659.5	15	Cameroon	264.1
6	Jordan	654.1	16	Yemen	257.6
7	Kenya	551.4	17	France	252.3
8	Chad	452.9	18	South Sudan	284.2
9	Uganda	385.5	19	Egypt	236.1
10	China	301.1	20	Russia	235.8

Origin of asylum applications to industrialised countries
'000, 2014

1	Syria	149.6	11	Russia	17.2
2	Iraq	68.7	12	Albania	17.0
3	Afghanistan	59.5	13	Ukraine	15.7
4	Serbia[b]	55.7	14	Mexico	14.1
5	Eritrea	48.4	15	Mali	13.4
6	Pakistan	26.3	16	Bangladesh	12.8
7	China	22.3	17	Gambia, The	12.1
8	Nigeria	22.1	18	El Salvador	10.6
9	Iran	20.2	19	Guatemala	9.2
10	Somalia	19.9	20	India	8.4

Asylum applications in industrialised countries
'000, 2014

1	Germany	173.1	9	Austria	28.1
2	United States	121.2	10	Netherlands	23.9
3	Turkey	87.8	11	Switzerland	22.1
4	Sweden	75.1	12	Serbia[b]	16.6
5	Italy	63.6	13	Denmark	14.8
6	France	59.0	14	Belgium	13.9
7	Hungary	41.4	15	Canada	13.5
8	United Kingdom	31.3	16	Norway	12.6

a According to UNHCR. Includes people in "refugee-like situations".
b Includes Kosovo.

The world economy

Biggest economies
GDP, $bn, 2014

1	United States	17,348	23	Argentina	545
2	China	10,431		Poland	545
3	Japan	4,596	25	Belgium	532
4	Germany	3,874	26	Taiwan	530
5	United Kingdom	2,992	27	Norway	501
6	France[a]	2,834	28	Austria	438
7	Brazil	2,417	29	Iran	416
8	Italy	2,142	30	Thailand	404
9	India	2,043	31	United Arab Emirates	399
10	Russia	2,030	32	Colombia	378
11	Canada	1,784	33	South Africa	350
12	Australia	1,442	34	Denmark	346
13	South Korea	1,410	35	Malaysia	338
14	Spain	1,384	36	Israel	306
15	Mexico	1,298		Singapore	306
16	Indonesia	891	38	Egypt	301
17	Netherlands	881	39	Hong Kong	291
18	Turkey	798	40	Philippines	285
19	Saudi Arabia	754	41	Finland	273
20	Switzerland	701	42	Chile	259
21	Nigeria	574	43	Ireland	251
22	Sweden	571	44	Venezuela	250

Biggest economies by purchasing power
GDP PPP, $bn, 2014

1	China	17,961	24	Poland	961
2	United States	17,348	25	Argentina	951
3	India	7,347	26	Pakistan	884
4	Japan	4,760	27	Netherlands	809
5	Russia	3,824	28	Malaysia	769
6	Germany	3,748	29	South Africa	707
7	Brazil	3,287	30	Philippines	693
8	Indonesia	2,685	31	Colombia	641
9	United Kingdom	2,594	32	United Arab Emirates	617
10	France[a]	2,591	33	Algeria	552
11	Mexico	2,150	34	Venezuela	541
12	Italy	2,133	35	Bangladesh	536
13	South Korea	1,784	36	Iraq	526
14	Saudi Arabia	1,612	37	Vietnam	513
15	Canada	1,597	38	Belgium	483
16	Spain	1,549	39	Switzerland	474
17	Turkey	1,515	40	Singapore	458
18	Iran	1,357	41	Sweden	450
19	Australia	1,100	42	Kazakhstan	420
20	Taiwan	1,080	43	Chile	410
21	Thailand	1,067	44	Hong Kong	401
22	Nigeria	1,053	45	Austria	397
23	Egypt	996	46	Romania	395

Note: For a list of 184 countries with their GDPs, see pages 250–53. "Advanced economies" refers to 39 countries as defined by the IMF.

a Includes overseas territories.   b IMF coverage.

Regional GDP

$bn, 2015		*% annual growth 2010–15*	
World	73,171	World	3.8
Advanced economies	44,388	Advanced economies	1.8
G7	34,067	G7	1.8
Euro area (19)	11,540	Euro area (19)	0.8
Other Asia	15,571	Other Asia	7.4
Latin America & Caribbean	5,052	Latin America & Caribbean	3.0
Other Europe & CIS	3,532	Other Europe & CIS	2.3
Middle East, N. Africa, Afghanistan & Pakistan	3,144	Middle East, N. Africa, Afghanistan & Pakistan	3.7
Sub-Saharan Africa	1,484	Sub-Saharan Africa	4.9

Regional purchasing power

GDP, % of total, 2015		*$ per person, 2015*	
World	100.0	World	15,730
Advanced economies	42.4	Advanced economies	45,692
G7	31.5	G7	47,258
Euro area (19)	11.9	Euro area (19)	40,220
Other Asia	30.6	Other Asia	9,892
Latin America & Caribbean	8.3	Latin America & Caribbean	15,377
Other Europe & CIS	7.9	Other Europe & CIS	19,296
Middle East, N. Africa, Afghanistan & Pakistan	7.6	Middle East, N. Africa, Afghanistan & Pakistan	13,330
Sub-Saharan Africa	3.1	Sub-Saharan Africa	3,817

Regional population

% of total (7.2bn), 2015		*No. of countries[b], 2015*	
World	100.0	World	189
Advanced economies	14.6	Advanced economies	39
G7	10.5	G7	7
Euro area (19)	4.7	Euro area (19)	19
Other Asia	48.7	Other Asia	29
Latin America & Caribbean	8.5	Latin America & Caribbean	32
Other Europe & CIS	6.4	Other Europe & CIS	24
Middle East, N. Africa, Afghanistan & Pakistan	9.0	Middle East, N. Africa, Afghanistan & Pakistan	22
Sub-Saharan Africa	12.8	Sub-Saharan Africa	45

Regional international trade

Exports of goods & services *% of total, 2015*		*Current-account balances* *$bn, 2015*	
World	100.0	World	231
Advanced economies	63.3	Advanced economies	303
G7	34.2	G7	-201
Euro area (19)	25.5	Euro area (19)	345
Other Asia	18.4	Other Asia	290
Latin America & Caribbean	5.1	Latin America & Caribbean	-181
Other Europe & CIS	6.3	Other Europe & CIS	19
Middle East, N. Africa, Afghanistan & Pakistan	5.3	Middle East, N. Africa, Afghanistan & Pakistan	-112
Sub-Saharan Africa	1.7	Sub-Saharan Africa	-88

Living standards

Highest GDP per person
$, 2014

1	Monaco	187,650	31	Hong Kong	40,298
2	Liechtenstein	157,040	32	New Caledonia	39,392
3	Luxembourg	116,745	33	Israel	38,500
4	Norway	97,227	34	Japan	36,249
5	Qatar	96,732	35	Italy	35,825
6	Macau	96,038	36	Martinique	31,049
7	Bermuda	89,795	37	Spain	29,908
8	Switzerland	85,397	38	Guadeloupe	29,721
9	Denmark	61,294	39	South Korea	28,166
10	Australia	61,042	40	Puerto Rico	28,123
11	Sweden	58,857	41	Guam[bc]	27,858
12	Channel Islands	56,147	42	Cyprus	26,188
13	Singapore	55,635	43	Réunion	26,036
14	United States	54,306	44	Malta	25,787
15	Ireland	53,648	45	Bahrain	24,849
16	Iceland	52,423	46	Saudi Arabia	24,407
17	Netherlands	52,212	47	Slovenia	23,992
18	Austria	51,378	48	Taiwan	22,574
19	Canada	50,123	49	Bahamas	22,219
20	Finland	49,779	50	Portugal	22,157
21	Virgin Islands (US)	48,455	51	Greece	21,448
22	Germany	48,042	52	Estonia	20,138
23	Belgium	47,424	53	Trinidad & Tobago	20,132
24	United Kingdom	46,504	54	French Polynesia	20,099
25	Kuwait	45,817	55	French Guiana	19,970
26	Andorra	45,033	56	Czech Republic	19,470
27	New Zealand	44,028	57	Equatorial Guinea	18,919
28	United Arab Emirates	43,963	58	Slovakia	18,501
29	France[a]	42,719	59	Oman	18,358
30	Brunei	40,978	60	Uruguay	16,807

Lowest GDP per person
$, 2014

1	Burundi	268		North Korea	696
2	Central African Rep.	359	18	Nepal	701
3	Malawi	363	19	Burkina Faso	710
4	Gambia, The	427	20	Uganda	728
5	Niger	432	21	Sierra Leone	752
6	Madagascar	453	22	Eritrea	793
7	Liberia	458	23	Haiti	824
8	Congo-Kinshasa	480	24	Mali	846
9	Somalia	543	25	Benin	905
10	Guinea	546	26	Zimbabwe	931
11	Ethiopia	573	27	Tanzania	953
12	Guinea-Bissau	617	28	Chad	1,026
13	Mozambique	619	29	Senegal	1,047
14	Afghanistan	646	30	Lesotho	1,053
15	Togo	648	31	Cambodia	1,095
16	Rwanda	696	32	Tajikistan	1,114

a Includes overseas territories.   b 2010   c Estimate.

Highest purchasing power
GDP per person in PPP (US = 100), 2014

1	Monaco	332.3	35	Japan	69.1
2	Qatar	259.9	36	Guadeloupe	68.5
3	Macau	259.0	37	Virgin Islands (US)	66.7
4	Luxembourg	174.7	38	Puerto Rico	66.1
5	Liechtenstein	158.0	39	New Zealand	66.0
6	Singapore	153.2	40	Italy	65.7
7	Brunei	145.4	41	South Korea	65.6
8	Kuwait	138.8	42	Equatorial Guinea	64.2
9	United Arab Emirates	125.1	43	Malta	63.7
10	Norway	124.2	44	Israel	63.1
11	Switzerland	106.2	45	Spain	61.7
12	Channel Islands	103.1	46	Trinidad & Tobago	60.7
13	Hong Kong	102.2	47	Martinique	57.2
14	Bermuda	100.4	48	Cyprus	57.1
15	United States	100.0	49	Czech Republic	55.2
16	Saudi Arabia	96.1	50	Slovenia	54.9
17	Ireland	93.1	51	Guam[bc]	54.4
18	Netherlands	88.3	52	Réunion	52.8
19	Austria	85.8	53	Slovakia	52.2
20	Australia	85.7	54	Estonia	51.5
21	Germany	85.6	55	Lithuania	50.7
22	Sweden	85.5	56	Portugal	50.1
23	Taiwan	84.7	57	Russia	49.1
24	Bahrain	84.1	58	Greece	47.5
25	Canada	82.6	59	Malaysia	47.4
	Denmark	82.6	60	French Polynesia	47.1
27	Iceland	81.2	61	Hungary	46.3
28	Andorra	80.0	62	Poland	45.8
29	Belgium	79.2	63	Kazakhstan	44.5
30	New Caledonia	78.7	64	Latvia	43.8
31	Finland	74.5	65	Bahamas	43.4
32	United Kingdom	74.3	66	Chile	42.5
33	France[a]	71.9	67	Argentina	40.7
34	Oman	70.8	68	Panama	38.9

Lowest purchasing power
GDP per person in PPP (US = 100), 2014

1	Somalia	0.78		North Korea	2.95
2	Central African Rep.	1.10	16	Eritrea	2.97
3	Burundi	1.36	17	Rwanda	3.07
4	Congo-Kinshasa	1.42	18	Burkina Faso	3.08
5	Liberia	1.55	19	Haiti	3.20
6	Niger	1.75	20	Zimbabwe	3.31
7	Mozambique	2.09	21	Afghanistan	3.54
8	Malawi	2.16	22	Mali	3.60
9	Guinea	2.22	23	South Sudan	3.63
10	Guinea-Bissau	2.59	24	Sierra Leone	3.66
11	Togo	2.64	25	Uganda	3.67
12	Madagascar	2.66	26	Benin	3.75
13	Ethiopia	2.76	27	Chad	4.02
14	Gambia, The	2.95	28	Senegal	4.28

The quality of life

Human development index[a]

Highest, 2014

1	Norway	94.4	32	Cyprus	85.0
2	Australia	93.5		Qatar	85.0
3	Switzerland	93.0	34	Andorra	84.5
4	Denmark	92.3	35	Slovakia	84.4
5	Netherlands	92.2	36	Poland	84.3
6	Germany	91.6	37	Lithuania	83.9
	Ireland	91.6		Malta	83.9
8	United States	91.5	39	Saudi Arabia	83.7
9	Canada	91.3	40	Argentina	83.6
	New Zealand	91.3	41	United Arab Emirates	83.5
11	Singapore	91.2	42	Chile	83.2
12	Hong Kong	91.0	43	Portugal	83.0
13	Liechtenstein	90.8	44	Hungary	82.8
14	Sweden	90.7	45	Bahrain	82.4
	United Kingdom	90.7	46	Latvia	81.9
16	Iceland	89.9	47	Croatia	81.8
17	South Korea	89.8	48	Kuwait	81.6
18	Israel	89.4	49	Montenegro	80.2
19	Luxembourg	89.2	50	Belarus	79.8
20	Japan	89.1		Russia	79.8
21	Belgium	89.0	52	Oman	79.3
22	France	88.8		Romania	79.3
23	Austria	88.5		Uruguay	79.3
24	Finland	88.3	55	Bahamas	79.0
25	Slovenia	88.0	56	Kazakhstan	78.8
26	Spain	87.6	57	Barbados	78.5
27	Italy	87.3	58	Bulgaria	78.2
28	Czech Republic	87.0	59	Panama	78.0
29	Greece	86.5	60	Malaysia	77.9
30	Estonia	86.1	61	Mauritius	77.7
31	Brunei	85.6	62	Trinidad & Tobago	77.2

Human development index[a]

Lowest, 2014

1	Niger	34.8	12	Liberia	43.0
2	Central African Rep.	35.0	13	Congo-Kinshasa	43.3
3	Eritrea	39.1	14	Gambia, The	44.1
4	Chad	39.2	15	Ethiopia	44.2
5	Burundi	40.0	16	Malawi	44.5
6	Burkina Faso	40.2	17	Ivory Coast	46.2
7	Guinea	41.1	18	Afghanistan	46.5
8	Sierra Leone	41.3	19	Senegal	46.6
9	Mozambique	41.6	20	South Sudan	46.7
10	Mali	41.9	21	Sudan	47.9
11	Guinea-Bissau	42.0	22	Benin	48.0

a GDP or GDP per person is often taken as a measure of how developed a country is, but its usefulness is limited as it refers only to economic welfare. The UN Development Programme combines statistics on average and expected years of schooling and life expectancy with income levels (now GNI per person, valued in PPP US$). The HDI is shown here scaled from 0 to 100; countries scoring over 80 are considered to have very high human development, 70–79 high, 55–69 medium and those under 55 low.

THE QUALITY OF LIFE 29

Inequality-adjusted human development index[a]
Highest, 2014

1	Norway	89.3		16	Belgium	82.0
2	Netherlands	86.1		17	Austria	81.6
	Switzerland	86.1		18	France	81.1
4	Australia	85.8		19	Slovakia	79.1
5	Denmark	85.6		20	Estonia	78.2
6	Germany	85.3		21	Japan	78.0
7	Iceland	84.6		22	Israel	77.5
	Sweden	84.6			Spain	77.5
9	Ireland	83.6		24	Italy	77.3
10	Finland	83.4		25	Hungary	76.9
11	Canada	83.2		26	Malta	76.7
12	Slovenia	82.9		27	Poland	76.0
	United Kingdom	82.9			United States	76.0
14	Czech Republic	82.3		29	Cyprus	75.8
15	Luxembourg	82.2			Greece	75.8

Gini coefficient[b]

Highest 2005–13

40 50 60 70

- South Africa
- Namibia
- Botswana
- Haiti
- Zambia
- Honduras
- C.A.R.
- Lesotho
- Colombia
- Brazil
- Guatemala
- Panama
- Swaziland
- Chile
- Rwanda
- Costa Rica
- Mexico
- Paraguay
- Kenya
- Gambia, The

Lowest 2005–13

0 10 20 30 40

- Ukraine
- Slovenia
- Sweden
- Iceland
- Czech Republic
- Belarus
- Slovakia
- Norway
- Denmark
- Romania
- Finland
- Afghanistan
- Kazakhstan
- Hungary
- Netherlands
- Albania
- Iraq
- Pakistan
- Serbia
- Austria

a Where there is inequality in the distribution of health, education and income, the IHDI of an average person in society is less than the ordinary HDI.
b A measure of the distribution of income within a country, where 100 is maximum inequality.

Economic growth

Highest economic growth
Average annual % increase in real GDP, 2004–14

1	Qatar	12.5	26	Sri Lanka	6.7
2	Azerbaijan	11.6	27	Papua New Guinea	6.6
3	Turkmenistan	11.1	28	Congo-Kinshasa	6.5
4	Ethiopia	10.8	29	Kazakhstan	6.4
	Macau	10.8		Tanzania	6.4
6	China	10.0	31	Bangladesh	6.2
7	Angola	9.9		Vietnam	6.2
8	Afghanistan	8.8	33	Peru	6.1
9	Panama	8.5	34	Burkina Faso	6.0
10	Mongolia	8.4		Niger	6.0
11	Myanmar	8.2	36	Indonesia	5.9
	Uzbekistan	8.2	37	Dominican Rep.	5.8
13	Laos	7.8		Malawi	5.8
	Rwanda	7.8		Singapore	5.8
	Sierra Leone	7.8	40	Georgia	5.7
16	India	7.7		Mauritania	5.7
17	Zambia	7.6	42	Belarus	5.5
18	Cambodia	7.5		Saudi Arabia	5.5
19	Nigeria	7.4	44	Chad	5.4
20	Ghana	7.3		Uruguay	5.4
	Mozambique	7.3	46	Philippines	5.3
22	Timor-Leste	7.0	47	Armenia	5.2
23	Tajikistan	6.9		Botswana	5.2
	Uganda	6.9		Cuba[a]	5.2
25	Liberia	6.8	50	Iraq	5.2

Lowest economic growth
Average annual % change in real GDP, 2004–14

1	South Sudan[b]	-14.1		Spain	0.6
2	Libya	-3.6	22	Euro area	0.7
3	Virgin Islands (US)	-2.4		North Korea	0.7
4	Greece	-2.0	24	Martinique[a]	0.8
5	Central African Rep.	-1.8	25	Barbados	0.9
6	Puerto Rico[a]	-1.7		France	0.9
7	Andorra[a]	-1.4		Guam	0.9
8	Bermuda[a]	-0.8		Hungary	0.9
	French Polynesia[c]	-0.8	29	Netherlands	1.0
10	Italy	-0.5	30	Belgium	1.1
11	Portugal	-0.3	31	Slovenia	1.2
12	Jamaica	0.1		United Kingdom	1.2
13	Croatia	0.3	33	Austria	1.3
	Ukraine	0.3		Germany	1.3
15	Brunei	0.4	35	Norway	1.4
	Denmark	0.4		Zimbabwe	1.4
17	Bahamas	0.6	37	United States	1.5
	Cyprus	0.6	38	Eritrea	1.6
	Finland	0.6	39	Sweden	1.7
	Japan	0.6	40	Equatorial Guinea	1.8

a 2004–13   b 2011–14   c 2005–14

Highest economic growth
Average annual % increase in real GDP, 1994–2004

1	Equatorial Guinea	46.4	11	Armenia	8.0
2	Sudan	15.8		Ireland	8.0
3	Liberia	13.2	13	Angola	7.9
4	Myanmar[a]	11.6	14	Sierra Leone	7.8
5	Rwanda	10.1		Turkmenistan	7.8
6	China	9.1	16	Cambodia	7.7
	Qatar	9.1		Chad	7.7
8	Bosnia & Herz.[b]	8.5		Trinidad & Tobago	7.7
9	Mozambique	8.3		West Bank & Gaza	7.7
10	Iraq	8.1	20	French Guiana[c]	7.4

Lowest economic growth
Average annual % change in real GDP, 1994–2004

1	Zimbabwe[d]	-6.3	11	Guinea-Bissau	1.0
2	Congo-Kinshasa	-1.1		Venezuela	1.0
3	North Korea	-0.1	13	Argentina	1.1
4	Burundi	0.2		Montenegro[a]	1.1
5	Uruguay	0.4		Japan	1.1
6	Central African Rep.	0.5	16	Bulgaria	1.2
	Channel Islands[d]	0.5		Ukraine	1.2
8	Libya	0.6	18	Gabon	1.3
9	Papua New Guinea	0.7		Germany	1.3
10	Jamaica	0.8		Moldova	1.3

Highest services growth
Average annual % increase in real terms, 2006–14

1	Ethiopia	13.5		Nigeria	9.5
2	Qatar	12.9	11	Timor-Leste[e]	9.4
3	Afghanistan	12.3		Zambia	9.4
	Macau	12.3	13	Rwanda	9.3
5	Uzbekistan	11.8	14	Zimbabwe	9.1
6	Tajikistan[e]	11.0	15	Congo-Kinshasa	8.4
7	China	9.9	16	Mozambique	8.3
8	India	9.8	17	Ghana	8.0
9	Mongolia	9.5	18	Panama	7.8

Lowest services growth
Average annual % change in real terms, 2006–14

1	Central African Rep.	-3.5	10	Croatia	0.2
2	Puerto Rico[e]	-3.1		Jamaica	0.2
3	Greece	-2.2	12	Denmark	0.3
4	Bermuda[f]	-1.5		Japan[e]	0.3
5	Ukraine	-1.0	14	Portugal	0.4
6	Italy	-0.3	15	Estonia	0.6
	North Korea	-0.3		Finland	0.6
8	Guam	0.0		Hungary	0.6
9	Virgin Islands (US)	0.1	18	Bahamas	0.9

a 1997–2004   b 1996–2004   c 2000–04   d 1998–2004   e 2006–13   f 2006–12
Note: Rankings of highest and lowest industrial growth 2006–14 can be found on page 44.

Trading places

Biggest exporters
% of total world exports (goods, services and income), 2014

1	Euro area (18)	16.29		22	Saudi Arabia	1.42
2	United States	11.75		23	Ireland	1.37
3	China	9.97		24	Australia	1.27
4	Germany	7.48		25	Sweden	1.16
5	Japan	4.07		26	Thailand	1.07
6	United Kingdom	4.01		27	Brazil	1.03
7	France	3.97		28	Hong Kong	1.02
8	Netherlands	3.90			Poland	1.02
9	South Korea	2.79		30	Austria	1.01
10	Italy	2.65		31	Malaysia	0.99
11	Canada	2.38		32	Norway	0.87
12	Russia	2.26		33	Turkey	0.83
13	Switzerland	2.22		34	Denmark	0.80
14	Spain	1.92		35	Indonesia	0.75
15	Belgium	1.90		36	Czech Republic	0.66
16	India	1.84		37	Vietnam	0.60
17	Mexico	1.60		38	Qatar	0.55
18	Singapore	1.57		39	Hungary	0.51
19	United Arab Emirates	1.49		40	Finland	0.47
20	Taiwan	1.48			Kuwait	0.47
21	Luxembourg	1.45		42	South Africa	0.43

Trade dependency
Trade[a] as % of GDP, 2014

Most			Least		
1	Slovakia	81.0	1	Sudan	8.5
2	United Arab Emirates	77.9	2	Bermuda	8.8
3	Vietnam	77.4	3	Brazil	9.4
4	Hungary	70.5	4	Central African Rep.	10.0
5	Liberia	69.3	5	Cuba	11.3
6	Czech Republic	68.7	6	United States	11.5
7	Lithuania	66.4	7	Argentina	12.5
8	Singapore	63.0	8	Nigeria	12.6
9	Equatorial Guinea	61.5	9	Syria	12.7
	Lesotho	61.5	10	Egypt	13.5
11	Belgium	60.7	11	Pakistan	13.8
12	Slovenia	60.0	12	Burundi	14.3
13	Estonia	59.8	13	Macau	14.5
14	Netherlands	59.4		Uganda	14.5
15	Malaysia	56.3	15	Hong Kong	14.6
16	Puerto Rico	56.0	16	Colombia	15.7
17	Taiwan	54.9	17	French Polynesia	15.9
18	Cambodia	54.0	18	Japan	16.3
19	Thailand	52.5	19	Iran	16.4
20	Bulgaria	52.4	20	Australia	16.5
21	Botswana	52.2		Myanmar	16.5

Notes: The figures are drawn wherever possible from balance of payment statistics, so have differing definitions from statistics taken from customs or similar sources. For Hong Kong and Singapore, only domestic exports and retained imports are used. Euro area data exclude intra-euro area trade.
a Average of imports plus exports of goods.

Biggest traders of goods[a]

% of world, 2015

Exports

	0 3 6 9 12 15
China	
United States	
Germany	
Japan	
Netherlands	
South Korea	
France	
Italy	
UK	
Canada	
Belgium	
Mexico	
Russia	
Switzerland	
Spain	
Taiwan	
India	
U.A.E.[b]	

Imports

	0 3 6 9 12 15
United States	
China	
Germany	
Japan	
UK	
France	
Netherlands	
Canada	
South Korea	
Italy	
Mexico	
India	
Belgium	
Spain	
Switzerland	
Taiwan	
U.A.E.[b]	
Australia[b]	

Biggest earners from services and income

% of world exports of services and income, 2014

1	Euro area (18)	19.72	24	Australia	1.12
2	United States	17.00	25	Norway	1.04
3	United Kingdom	6.63	26	Taiwan	0.97
4	Germany	5.95	27	Poland	0.70
5	France	5.37	28	Thailand	0.69
6	Netherlands	5.27	29	Macau	0.64
7	China	4.93		Malaysia	0.64
8	Japan	4.40	31	Turkey	0.61
9	Luxembourg	4.05	32	Brazil	0.59
10	Switzerland	3.00	33	Greece	0.56
11	Hong Kong	2.98	34	Finland	0.55
12	Ireland	2.40	35	Israel	0.49
13	Singapore	2.29	36	Portugal	0.48
14	Spain	2.21	37	United Arab Emirates	0.46
15	Italy	2.17	38	Saudi Arabia	0.44
16	Belgium	2.12	39	Hungary	0.43
17	India	1.85	40	Philippines	0.38
18	Canada	1.81	41	Czech Republic	0.36
19	South Korea	1.54		Mexico	0.36
20	Sweden	1.49	43	Indonesia	0.28
21	Russia	1.24		Malta	0.28
22	Austria	1.17	45	South Africa	0.27
23	Denmark	1.15			

a Individual countries only.   b Estimate.

Balance of payments: current account

Largest surpluses
$m, 2014

1	Euro area (18)	315,010		26	Philippines	10,756
2	Germany	280,339		27	Azerbaijan	10,209
3	China	219,678		28	Vietnam	9,359
4	South Korea	84,373		29	Ireland	8,914
5	Netherlands	83,532		30	Austria	8,291
6	Saudi Arabia	73,758		31	Puerto Rico	5,083
7	Taiwan	65,335		32	Brunei	4,750
8	Switzerland	61,539		33	Kazakhstan	4,643
9	Norway	59,762		34	Oman	4,056
10	Russia	58,432		35	Hong Kong	3,788
11	United Arab Emirates	54,610		36	Venezuela	3,598
12	Kuwait	53,968		37	Luxembourg	3,549
13	Singapore	53,176		38	Slovenia	3,451
14	Qatar	49,410		39	Hungary	2,710
15	Italy	38,512		40	Botswana	2,496
16	Sweden	30,555		41	Papua New Guinea	1,932
17	Iraq	24,428		42	Trinidad & Tobago	1,822
18	Japan	24,021		43	Lithuania	1,685
19	Denmark	21,421		44	Cuba	1,524
20	Macau	21,082		45	Nigeria	1,268
21	Iran	15,861		46	Portugal	1,209
22	Thailand	15,413		47	Bahrain	1,124
23	Malaysia	14,472		48	Timor-Leste	1,106
24	Israel	12,927		49	Bermuda	816
25	Spain	12,808		50	Bulgaria	693

Largest deficits
$m, 2014

1	United States	-389,525		22	Egypt	-5,972
2	United Kingdom	-151,882		23	Mozambique	-5,797
3	Brazil	-104,181		24	Belarus	-5,222
4	Australia	-44,138		25	Tanzania	-5,021
5	Turkey	-43,552		26	Greece	-4,872
6	Canada	-40,562		27	Sudan	-4,852
7	Indonesia	-27,516		28	Panama	-4,794
8	France	-27,481		29	Ukraine	-4,596
9	India	-27,452		30	Morocco	-4,447
10	Mexico	-24,846		31	Tunisia	-4,302
11	Colombia	-19,593		32	Angola	-3,722
12	South Africa	-19,086		33	Ghana	-3,698
13	Lebanon	-12,207		34	Syria	-3,667
14	Poland	-11,124		35	Pakistan	-3,544
15	Algeria	-9,682		36	Chile	-3,316
16	Argentina	-8,075		37	Congo-Kinshasa	-3,040
17	Peru	-8,031		38	Finland	-2,686
18	Afghanistan	-6,855		39	Uruguay	-2,678
19	Ethiopia	-6,418		40	Uganda	-2,674
20	Kenya	-6,339		41	Serbia	-2,635
21	New Zealand	-6,137		42	Libya	-2,534

Note: Euro area data exclude intra-euro area trade.

Largest surpluses as % of GDP
$m, 2014

1	Timor-Leste	78.1		Vietnam	5.0
2	Macau	38.0	27	Puerto Rico	4.9
3	Kuwait	33.0	28	Malaysia	4.3
4	Brunei	27.8	29	Israel	4.2
5	Qatar	23.5	30	Philippines	3.8
6	Singapore	17.3		Thailand	3.8
7	Botswana	15.8	32	Iran	3.7
8	Bermuda	14.6	33	Ireland	3.6
9	United Arab Emirates	13.7	34	Lithuania	3.5
10	Azerbaijan	13.6	35	French Polynesia	3.4
11	Taiwan	12.3		Malta	3.4
12	Norway	12.0	37	Bahrain	3.3
13	Papua New Guinea	11.4	38	Iceland	3.2
14	Iraq	10.9	39	Russia	3.1
15	Saudi Arabia	9.8	40	Nepal	2.5
16	Netherlands	9.5	41	Euro area (18)	2.3
17	Switzerland	8.8	42	China	2.1
18	Germany	7.2		Kazakhstan	2.1
19	Slovenia	7.0	44	Hungary	2.0
20	Denmark	6.3	45	Austria	1.9
	Trinidad & Tobago	6.3		Cuba	1.9
22	South Korea	6.0	47	Italy	1.8
23	Luxembourg	5.5	48	Venezuela	1.4
24	Sweden	5.4	49	Hong Kong	1.3
25	Oman	5.0		Swaziland	1.3

Largest deficits as % of GDP
$m, 2014

1	Liberia	-60.5	24	West Bank & Gaza	-10.9
2	Mozambique	-36.4	25	Syria	-10.7
3	Afghanistan	-34.2	26	Equatorial Guinea	-10.6
4	Mauritania	-30.3	27	Lesotho	-10.5
5	Sierra Leone	-27.2	28	Kenya	-10.4
6	Lebanon	-26.7		Panama	-10.4
7	Malawi	-25.3		Tanzania	-10.4
8	Kyrgyzstan	-25.1	31	Fiji	-10.3
9	Bahamas	-22.3	32	Chad	-10.2
10	Burundi	-18.0		Tajikistan	-10.2
11	Guinea	-17.9	34	Cambodia	-9.9
12	Zimbabwe	-15.9		Uganda	-9.9
13	Haiti	-15.7	36	Laos	-9.8
14	Montenegro	-15.2	37	Ghana	-9.6
15	Gambia, The	-14.5	38	Benin	-9.2
16	Rwanda	-13.3		Congo-Kinshasa	-9.2
17	Albania	-12.9	40	Senegal	-8.8
18	Togo	-12.7		Tunisia	-8.8
19	Guyana	-12.4	42	Barbados	-8.5
20	Mongolia	-11.7		Moldova	-8.5
21	Namibia	-11.6	44	Jamaica	-8.1
22	Ethiopia	-11.5	45	Burkina Faso	-8.0
23	Georgia	-11.1		Suriname	-8.0

Official reserves[a]

$m, end-2015

1	China	3,405,253	16	Thailand	156,460
2	Japan	1,233,098	17	Algeria	150,595
3	Euro area (18)	701,553	18	France	138,199
4	Saudi Arabia	626,990	19	Italy	130,592
5	Switzerland	602,402	20	United Kingdom	129,601
6	Taiwan	440,468	21	Turkey	111,977
7	United States	383,728	22	Indonesia	105,929
8	Russia	368,043	23	Malaysia	95,282
9	South Korea	366,707	24	Poland	94,903
10	Hong Kong	358,823	25	United Arab Emirates	93,929
11	Brazil	356,465	26	Libya[b]	93,615
12	India	353,319	27	Israel	90,575
13	Singapore	251,876	28	Philippines	80,640
14	Mexico	177,597	29	Canada	79,754
15	Germany	173,731	30	Iraq[b]	66,369

Official gold reserves

Market prices, $m, end-2015

1	Euro area (18)	367,680	14	Portugal	13,036
2	United States	277,189	15	Saudi Arabia	11,005
3	Germany	115,224	16	United Kingdom	10,575
4	Italy	83,559	17	Lebanon	9,775
5	France	83,006	18	Spain	9,596
6	China	60,060	19	Austria	9,542
7	Russia	48,208	20	Belgium	7,750
8	Switzerland	35,443	21	Kazakhstan	7,560
9	Japan	26,079	22	Philippines	6,676
10	Netherlands	20,872	23	Algeria	5,918
11	India	19,008	24	Thailand	5,194
12	Turkey	17,569	25	Singapore	4,342
13	Taiwan	14,437			

Workers' remittances

Inflows, $m, 2014

1	India	70,389	16	Lebanon	7,446
2	China	62,332	17	Ukraine	7,354
3	Philippines	28,403	18	Italy	7,256
4	France	24,968	19	Poland	7,134
5	Mexico	24,460	20	Morocco	7,053
6	Nigeria	20,921	21	Sri Lanka	7,037
7	Egypt	19,570	22	United States	6,878
8	Germany	17,629	23	South Korea	6,481
9	Pakistan	17,066	24	Uzbekistan	6,206
10	Bangladesh	14,969	25	Nepal	5,878
11	Vietnam	12,000	26	Guatemala	5,837
12	Belgium	11,494	27	Thailand	5,655
13	Spain	10,744	28	Dominican Rep.	4,811
14	Indonesia	8,551	29	Hungary	4,331
15	Russia	7,777	30	Portugal	4,275

a Foreign exchange, SDRs, IMF position and gold at market prices.   b 2014

Exchange rates

The Economist's Big Mac index

Local currency under(-)/over(+) valuation against the dollar[a], January 2016, %

Big Mac price, $[b]

	Big Mac price, $[b]
Switzerland	6.44
Sweden	5.23
Norway	5.21
United States[c]	4.93
Denmark	4.32
Israel	4.29
United Kindom	4.22
Canada	4.14
Euro area[d]	4.00
New Zealand	3.91
Australia	3.74
South Korea	3.59
United Arab Emirates	3.54
Turkey	3.41
Brazil	3.35
Singapore	3.27
Saudi Arabia	3.20
Japan	3.12
Thailand	3.09
Czech Republic	2.98
Chile	2.94
Pakistan	2.86
Mexico	2.81
Philippines	2.79
China[e]	2.68
Hong Kong	2.48
Colombia	2.43
Argentina	2.39
Poland	2.37
Indonesia	2.19
Egypt	2.16
Taiwan	2.08
India[f]	1.90
Malaysia	1.82
South Africa	1.77
Russia	1.53

a Based on purchasing-power parity: local price of a Big Mac burger divided by United States price. b At market exchange rates. c Average of four cities.
d Weighted average of prices in euro area. e Average of five cities. f Maharaja Mac.

Inflation

Consumer-price inflation

Highest, 2015, %

1	Venezuela[a]	121.7
2	South Sudan[a]	52.8
3	Ukraine	48.7
4	Yemen[a]	30.0
5	Malawi	21.9
6	Ghana[a]	17.2
7	Sudan	16.9
8	Russia	15.5
9	Belarus[a]	13.5
10	Iran	12.0
11	Myanmar	11.5
12	Egypt	11.0
13	Argentina[b]	10.6
14	Angola	10.3
15	Ethiopia	10.1
	Zambia	10.1
17	Moldova	9.6
18	Brazil[a]	9.0
	Eritrea[a]	9.0
	Nigeria	9.0
	Sierra Leone	9.0
22	Uruguay	8.7

Lowest, 2015, %

1	Lebanon	-3.7
2	Zimbabwe[a]	-2.4
3	Afghanistan	-1.5
	Cyprus	-1.5
5	Bulgaria	-1.1
	Greece	-1.1
	Switzerland	-1.1
8	Bosnia & Herz.	-1.0
9	Jordan	-0.9
	Poland	-0.9
	Thailand	-0.9
12	El Salvador	-0.7
	Lithuania	-0.7
14	Israel	-0.6
	Romania	-0.6
16	Croatia[a]	-0.5
	Kosovo	-0.5
	Singapore[a]	-0.5
	Slovenia	-0.5
	Spain	-0.5
21	Brunei	-0.4

Highest average annual consumer-price inflation, 2010–15, %

1	Venezuela[a]	50.5
2	Belarus[a]	31.1
3	Sudan	28.5
4	Iran	22.6
5	South Sudan[ac]	22.5
6	Malawi	20.4
7	Ethiopia	16.1
8	Yemen[a]	15.4
9	Guinea	13.2
10	Ukraine	12.5
11	Sierra Leone	11.8
12	Ghana[a]	11.7
13	Uzbekistan[a]	10.7
14	Argentina[ad]	10.1
15	Angola	10.0
	Mongolia[a]	10.0
17	Nigeria	9.7
18	Tanzania	9.6
19	Egypt	9.5
20	Uganda	9.4
21	Burundi	9.0
	Pakistan	9.0
23	Nepal	8.8

Lowest average annual consumer-price inflation, 2010–15, %

1	Switzerland	-0.4
2	Brunei	0.0
3	Greece	0.1
4	Bosnia & Herz.	0.7
	Bulgaria	0.7
	Japan	0.7
	Sweden	0.7
8	Ireland	0.8
9	Senegal[a]	0.9
10	Cyprus	1.0
	Taiwan	1.0
12	Niger	1.1
13	France	1.2
	Morocco[a]	1.2
	Slovenia	1.2
	Zimbabwe	1.2
17	Israel	1.3
	Spain	1.3
19	Croatia	1.4
	Denmark	1.4
	Germany	1.4
	Portugal	1.4

a Estimate.   b 2013   c 2011–15   d 2010–13

Commodity prices

End 2015, % change on a year earlier		2010–15, % change		
1	Tea	49.2	1	Beef (US)	26.4
2	Wool (Aus)	19.5	2	Wool (Aus)	22.7
3	Wool (NZ)	10.5	3	Wool (NZ)	14.2
4	Cocoa	8.6	4	Cocoa	4.6
5	Cotton	0.8	5	Beef (Aus)	3.5
6	Lead	-2.8	6	Tea	1.1
7	Sugar	-3.5	7	Hides	-4.4
8	Coconut oil	-6.7	8	Timber	-21.7
9	Soya oil	-7.2	9	Gold	-22.8
10	Corn	-10.8	10	Lamb	-26.5
11	Gold	-11.3	11	Lead	-27.7
12	Rice	-14.8	12	Soya meal	-30.3
13	Soyabeans	-16.2	13	Zinc	-31.4
14	Aluminium	-16.3	14	Aluminium	-36.1
15	Rubber	-18.4	15	Rice	-36.7
16	Palm oil	-18.6	16	Soyabeans	-36.8
17	Beef (US)	-19.5	17	Coconut oil	-37.0
18	Lamb	-20.0	18	Wheat	-40.4
19	Coffee	-20.2	19	Coffee	-41.8
20	Wheat	-21.0	20	Corn	-41.9
21	Tin	-23.1	21	Tin	-45.7
22	Timber	-23.6	22	Soya oil	-46.3
23	Copper	-26.0	23	Copper	-50.1
24	Soya meal	-27.1	24	Sugar	-52.8
	Zinc	-27.1	25	Palm oil	-55.8
26	Oil[a]	-29.6	26	Oil[a]	-58.5

House prices

Q1 2016[b], % change on a year earlier		Q1 2010–Q1 2016[b], % change		
1	Turkey	18.6	1	Brazil	113.3
2	New Zealand	14.7	2	Turkey	104.9
3	Sweden	13.7	3	Hong Kong	97.9
4	Colombia	9.4	4	Indonesia	68.7
5	Austria	9.3	5	Colombia	61.3
6	Ireland	8.8	6	Estonia	60.7
7	Australia	8.7	7	Israel	51.5
8	Iceland	8.2	8	India	41.7
9	United Kingdom	7.7	9	Sweden	40.3
10	Israel	7.6	10	Iceland	39.6
11	Denmark	7.2	11	New Zealand	39.5
12	Mexico	6.8	12	Austria	39.4
13	Latvia	6.3	13	Chile	35.9
14	Canada	5.9		Germany	35.9
	Slovakia	5.9	15	Norway	34.7
16	Germany	5.6	16	South Africa	32.2
17	Luxembourg	5.3	17	Mexico	32.0
18	Estonia	5.1	18	Latvia	30.2
	Hungary	5.1	19	United Kingdom	29.5
	United States	5.1	20	Canada	29.2

a West Texas Intermediate.   b Or latest.

Debt

Highest foreign debt[a]

$bn, 2014

1	China	959.5	26	Venezuela	107.3
2	Russia	599.1	27	Colombia	102.3
3	Brazil	556.9	28	Israel	96.2
4	Singapore[b]	467.6	29	Philippines	77.7
5	India	463.2	30	Vietnam	71.9
6	Mexico	432.6	31	Peru	66.5
7	Turkey	408.2	32	Pakistan	62.2
8	South Korea	370.4	33	Iraq	58.1
9	Poland	337.8	34	Croatia	56.5
10	Indonesia	293.4	35	Bulgaria	48.7
11	Hong Kong	229.2	36	Sudan	48.1
12	Malaysia	210.8	37	Sri Lanka	43.6
13	United Arab Emirates	192.5	38	Morocco	42.8
14	Taiwan	177.9	39	Belarus	40.0
15	Saudi Arabia	166.1	40	Egypt	39.6
16	Kazakhstan	157.6	41	Kuwait	35.3
17	Chile	149.7	42	Bangladesh	34.9
18	Hungary	145.3	43	Lebanon	34.4
19	South Africa	144.0	44	Serbia	33.1
20	Argentina	139.6	45	Angola	28.4
21	Qatar	137.4	46	Nigeria	26.9
22	Thailand	135.8	47	Dominican Rep.	26.7
23	Ukraine	130.7	48	Tunisia	26.4
24	Czech Republic	125.3	49	Ecuador	26.3
25	Romania	111.3	50	Cuba	25.2

Highest foreign debt burden[a]

Total foreign debt as % of GDP, 2014

1	Mongolia	173.3	19	Zimbabwe	74.5
2	Singapore[b]	152.6	20	Kazakhstan	71.5
3	Jamaica	123.8	21	Mauritania	70.3
4	Papua New Guinea	118.5	22	Lebanon	69.4
5	Hungary	105.0	23	Jordan	67.7
6	Ukraine	99.2	24	Qatar	65.4
7	Croatia	98.8	25	Sudan	65.2
8	Kyrgyzstan	98.0	26	Macedonia	64.0
9	Laos	91.5	27	Malaysia	62.4
10	Mauritius	89.5	28	Gambia, The	62.0
11	Moldova	89.3		Poland	62.0
12	Nicaragua	86.8	30	Czech Republic	61.1
13	Bulgaria	85.9	31	Albania	59.8
14	Georgia	84.3	32	Chile	57.8
15	Hong Kong	78.7		El Salvador	57.8
16	Armenia	78.5	34	Bosnia & Herz.	57.2
17	Estonia	75.8	35	Bahrain	55.8
18	Serbia	74.9		Romania	55.8

a Foreign debt is debt owed to non-residents and repayable in foreign currency; the figures shown include liabilities of government, public and private sectors. Longer-established developed countries have been excluded.

b The calculation of Singapore's debt has changed from previous editions and now includes all financial sector and intra-firm debt.

Highest foreign debt[a]
As % of exports of goods and services, 2014

1	Sudan	649.4	15	Ukraine	166.1
2	Mongolia	312.6	16	Nicaragua	165.6
3	Laos	303.5	17	Tanzania	162.3
4	Central African Rep.	282.6	18	Chile	161.6
5	Jamaica	254.9	19	Albania	158.7
6	Zimbabwe	232.4	20	Argentina	156.8
7	Papua New Guinea	222.8	21	Mozambique	156.3
8	Ethiopia	220.6	22	Kyrgyzstan	149.6
9	Burundi	214.4	23	Mauritania	145.5
10	Brazil	199.2	24	Niger	144.4
11	Croatia	191.1	25	Serbia	143.8
12	Sri Lanka	182.3	26	Colombia	142.2
13	Turkey	181.5	27	Rwanda	140.8
14	Kazakhstan	176.9	28	Indonesia	140.0

Highest debt service ratio[c]
Average, %, 2014

1	Zimbabwe	72.7	15	Russia	22.4
2	Serbia	40.2	16	Indonesia	22.1
3	Syria	38.9	17	Armenia	21.6
4	Kazakhstan	35.7	18	Brazil	21.4
5	Croatia	32.5	19	Sudan	20.6
6	Ukraine	32.4	20	Mongolia	20.4
7	Romania	27.8	21	Venezuela	19.1
8	Balkans	26.8	22	Georgia	18.9
9	Mauritius	26.3	23	Costa Rica	18.8
10	Hungary	25.9	24	Paraguay	18.7
11	Chile	25.0	25	Colombia	18.4
12	Turkey	24.9	26	Macedonia	16.4
13	Poland	24.2	27	India	16.3
14	Jamaica	23.0	28	Argentina	15.8

Household debt[d]
As % of net disposable income, 2014

1	Denmark	304.9	13	Spain	127.3
2	Netherlands	273.6	14	Finland	126.6
3	Norway	224.3	15	Greece	115.0
4	Ireland	207.4	16	United States	113.4
5	Australia	205.5	17	Belgium	111.9
6	Switzerland[e]	197.9	18	France	104.7
7	Sweden	173.4	19	Germany	93.6
8	Canada	166.4	20	Italy	90.1
9	South Korea	164.2	21	Austria	89.1
10	United Kingdom	156.2	22	Estonia	83.5
11	Portugal	140.9	23	Czech Republic	68.9
12	Japan[e]	129.5	24	Slovakia	62.3

c Debt service is the sum of interest and principal repayments (amortisation) due on outstanding foreign debt. The debt service ratio is debt service as a percentage of exports of goods, non-factor services, primary income and workers' remittances.
d OECD countries. e 2012

Aid

Largest recipients of bilateral and multilateral aid
$m, 2014

1	Afghanistan	4,823.3	26	Ghana	1,126.4
2	Vietnam	4,217.9	27	Burkina Faso	1,119.9
3	Syria	4,198.0	28	Somalia	1,109.4
4	Pakistan	3,611.9	29	Senegal	1,106.9
5	Ethiopia	3,585.1	30	Haiti	1,083.5
6	Egypt	3,532.2	31	South Africa	1,070.4
7	Turkey	3,441.8	32	Rwanda	1,034.0
8	India	2,983.6	33	Zambia	994.6
9	Jordan	2,699.1	34	Malawi	930.2
10	Kenya	2,665.1	35	Ivory Coast	922.5
11	Tanzania	2,648.0	36	Tunisia	921.3
12	West Bank & Gaza	2,486.5	37	Niger	917.8
13	Nigeria	2,476.2	38	Brazil	911.6
14	Bangladesh	2,418.0	39	Sierra Leone	910.6
15	Congo-Kinshasa	2,398.2	40	Nepal	880.1
16	Morocco	2,247.0	41	Sudan	871.9
17	Mozambique	2,103.4	42	Cameroon	852.3
18	South Sudan	1,964.2	43	Lebanon	819.6
19	Uganda	1,632.9	44	Mexico	806.7
20	Ukraine	1,403.7	45	Cambodia	799.4
21	Myanmar	1,380.1	46	Zimbabwe	757.8
22	Iraq	1,369.8	47	Liberia	744.3
23	Mali	1,233.6	48	Philippines	675.7
24	Colombia	1,221.3	49	Bolivia	671.8
25	Yemen	1,164.2	50	Bosnia & Herz.	632.0

$ per person, 2014

1	West Bank & Gaza	579.0	25	Rwanda	91.2
2	Jordan	408.5	26	Armenia	88.3
3	Kosovo	317.9	27	Tunisia	83.8
4	Guyana	208.5	28	Papua New Guinea	77.4
5	Timor-Leste	203.8	29	Mozambique	77.3
6	Syria	189.5	30	Honduras	75.8
7	Lebanon	180.3	31	Senegal	75.4
8	Liberia	169.3	32	Mali	72.2
9	Bosnia & Herz.	165.5	33	Nicaragua	71.6
10	South Sudan	164.9	34	Laos	70.6
11	Montenegro	163.9	35	Swaziland	67.7
12	Afghanistan	152.5	36	Morocco	66.2
13	Moldova	145.5	37	Gabon	66.0
14	Sierra Leone	144.2	38	Mauritania	64.8
15	Central African Rep.	127.0	39	Burkina Faso	63.7
16	Georgia	125.0	40	Bolivia	63.6
17	Mongolia	108.1	41	Zambia	63.3
18	Kyrgyzstan	107.0	42	Guinea-Bissau	60.4
19	Somalia	105.5	43	Kenya	59.4
20	Fiji	103.8	44	Benin	56.7
21	Haiti	102.5	45	Malawi	55.7
22	Macedonia	101.5	46	Cambodia	52.2
23	Albania	96.8	47	Serbia	52.0
24	Namibia	94.3	48	Gambia, The	51.7

Largest bilateral and multilateral donors[a]

$bn, 2014

	$bn (0–35)	% of GDP
United States		0.19
United Kingdom		0.70
Germany		0.42
Saudi Arabia		1.80
France		0.37
Japan		0.19
Sweden		1.09
Netherlands		0.64
Norway		1.00
United Arab Emirates		1.26
Australia		0.31
Canada		0.24
Italy		0.19
Turkey		0.45
Switzerland		0.50
Denmark		0.86
Belgium		0.46
Spain		0.13
South Korea		0.13
Finland		0.59

Biggest changes to aid

$m, 2010–14

	Increases			Decreases	
1	Syria	4,063	1	Haiti	-1,953
2	Egypt	2,943	2	Indonesia	-1,778
3	Turkey	2,395	3	Afghanistan	-1,649
4	South Sudan	1,964	4	China	-1,605
5	Jordan	1,748	5	Congo-Brazzaville	-1,209
6	Vietnam	1,279	6	Sudan	-1,156
7	Morocco	1,257	7	Congo-Kinshasa	-1,083
8	Kenya	1,041	8	Iraq	-809
9	Myanmar	1,025	9	Liberia	-669
10	Bangladesh	1,014	10	Ghana	-564
11	Ukraine	752	11	Panama	-322
12	Peru	624	12	Tanzania	-309
13	Somalia	604	13	Serbia	-289
14	Pakistan	592	14	Nicaragua	-232
15	Colombia	547	15	Togo	-196

a China also provides aid, but does not disclose amounts.

Industry and services

Largest industrial output
$bn, 2014

1	China	4,423	23	Norway	171
2	United States[a]	3,212	24	Netherlands	168
3	Japan[a]	1,280	25	Iran	159
4	Germany	1,055		Poland	159
5	Russia	570	27	Thailand	149
6	India	568	28	Qatar	143
7	United Kingdom	558	29	Nigeria	136
8	France	493	30	Malaysia	135
9	South Korea	492	31	Iraq	133
10	Brazil	469	32	Sweden	131
11	Italy	451	33	Argentina	130
12	Saudi Arabia	425	34	Colombia	125
13	Mexico	422	35	Kuwait	115
14	Canada[b]	420	36	Austria	109
15	Indonesia	372		Egypt	109
16	Australia	368	38	Belgium	105
17	Spain	282	39	Puerto Rico[a]	99
18	United Arab Emirates	220	40	South Africa	93
19	Turkey	193	41	Algeria	90
20	Switzerland	178	42	Philippines	89
21	Taiwan	177	43	Chile	83
22	Venezuela[c]	172	44	Kazakhstan	74

Highest growth in industrial output
Average annual % increase in real terms, 2006–14

1	Timor-Leste[d]	28.9	11	Rwanda	9.3
2	Sierra Leone	23.6	12	Bangladesh	8.3
3	Liberia	19.9	13	Tanzania	8.2
4	Ethiopia	14.4	14	Azerbaijan	8.1
5	Laos	12.9	15	Mongolia	8.0
6	Panama	11.5	16	Zambia	7.5
7	Ghana	11.0	17	Burkina Faso	7.4
	Qatar	11.0		Cambodia	7.4
9	China	10.2		Iraq	7.4
10	Niger	10.1	20	Lebanon	6.9

Lowest growth in industrial output
Average annual % change in real terms, 2006–14

1	Greece	-8.4	12	Latvia	-2.1
2	Cyprus	-7.3	13	Denmark	-1.8
3	Bermuda[e]	-6.1	14	Ireland	-1.7
4	Central African Rep.	-4.8		Ukraine	-1.7
5	Spain	-3.8	16	Puerto Rico[d]	-1.1
6	Croatia	-2.8		United Kingdom	-1.1
7	Brunei	-2.7	18	France	-0.9
8	Italy	-2.5		Moldova	-0.9
9	Jamaica	-2.3	20	Norway	-0.8
10	Finland	-2.2	21	Hungary	-0.7
	Portugal	-2.2			

a 2013   b 2010   c 2012   d 2006–13   e 2006–12

Largest manufacturing output
$bn, 2014

1	China	3,713	21	Australia	93
2	United States[a]	1,944	22	Poland	89
3	Japan[a]	905	23	Sweden	83
4	Germany	788	24	Saudi Arabia	81
5	South Korea	390	25	Malaysia	77
6	India	322	26	Austria	72
7	Italy	297	27	Argentina	66
8	France	284	28	Belgium	65
9	United Kingdom	283	29	Philippines	59
10	Russia	248	30	Nigeria	55
11	Brazil	219	31	Singapore	54
12	Mexico	217	32	Czech Republic	49
13	Indonesia	187		Iran	49
14	Spain	167	34	Puerto Rico[a]	48
15	Canada[b]	162		Venezuela[c]	48
16	Taiwan	157	36	Egypt	45
17	Switzerland	129		Ireland	45
18	Turkey	126	38	Colombia	42
19	Thailand	112		South Africa	42
20	Netherlands	96	40	Denmark	41

Largest services output
$bn, 2014

1	United States[a]	12,227	27	Norway	269
2	China	4,982	28	Hong Kong	260
3	Japan[a]	3,543	29	Denmark	225
4	Germany	2,401	30	Iran	218
5	United Kingdom	2,087		Singapore	218
6	France	1,999	32	South Africa	214
7	Italy	1,429	33	Thailand	213
8	Brazil	1,424	34	Colombia	200
9	India	982	35	United Arab Emirates	177
10	Australia	959	36	Malaysia	173
11	Russia	955	37	Greece	167
12	Spain	944	38	Finland	166
13	Mexico	765		Ireland	166
14	South Korea	764	40	Philippines	163
15	Netherlands	609	41	Venezuela[b]	154
16	Switzerland	496	42	Portugal	153
17	Turkey	461	43	Chile	145
18	Indonesia	375	44	Pakistan	126
19	Belgium	367	45	Egypt	125
	Sweden	367	46	Kazakhstan	121
21	Taiwan	336	47	Romania	118
22	Nigeria	312	48	Czech Republic	110
23	Poland	311	49	Peru[c]	98
24	Saudi Arabia	307	50	Bangladesh	93
25	Argentina	286	51	Algeria	86
26	Austria	275	52	Iraq	81

a 2013 b 2010 c 2012

Agriculture and fisheries

Largest agricultural output
$bn, 2014

1	China	950	16	Iran	39
2	India	336	17	Argentina	38
3	United States[a]	226	18	Vietnam	34
4	Indonesia	119	19	Australia	33
5	Nigeria	114	20	Philippines	32
6	Brazil	111		Spain	32
7	Russia	66	22	Malaysia	30
8	Japan[a]	59		South Korea	30
9	Pakistan	58	24	Bangladesh	27
10	Turkey	57	25	Germany	24
11	France	42	26	Canada[b]	23
	Italy	42	27	Algeria	22
	Thailand	42		Colombia	22
14	Egypt	40	29	Ethiopia	21
	Mexico	40		Sudan	21

Most economically dependent on agriculture
% of GDP from agriculture, 2014

1	Central African Rep.	58.2	15	Cambodia	30.4
2	Sierra Leone	56.0	16	Kenya	30.3
3	Chad	52.6	17	Sudan	29.2
4	Guinea-Bissau	43.9	18	Laos	27.7
5	Ethiopia	41.9	19	Tajikistan[a]	27.4
6	Togo	41.7	20	Uganda	27.2
7	Mali	39.5	21	Madagascar	26.5
8	Burundi	39.3	22	Mozambique	25.2
9	Niger	36.7	23	Pakistan	25.0
10	Burkina Faso	34.2	24	Gambia, The[a]	23.6
11	Nepal	33.7	25	Afghanistan	23.5
12	Malawi	33.3		Benin	23.5
13	Rwanda	33.1	27	Mauritania	22.8
14	Tanzania	31.5	28	Albania	22.6

Least economically dependent on agriculture
% of GDP from agriculture, 2014

1	Macau[c]	0.0	14	Japan[a]	1.2
	Singapore	0.0	15	Oman	1.3
3	Hong Kong	0.1	16	Austria	1.4
	Qatar	0.1		Denmark	1.4
5	Luxembourg	0.3		Sweden	1.4
6	Kuwait	0.4		United States[a]	1.4
7	Trinidad & Tobago[a]	0.6	20	Canada[b]	1.5
8	Belgium	0.7	21	Ireland	1.6
	Brunei[a]	0.7	22	France	1.7
	Germany	0.7		Norway	1.7
	United Kingdom	0.7	24	Bahamas	1.8
12	Bermuda[c]	0.8		Netherlands	1.8
	Switzerland	0.8		Taiwan	1.8

a 2013   b 2010   c 2012

Biggest producers
'000 tonnes, 2013 or 2014

Cereals

1	China	557,407	6	Indonesia	89,855
2	United States	442,933	7	Ukraine	63,377
3	India	293,993	8	France	56,151
4	Russia	103,154	9	Argentina	55,506
5	Brazil	101,398	10	Bangladesh	55,070

Meat

1	China	83,462	6	India	6,215
2	United States	42,642	7	Mexico	6,122
3	Brazil	26,011	8	France	5,560
4	Russia	8,544	9	Spain	5,424
5	Germany	8,201	10	Argentina	5,210

Fruit

1	China	151,838	6	Mexico	17,553
2	India	82,632	7	Italy	16,371
3	Brazil	37,774	8	Indonesia	16,003
4	United States	26,986	9	Philippines	15,887
5	Spain	17,699	10	Turkey	15,341

Vegetables

1	China	580,702	6	Egypt	19,591
2	India	121,015	7	Russia	15,485
3	United States	34,280	8	Vietnam	14,976
4	Turkey	28,281	9	Mexico	13,238
5	Iran	23,652	10	Italy	13,049

Roots and tubers

1	China	173,307	5	Thailand	30,218
2	Nigeria	107,835	6	Brazil	27,705
3	India	55,622	7	Indonesia	27,135
4	Russia	31,501	8	Ghana	25,079

Fisheries and aquaculture production
Fish, crustaceans and molluscs, million tonnes, 2014

1	China	61.5	15	South Korea	2.2
2	Indonesia[a]	10.6	16	Malaysia	1.7
3	India	9.6	17	Mexico	1.6
4	Vietnam	6.3	18	Egypt[a]	1.5
5	United States	5.4	19	Morocco	1.4
6	Myanmar	5.0		Spain	1.4
7	Russia	4.4		Taiwan	1.4
8	Japan	4.3	22	Brazil	1.3
9	Peru	3.7	23	Iceland	1.1
10	Norway	3.6		Nigeria	1.1
11	Bangladesh[a]	3.5	25	Canada	1.0
12	Chile	3.4		Ecuador	1.0
13	Philippines	3.1		United Kingdom	1.0
14	Thailand	2.6	28	Iran	0.9

a Estimate.

Commodities

Wheat

Top 10 producers, 2014–15
'000 tonnes

1	EU28	156,115
2	China	126,208
3	India	95,850
4	Russia	59,100
5	United States	55,147
6	Canada	29,420
7	Pakistan	25,980
8	Ukraine	24,740
9	Australia	23,076
10	Turkey	19,000

Top 10 consumers, 2014–15
'000 tonnes

1	EU28	123,600
2	China	123,400
3	India	93,290
4	Russia	36,570
5	United States	31,610
6	Pakistan	25,120
7	Turkey	20,460
8	Egypt	19,240
9	Iran	18,250
10	Ukraine	11,950

Rice[a]

Top 10 producers, 2014–15
'000 tonnes

1	China	144,560
2	India	105,480
3	Indonesia	35,560
4	Bangladesh	34,500
5	Vietnam	28,234
6	Thailand	18,750
7	Myanmar	12,600
8	Philippines	11,915
9	Brazil	8,465
10	Japan	7,849

Top 10 consumers, 2014–15
'000 tonnes

1	China	148,000
2	India	98,600
3	Indonesia	38,300
4	Bangladesh	35,200
5	Vietnam	22,100
6	Philippines	13,200
7	Thailand	11,000
8	Myanmar	10,650
9	Japan	8,315
10	Brazil	7,930

Sugar[b]

Top 10 producers, 2014
'000 tonnes

1	Brazil	35,530
2	India	26,030
3	EU28	17,790
4	China	12,530
5	Thailand	9,280
6	United States	7,200
7	Mexico	6,240
8	Pakistan	6,200
9	Australia	4,660
10	Russia	4,600

Top 10 consumers, 2014
'000 tonnes

1	India	24,060
2	EU28	19,190
3	China	15,030
4	Brazil	12,000
5	United States	10,060
6	Indonesia	6,070
7	Russia	5,400
8	Pakistan	4,740
9	Mexico	4,310
10	Egypt	3,170

Coarse grains[c]

Top 5 producers, 2014–15
'000 tonnes

1	United States	377,669
2	China	223,946
3	EU28	170,612
4	Brazil	87,261
5	India	42,870

Top 5 consumers, 2014–15
'000 tonnes

1	United States	311,692
2	China	234,950
3	EU28	161,741
4	Brazil	60,209
5	Mexico	42,740

a Milled. b Raw.
c Includes: maize (corn), barley, sorghum, oats, rye, millet, triticale and other.
d Tonnes at 65 degrees brix.

Tea

Top 10 producers, 2013		*Top 10 consumers, 2014*	
'000 tonnes		*'000 tonnes*	
1 China	1,924	1 China	1,672
2 India	1,209	2 India	1,021
3 Kenya	432	3 Turkey	247
4 Sri Lanka	340	4 Russia	164
5 Vietnam	214	5 Pakistan	138
6 Turkey	212	6 United States	128
7 Iran	160	7 Japan	114
8 Indonesia	148	8 United Kingdom	107
9 Argentina	105	9 Egypt	103
10 Japan	85	10 Iran	87

Coffee

Top 10 producers, 2014–15		*Top 10 consumers, 2014*	
'000 tonnes		*'000 tonnes*	
1 Brazil	2,594	1 EU28	2,547
2 Vietnam	1,650	2 United States	1,426
3 Colombia	810	3 Brazil	1,216
4 Indonesia	660	4 Japan	450
5 Ethiopia	384	5 Indonesia	250
6 India	350	6 Russia	241
7 Honduras	345	7 Canada	235
8 Uganda	285	8 Ethiopia	219
9 Mexico	234	9 Philippines	161
10 Guatemala	204	10 Mexico	141

Cocoa

Top 10 producers, 2014–15		*Top 10 consumers, 2013–14*	
'000 tonnes		*'000 tonnes*	
1 Ivory Coast	1,796	1 United States	768
2 Ghana	740	2 Germany	335
3 Indonesia	325	3 France	230
4 Ecuador	250	4 United Kingdom	223
5 Cameroon	232	5 Brazil	206
6 Brazil	230	6 Russia	201
7 Nigeria	195	7 Japan	170
8 Peru	83	8 Spain	115
9 Dominican Rep.	82	9 Italy	95
10 Colombia	51	10 Canada	89

Orange juice[d]

Top 5 producers, 2014–15		*Top 5 consumers, 2014–15*	
'000 tonnes		*'000 tonnes*	
1 Brazil	974	1 EU28	841
2 United States	438	2 United States	672
3 Mexico	121	3 China	100
4 EU28	107	4 Canada	89
5 South Africa	41	5 Japan	68

Copper

Top 10 producers[a], 2014		*Top 10 consumers[b], 2014*	
'000 tonnes		*'000 tonnes*	
1 Chile	5,750	1 China	11,303
2 China	1,632	2 United States	1,767
3 United States	1,383	3 Germany	1,162
4 Peru	1,380	4 Japan	1,072
5 Congo-Kinshasa	996	5 South Korea	759
6 Australia	965	6 Italy	622
7 Zambia	756	7 Russia	568
8 Russia	720	8 Taiwan	465
9 Canada	696	9 Turkey	453
10 Mexico	514	10 India	434

Lead

Top 10 producers[a], 2014		*Top 10 consumers[b], 2014*	
'000 tonnes		*'000 tonnes*	
1 China	2,853	1 China	4,718
2 Australia	728	2 United States	1,670
3 United States	385	3 South Korea	601
4 Peru	278	4 India	521
5 Mexico	250	5 Germany	337
6 Russia	194	6 Italy	258
7 India	105	7 Japan	254
8 Poland	77	8 Spain	245
9 Bolivia	76	9 Brazil	229
10 Sweden	71	10 United Kingdom	208

Zinc

Top 10 producers[a], 2014		*Top 10 consumers[c], 2014*	
'000 tonnes		*'000 tonnes*	
1 China	5,200	1 China	6,420
2 Australia	1,560	2 United States	962
3 Peru	1,319	3 South Korea	644
4 United States	832	4 India	638
5 India	729	5 Japan	503
6 Mexico	660	6 Germany	477
7 Bolivia	449	7 Belgium	388
8 Kazakhstan	386	8 Italy	242
9 Canada	353	Russia	242
10 Ireland	283	10 Brazil	241

Tin

Top 5 producers[a], 2014		*Top 5 consumers[b], 2014*	
'000 tonnes		*'000 tonnes*	
1 China	177.3	1 China	192.6
2 Indonesia	69.6	2 United States	28.8
3 Peru	23.1	3 Japan	27.1
4 Bolivia	19.8	4 Germany	18.8
5 Myanmar	17.5	5 South Korea	13.8

Nickel

Top 10 producers[a], 2014
'000 tonnes

1	Philippines	410.8			

Top 10 consumers[b], 2014
'000 tonnes

Rank	Producer	Amount		Rank	Consumer	Amount
1	Philippines	410.8		1	China	760.9
2	Russia	264.0		2	Japan	157.4
3	Australia	244.7		3	United States	152.4
4	Canada	235.0		4	South Korea	99.8
5	New Caledonia	178.1		5	Taiwan	65.8
6	Indonesia	145.5		6	Germany	62.2
7	China	92.4		7	Italy	60.0
8	Brazil	85.6		8	Spain	32.6
9	South Africa	55.0		9	South Africa	31.5
10	Cuba	50.0		10	Belgium	29.1

Aluminium

Rank	*Top 10 producers[d], 2014* '000 tonnes			Rank	*Top 10 consumers[e], 2014* '000 tonnes	
1	China	27,517		1	China	27,204
2	Russia	3,488		2	United States	5,250
3	Canada	2,858		3	Germany	2,289
4	United Arab Emirates	2,296		4	Japan	2,034
5	India	1,767		5	India	1,523
6	United States	1,710		6	South Korea	1,282
7	Australia	1,704		7	Brazil	1,027
8	Norway	1,331		8	Turkey	915
9	Brazil	962		9	United Arab Emirates	835
10	Bahrain	931		10	Italy	810

Precious metals

Rank	*Gold [a]* *Top 10 producers, 2014* tonnes			Rank	*Silver [a]* *Top 10 producers, 2014* tonnes	
1	China	451.8		1	Mexico	5,766
2	Australia	274.0		2	Peru	3,777
3	Russia	249.1		3	China	3,673
4	United States	210.1		4	Australia	1,847
5	Canada	152.1		5	Chile	1,572
6	South Africa	151.6		6	Russia	1,412
7	Peru	141.3		7	Bolivia	1,345
8	Ghana	135.8		8	Poland	1,200
9	Mexico	117.8		9	United States	1,180
10	Uzbekistan	102.0		10	Kazakhstan	982

Rank	*Platinum* *Top 3 producers, 2014* tonnes			Rank	*Palladium* *Top 3 producers, 2014* tonnes	
1	South Africa	110.3		1	Russia	81.3
2	Russia	22.1		2	South Africa	66.2
3	United States/Canada	10.6		3	United States/Canada	28.4

a Mine production.   b Refined consumption.   c Slab consumption.
d Primary refined production.   e Primary refined consumption.

Rubber (natural and synthetic)

Top 10 producers, 2014		*Top 10 consumers, 2014*	
'000 tonnes		*'000 tonnes*	
1 Thailand	4,553	1 China	8,987
2 China	3,735	2 EU28	3,486
3 Indonesia	3,211	3 United States	2,787
4 EU28	2,428	4 Japan	1,665
5 United States	2,312	5 India	1,533
6 Japan	1,599	6 Thailand	1,020
7 South Korea	1,517	7 Brazil	922
8 Russia	1,316	8 Indonesia	843
9 Vietnam	954	9 Germany	810
10 Germany	881	10 Malaysia	802

Cotton

Top 10 producers, 2014–15		*Top 10 consumers, 2014–15*	
'000 tonnes		*'000 tonnes*	
1 China	6,480	1 China	7,479
2 India	6,460	2 India	5,359
3 United States	3,553	3 Pakistan	2,506
4 Pakistan	2,305	4 Turkey	1,486
5 Brazil	1,551	5 Bangladesh	937
6 Uzbekistan	885	6 Vietnam	903
7 Turkey	754	7 Brazil	797
8 Australia	516	8 United States	778
9 Turkmenistan	330	9 Indonesia	711
10 Mexico	302	10 Mexico	405

Major oil seeds[a]

Top 5 producers, 2014–15		*Top 5 consumers, 2014–15*	
'000 tonnes		*'000 tonnes*	
1 United States	115,440	1 China	136,265
2 Brazil	100,101	2 United States	63,935
3 Argentina	64,336	3 EU28	50,915
4 China	47,270	4 Argentina	48,645
5 India	29,390	5 Brazil	45,650

Major vegetable oils[b]

Top 5 producers, 2014–15		*Top 5 consumers, 2014–15*	
'000 tonnes		*'000 tonnes*	
1 Indonesia	33,000	1 China	28,102
2 China	20,313	2 EU28	22,675
3 Malaysia	19,956	3 India	17,230
4 EU28	16,405	4 United States	12,256
5 Untied States	10,576	5 Indonesia	7,649

a Soyabeans, rapeseed (canola), cottonseed, sunflowerseed and groundnuts (peanuts).
b Palm, soyabean, rapeseed and sunflowerseed oil.
c Includes crude oil, shale oil, oil sands and natural gas liquids.   d Opec member.

Oil[c]

Top 10 producers, 2015
'000 barrels per day

1	United States	12,704
2	Saudi Arabia[d]	12,014
3	Russia	10,980
4	Canada	4,385
5	China	4,309
6	Iraq[d]	4,031
7	Iran[d]	3,920
8	United Arab Emirates[d]	3,902
9	Kuwait[d]	3,096
10	Venezuela[d]	2,626

Top 10 consumers, 2015
'000 barrels per day

1	United States	19,396
2	China	11,968
3	India	4,159
4	Japan	4,150
5	Saudi Arabia[d]	3,895
6	Brazil	3,157
7	Russia	3,113
8	South Korea	2,575
9	Germany	2,338
10	Canada	2,322

Natural gas

Top 10 producers, 2015
Billion cubic metres

1	United States	767.3
2	Russia	573.3
3	Iran[d]	192.5
4	Qatar[d]	181.4
5	Canada	163.5
6	China	138.0
7	Norway	117.2
8	Saudi Arabia[d]	106.4
9	Algeria[d]	83.0
10	Indonesia[d]	75.0

Top 10 consumers, 2015
Billion cubic metres

1	United States	778.0
2	Russia	391.5
3	China	197.3
4	Iran[d]	191.2
5	Japan	113.4
6	Saudi Arabia[d]	106.4
7	Canada	102.5
8	Mexico	83.2
9	Germany	74.6
10	United Arab Emirates[d]	69.1

Coal

Top 10 producers, 2015
Million tonnes oil equivalent

1	China	1,827.0
2	United States	455.2
3	India	283.9
4	Australia	275.0
5	Indonesia	241.1
6	Russia	184.5
7	South Africa	142.9
8	Colombia	55.6
9	Poland	53.7
10	Kazakhstan	45.8

Top 10 consumers, 2015
Million tonnes oil equivalent

1	China	1,920.4
2	United States	396.3
3	India	407.2
4	Japan	119.4
5	Russia	88.7
6	South Africa	85.0
7	South Korea	84.5
8	Indonesia	80.3
9	Germany	78.3
10	Poland	49.8

Oil reserves[c]

Top proved reserves, end 2015
% of world total

1	Venezuela[d]	17.7	6	Kuwait[d]	6.0
2	Saudi Arabia[d]	15.7		Russia	6.0
3	Canada	10.1	8	United Arab Emirates[d]	5.8
4	Iran[d]	9.3	9	United States	3.2
5	Iraq[d]	8.4	10	Libya[d]	2.8

Energy

Largest producers
Million tonnes of oil equivalent, 2013

1	China	2,614	16	Norway	192
2	United States	1,881	17	Kuwait	171
3	Russia	1,340	18	Kazakhstan	169
4	Saudi Arabia	615	19	South Africa	166
5	India	523	20	Iraq	158
6	Indonesia	460	21	Algeria	138
7	Canada	435	22	France	136
8	Australia	344	23	Colombia	126
9	Iran	299	24	Germany	120
10	Nigeria	256	25	United Kingdom	110
11	Brazil	253	26	Angola	98
12	Qatar	224	27	Malaysia	95
13	Mexico	217	28	Ukraine	86
14	United Arab Emirates	202	29	Egypt	83
15	Venezuela	192	30	Thailand	78

Largest consumers
Million tonnes of oil equivalent, 2013

1	China	3,022	16	Italy	155
2	United States	2,188	17	South Africa	141
3	India	775	18	Nigeria	134
4	Russia	731		Thailand	134
5	Japan	455	20	Australia	129
6	Germany	318	21	Spain	117
7	Brazil	294		Turkey	117
8	South Korea	264	23	Ukraine	116
9	Canada	253	24	Poland	98
	France	253	25	Malaysia	89
11	Iran	228	26	Pakistan	86
12	Indonesia	214	27	Kazakhstan	82
13	Saudi Arabia	192	28	Argentina	81
14	Mexico	191	29	Egypt	78
	United Kingdom	191	30	Netherlands	77

Energy efficiency[a]
GDP per unit of energy use, 2013

Most efficient			Least efficient		
1	South Sudan	32.8	1	Trinidad & Tobago	2.1
2	Hong Kong	26.6	2	Zimbabwe	2.2
3	Sri Lanka	21.0	3	Congo-Kinshasa	2.3
4	Cuba	19.4		Iceland	2.3
5	Colombia	18.4	5	Mozambique	2.5
6	Panama	18.0	6	Ethiopia	2.6
7	Malta	16.6	7	Turkmenistan	2.7
	Switzerland	16.6	8	Togo	2.9
9	Dominican Rep.	16.3	9	Ukraine	3.3
	Ireland	16.3	10	Uzbekistan	3.5
11	Singapore	16.1			

a 2011 PPP $ per kg of oil equivalent.

Net energy importers
% of commercial energy use, 2013 or latest

Highest			Lowest		
1	Hong Kong	99	1	South Sudan	-672
	Malta	99	2	Angola	-538
3	Singapore	98	3	Congo-Brazzaville	-513
4	Jordan	97	4	Norway	-486
	Lebanon	97	5	Gabon	-478
	Luxembourg	97	6	Brunei	-458
7	Cyprus	94	7	Qatar	-457
	Japan	94	8	Kuwait	-386
9	Moldova	90	9	Azerbaijan	-328
	Morocco	90	10	Colombia	-297
11	Dominican Rep.	86	11	Libya	-263
12	Belarus	85	12	Saudi Arabia	-220

Largest consumption per person
Kg of oil equivalent, 2013

1	Qatar	19,120	12	Saudi Arabia	6,363
2	Iceland	18,177	13	Oman	6,232
3	Trinidad & Tobago	14,538	14	Finland	6,075
4	Bahrain	10,172	15	Australia	5,586
5	Kuwait	9,757	16	South Korea	5,253
6	United Arab Emirates	7,691	17	Sweden	5,132
7	Brunei	7,393	18	Russia	5,093
8	Luxembourg	7,310	19	Belgium	5,039
9	Canada	7,202	20	Turkmenistan	5,012
10	United States	6,914	21	Singapore	4,833
11	Norway	6,439	22	Kazakhstan	4,787

Sources of electricity
% of total, 2013 or latest

Oil			Gas		
1	South Sudan	99.6	1	Bahrain	100.0
2	Benin	99.4		Qatar	100.0
	Eritrea	99.4		Turkmenistan	100.0
4	Malta	98.3	4	Trinidad & Tobago	99.6
5	Lebanon	93.4	5	Brunei	99.0

Hydropower			Nuclear power		
1	Albania	100.0	1	France	74.7
	Paraguay	100.0	2	Slovakia	55.1
3	Nepal	99.7	3	Belgium	51.9
	Tajikistan	99.7	4	Hungary	50.8
	Zambia	99.7	5	Sweden	43.4

Coal			Renewables excl. hydropower		
1	Kosovo	97.6	1	Denmark	46.0
2	South Africa	93.7	2	Nicaragua	41.4
3	Mongolia	92.9	3	El Salvador	33.5
4	Botswana	87.3	4	Portugal	31.1
5	Poland	85.2	5	Iceland	29.0

Labour markets

Labour-force participation
% of working-age population[a] working or looking for work, 2015

Highest

1	Madagascar	86.4
2	Uganda	85.0
3	Rwanda	84.9
4	Qatar	84.6
5	Eritrea	83.9
6	Burundi	83.7
7	Burkina Faso	83.5
8	Ethiopia	83.0
	Nepal	83.0
10	Zimbabwe	82.4
11	Guinea	82.3
12	Equatorial Guinea	82.0
13	Malawi	81.0
14	Cambodia	80.9
	Togo	80.9
16	United Arab Emirates	80.1
17	North Korea	79.5
18	Mozambique	79.1
19	Tanzania	78.6
20	Vietnam	78.3
21	Central African Rep.	78.0
	Myanmar	78.0
23	Botswana	77.4
	Laos	77.4
25	Gambia, The	77.3
26	Ghana	77.0
27	Cameroon	76.0
28	Zambia	75.3

Lowest

1	Jordan	40.0
2	Timor-Leste	41.3
3	Syria	41.7
4	Moldova	42.0
5	Iraq	42.4
	Puerto Rico	42.4
7	Algeria	43.7
	West Bank & Gaza	43.7
9	Iran	44.5
10	Bosnia & Herz.	46.1
11	Lebanon	47.0
12	Mauritania	47.2
13	Tunisia	47.7
14	Sudan	48.1
15	Italy	48.4
16	Gabon	48.8
17	Montenegro	48.9
18	Morocco	49.2
19	Egypt	49.4
20	Yemen	49.6
21	Albania	50.3
	Turkey	50.3
23	Martinique	51.2
24	Serbia	51.5
25	Greece	51.7
26	Sri Lanka	51.8
	Swaziland	51.8

Most male workforce
Highest % men in workforce, 2015

1	United Arab Emirates	87.9
2	Oman	87.1
3	Syria	85.5
4	Qatar	85.0
5	Saudi Arabia	84.9
6	Jordan	82.7
7	Afghanistan	82.5
8	Iraq	82.2
9	Iran	81.9
10	Algeria	80.8
11	Bahrain	80.1
12	West Bank & Gaza	79.8
13	Pakistan	77.9
14	Egypt	77.0
15	India	75.8
16	Lebanon	75.2

Most female workforce
Highest % women in workforce, 2015

1	Martinique	55.5
2	Mozambique	54.5
	Rwanda	54.5
4	Burundi	51.7
5	Guadeloupe	51.5
6	Togo	51.3
7	Laos	51.1
8	Nepal	50.8
9	Malawi	50.6
10	Congo-Kinshasa	50.1
	Ghana	50.1
12	Lithuania	50.0
13	Myanmar	49.8
14	Barbados	49.7
15	Latvia	49.6
16	Sierra Leone	49.5

a Aged 15 and over.

Highest rate of unemployment

% of labour force[a], 2015

1	Mauritania	31.1	23	Iraq	16.9
2	Bosnia & Herz.	30.3	24	Armenia	16.3
3	Réunion	30.2	25	Croatia	16.1
4	Gambia, The	30.1		French Polynesia	16.1
5	Lesotho	27.5	27	Yemen	15.9
6	Macedonia	26.9	28	New Caledonia	15.8
7	Guadeloupe	26.2	29	Cyprus	15.6
8	West Bank & Gaza	25.9	30	Tunisia	14.8
9	Swaziland	25.6	31	Bahamas	14.4
10	Namibia	25.5		Dominican Rep.	14.4
11	South Africa	25.1	33	Jamaica	13.7
12	Greece	24.9	34	Puerto Rico	13.6
13	French Guiana	23.8		Sudan	13.6
14	Martinique	23.2	36	Jordan	12.8
15	Spain	22.4	37	Barbados	12.3
16	Mozambique	22.3		Georgia	12.3
17	Libya	20.6		Syria	12.3
18	Gabon	20.5	40	Egypt	12.1
19	Serbia	19.0		Italy	12.1
20	Botswana	18.6		Portugal	12.1
21	Montenegro	18.2	43	Slovakia	11.3
22	Albania	17.3	44	Guyana	11.2

Highest rate of youth unemployment

% of labour force[a] aged 15–24, 2015

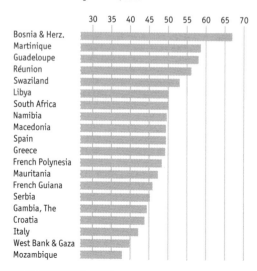

a ILO definition.

Minimum wage
As % of the median wage of full-time workers[a], 2014

1	Turkey	67.7	15	Lithuania	49.4
2	Chile	67.6	16	United Kingdom	48.0
3	France	61.1	17	Netherlands	47.7
4	Slovenia	60.9	18	Slovakia	47.5
5	New Zealand	59.6	19	Greece	46.1
6	Portugal	57.5	20	South Korea	45.8
7	Luxembourg	56.6	21	Canada	45.1
8	Israel	56.3	22	Ireland	43.1
9	Hungary	53.6	23	Estonia	41.5
10	Australia	53.3	24	Spain	41.4
11	Romania	53.1	25	Japan	38.9
12	Latvia	50.8	26	Mexico	37.5
13	Belgium	50.5	27	Czech Republic	36.8
14	Poland	50.2	28	United States	36.7

Average hours worked
Per employed person per week, 2014

1	Qatar	50.0	14	Kosovo	41.7
2	Pakistan	47.8		Macedonia	41.7
3	Turkey	47.1	16	Sri Lanka	41.6
4	Macau	47.0	17	Dominican Rep.	41.3
5	Malaysia	46.1	18	Bosnia & Herz.	41.0
6	South Africa	45.0	19	Greece	40.9
7	Thailand	44.9	20	Poland	40.4
8	Singapore	44.3	21	Bulgaria	40.1
9	Hong Kong	44.0	22	Iceland	39.9
10	South Africa	43.8	23	Chile	39.4
11	Guatemala	43.3		Czech Republic	39.4
12	Mexico	42.4		Serbia	39.4
13	Algeria	42.2			

Poverty pay
% of workers paid $2 or less per day, 2014

1	Madagascar	94.8	16	Mozambique	65.6
2	Liberia	93.1	17	Bangladesh	65.3
3	Central African Rep.	91.4	18	Tanzania	64.9
4	Burundi	89.3	19	Benin	64.5
5	Congo-Kinshasa	89.0	20	Zimbabwe	64.2
6	Afghanistan	88.6	21	Togo	63.3
7	Malawi	83.3	22	Sierra Leone	62.8
8	Guinea-Bissau	80.6	23	Laos	59.7
9	Mali	79.6	24	Burkina Faso	58.8
10	Zambia	73.7	25	Senegal	57.8
11	Guinea	73.2	26	Uganda	55.5
12	Rwanda	71.6	27	India	54.8
13	Eritrea	71.3	28	Chad	53.6
14	Nigeria	70.7	29	Ethiopia	53.3
15	Niger	68.2		Congo-Brazzaville	53.3

a OECD countries.

Business costs and foreign direct investment

Office rents

Rent, taxes and operating expenses, Q3 2015, $ per sq. ft.

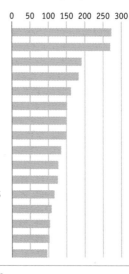

	0 50 100 150 200 250 300
London (West End), UK	
Hong Kong (Central)	
Beijing (Finance St.), China	
Beijing (CBD), China	
Hong Kong (West Kowloon)	
New Delhi (CBD), India	
Tokyo (Marunouchi Otemachi), Japan	
London (City), UK	
Shanghai (Pudong), China	
New York (Midtown Manhattan), US	
Moscow, Russia	
San Francisco (Downtown), US	
Shanghai (Puxi), China	
Paris, France	
Boston (Downtown), US	
Singapore	

Foreign direct investment[a]

Inflows, $m, 2014

1	China	128,500
2	Hong Kong	103,254
3	United States	92,397
4	United Kingdom	72,241
5	Singapore	67,523
6	Brazil	62,495
7	Canada	53,864
8	Australia	51,854
9	India	34,417
10	Netherlands	30,253
11	Chile	22,949
12	Spain	22,904
13	Mexico	22,795
14	Indonesia	22,580
15	Switzerland	21,914
16	Russia	20,958
17	Finland	18,625
18	Colombia	16,054
19	France	15,191
20	Poland	13,883
21	Thailand	12,566
22	Turkey	12,146

Outflows, $m, 2014

1	United States	336,943
2	Hong Kong	142,700
3	China	116,000
4	Japan	113,629
5	Germany	112,227
6	Russia	56,438
7	Canada	52,620
8	France	42,869
9	Netherlands	40,809
10	Singapore	40,660
11	Ireland	31,795
12	Spain	30,688
13	South Korea	30,558
14	Italy	23,451
15	Norway	19,247
16	Switzerland	16,798
17	Malaysia	16,445
18	Kuwait	13,108
19	Chile	12,999
20	Taiwan	12,697
21	Sweden	12,156
22	Denmark	10,952

Note: CBD is Central Business District.
a Investment in companies in a foreign country.

Business creativity and research

Entrepreneurial activity

Percentage of population aged 18–64 who are either a nascent entrepreneur[a] or owner-manager of a new business, average 2010–15

Highest			Lowest		
1	Senegal	38.6	1	Bulgaria	3.5
2	Zambia	38.0	2	Suriname	3.6
3	Nigeria	36.6	3	Italy	3.9
4	Bolivia	33.0	4	Japan	4.0
5	Ghana	32.1		Kosovo	4.0
6	Uganda	31.9	6	Morocco	4.4
7	Malawi	31.8	7	Russia	4.7
8	Cameroon	31.4	8	Denmark	4.8
9	Lebanon	30.2	9	Germany	5.0
10	Ecuador	30.0	10	Belgium	5.2
11	Botswana	28.6	11	France	5.3
12	Angola	25.8	12	Malaysia	5.4
13	Burkina Faso	25.7		Slovenia	5.4
	Namibia	25.7		Spain	5.4
15	Peru	24.1	15	Finland	5.9
16	Chile	23.4	16	United Arab Emirates	6.2
17	Colombia	21.2	17	Norway	6.5
18	Indonesia	19.1		Sweden	6.5
19	Thailand	18.6	19	Greece	6.7
20	Philippines	18.0		Switzerland	6.7
21	El Salvador	17.4	21	Macedonia	6.9
22	Trinidad & Tobago	17.3	22	Tunisia	7.0
23	Brazil	17.2	23	Belize	7.1
	Guatemala	17.2	24	Georgia	7.2

Brain drain[b]

Highest, 2015			Lowest, 2015		
1	Serbia	1.7	1	Switzerland	5.8
	Venezuela	1.7	2	Qatar	5.7
3	Moldova	1.9		United States	5.7
	Myanmar	1.9	4	Norway	5.5
5	Bosnia & Herz.	2.0		United Arab Emirates	5.5
	Burundi	2.0	6	Singapore	5.4
7	Bulgaria	2.1	7	Finland	5.3
	Croatia	2.1		Malaysia	5.3
	Haiti	2.1		United Kingdom	5.3
10	Romania	2.3	10	Hong Kong	5.2
	Mauritania	2.3	11	Netherlands	5.1
12	Macedonia	2.4	12	Luxembourg	5.0
	Zimbabwe	2.4	13	Canada	4.9
14	Algeria	2.5		Germany	4.9
	Guinea	2.5		Sweden	4.9
	Hungary	2.5	16	Chile	4.8
	Kyrgyzstan	2.5		Bahrain	4.8
	Slovakia	2.5	18	Panama	4.7

a An individual who has started a new firm which has not paid wages for over three months.
b Scores: 1 = talented people leave for other countries; 7 = they stay and pursue opportunities in the country.

Total expenditure on R&D

$bn, 2014

1	United States[a]	457.0
2	China	211.9
3	Japan	164.9
4	Germany	109.9
5	France	63.8
6	South Korea	60.5
7	United Kingdom	50.8
8	Brazil[a]	39.7
9	Australia[a]	32.3
10	Canada	28.8
11	Italy	27.6
12	Russia	22.1
13	Switzerland[b]	19.7
14	India	18.3
15	Sweden	18.1
16	Netherlands	17.3
17	Spain	16.9
18	Taiwan	15.9
19	Belgium	13.1
20	Austria	13.0

% of GDP, 2014

1	South Korea	4.29
2	Israel	4.13
3	Japan	3.59
4	Finland	3.17
5	Sweden	3.16
6	Denmark	3.05
7	Taiwan	3.00
8	Austria	2.99
9	Switzerland[b]	2.97
10	Germany	2.84
11	United States[a]	2.74
12	Belgium	2.46
13	Slovenia	2.39
14	Venezuela[c]	2.37
15	France	2.26
16	Australia[a]	2.15
17	China	2.04
18	Singapore[a]	2.01
19	Czech Republic	2.00
20	Netherlands	1.97

Innovation index[d]

2015, 100=maximum score ● Overall ○ Inputs ● Outputs

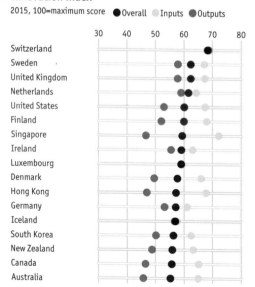

a 2013 b 2012 c 2011
d The innovation index averages countries' capacity for innovation (inputs) and success in innovation (outputs), based on 79 indicators.

Businesses and banks

Largest non-financial companies

By market capitalisation, $bn, end December 2015

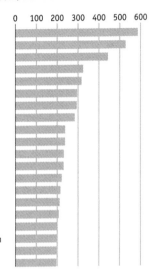

	0	100	200	300	400	500	600

- Apple, US
- Alphabet, US
- Microsoft, US
- Exxon Mobil, US
- Amazon, US
- Facebook, US
- General Electric, US
- Johnson & Johnson, US
- Roche, Switzerland
- Nestlé, Switzerland
- Novartis, Switzerland
- China Mobile, China
- PetroChina, China
- Procter & Gamble, US
- AT&T, US
- Toyota Motor, Japan
- Alibaba, China
- Anheuser-Busch, Belgium
- Pfizer, US
- Walmart, US

By net profit, $bn, 2015

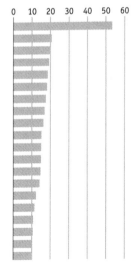

	0	10	20	30	40	50	60

- Apple, US
- Surgutneftegas, Russia
- Exxon Mobil, US
- Toyota Motor, Japan
- Samsung Electronics, S. Korea
- Novartis, Switzerland
- China Mobile, China
- Gilead Sciences, US
- Alphabet, US
- Nestlé, Switzerland
- Walmart, US
- GlaxoSmithKline, UK
- Johnson & Johnson, US
- IBM, US
- Microsoft, US
- Intel, US
- Merck, US
- KEPCO, S. Korea
- Verizon Communications, US
- TSMC, Taiwan

Largest banks
By market capitalisation, $bn, end December 2015

1	Wells Fargo	United States	277.7
2	JPMorgan Chase	United States	243.1
3	Industrial & Commercial Bank of China	China	242.8
4	Bank of America	United States	175.2
5	China Construction Bank	China	173.3
6	Bank of China	China	167.6
7	Agricultural Bank of China	China	159.0
8	HSBC	United Kingdom	155.5
9	Citigroup	United States	154.2
10	Commonwealth Bank of Australia	Australia	106.5
11	Mitsubishi UFJ	Japan	89.2
12	Westpac Banking	Australia	81.6
13	Royal Bank of Canada	Canada	81.2
14	Lloyds Banking Group	United Kingdom	79.6
15	UBS	Switzerland	76.9

By assets, $bn, end December 2015

1	Industrial & Commercial Bank of China	China	3,476
2	China Construction Bank	China	2,882
3	Agricultural Bank of China	China	2,785
4	Bank of China	China	2,622
5	HSBC	United Kingdom	2,549
6	JPMorgan Chase	United States	2,417
7	BNP Paribas	France	2,385
8	Bank of America	United States	2,153
9	Deutsche Bank	Germany	1,923
10	Barclays	United Kingdom	1,871
11	Citigroup	United States	1,808
12	Wells Fargo	United States	1,751
13	Japan Post	Japan	1,732
14	Crédit Agricole	France	1,704
15	Mizuho	Japan	1,606

Largest sovereign-wealth funds
By assets, $bn, April 2016

1	Government Pension Fund, Norway	848
2	Abu Dhabi Investment Authority, UAE	773
3	China Investment Corporation	747
4	SAMA Foreign Holdings, Saudi Arabia	632
5	Kuwait Investment Authority	592
6	SAFE Investment Company, China[a]	474
7	Hong Kong Monetary Authority Investment Portfolio	442
8	Government of Singapore Investment Corporation	344
9	Qatar Investment Authority	256
10	China National Social Security Fund	236

Note: Countries listed refer to the company's domicile.
a Estimate.

Stockmarkets

Largest market capitalisation
$bn, end 2015

1	NYSE	17,787
2	Nasdaq – US	7,281
3	Japan Exchange Group	4,895
4	Shanghai SE	4,549
5	London SE Group	3,879
6	Shenzhen SE	3,639
7	Euronext	3,306
8	Hong Kong Exchanges	3,185
9	Deutsche Börse	1,716
10	TMX Group	1,592
11	SIX Swiss Exchange	1,519
12	BSE India	1,516
13	National Stock Exchange of India	1,485
14	NASDAQ OMX Nordic Exchange[a]	1,268
15	Korea Exchange[b]	1,231
16	Australian Securities Exchange[c]	1,187
17	BME Spanish Exchanges	787
18	Taiwan SE Corp.	745
19	Johannesburg SE	736
20	Singapore Exchange	640
21	BM&F BOVESPA	491
22	Saudi SE – Tadawul	421
23	Mexican Exchange	402
24	Moscow Exchange	393
25	Bursa Malaysia	383
26	Indonesia SE	353
27	Stock Exchange of Thailand	349
28	Tel-Aviv SE	244
29	Philippine SE	239
30	Oslo Bors	194
31	Santiago SE	190
32	Borsa Istanbul	189
33	Qatar SE	143
34	Warsaw SE	138
35	Irish SE	128
36	Abu Dhabi Securities Exchange	112
37	Wiener Börse	96
38	Tehran SE	89
39	Colombia SE	86
40	Dubai Financial Market	84

Stockmarket gains and losses
$ terms, % change December 31st 2014 to December 31st 2015

Largest gains

1	Colombia (IGBC)	36.1
2	Greece (Athex Comp)	30.9
3	Egypt (Case 30)	27.4
4	Saudi Arabia (Tadawul)	20.6
5	Turkey (BIST)	19.5
6	Singapore (STI)	16.7
7	Thailand (SET)	16.3
8	Brazil (BVSP)	15.4
9	Indonesia (JSX)	13.8
10	Canada (S&P TSX)	12.5
11	Taiwan (TWI)	11.6
12	Poland (WIG)	10.6
13	Spain (Madrid SE)	8.0
14	Hong Kong (Hang Seng)	7.7
15	India (BSE)	5.3
16	United Kingdom (FTSE 100)	5.2
17	Malaysia (KLSE)	4.1
18	Chile (IGPA)	4.0
19	United States (DJIA)	2.3
20	Switzerland (SMI)	1.9

Largest losses

1	Venezuela (IBC)	-73.5
2	China (SSEB, $ terms)	-34.9
3	Hungary (BUX)	-30.5
4	Argentina (MERV)	-26.5
5	Denmark (OMXCB)	-25.5
6	Russia (RTS, $ terms)	-14.2
7	Belgium (Bel 20)	-11.2
	Italy (FTSE/MIB)	-11.2
9	Austria (ATX)	-9.9
10	Japan (Topix)	-9.0
11	Germany (DAX)[d]	-8.7
12	China (SSEA)	-8.5
13	Japan (Nikkei 225)	-8.3
14	France (CAC 40)	-7.9
15	United States (NAScomp)	-5.4
16	Euro area (FTSE Euro 100)	-5.2
17	Europe (FTSEurofirst 300)	-4.8
18	Norway (OSEAX)	-4.5
19	Netherlands (AEX)	-3.9
20	Euro area (EURO STOXX 50)	-3.7

a Copenhagen, Helsinki, Iceland, Stockholm, Tallinn, Riga and Vilnius stock exchanges.
b Includes Kosdaq. c Includes investment funds. d Total return index.

Value traded[a]

$bn, 2015

1	Nasdaq – US	32,984		17	NASDAQ OMX Nordic Exchange[d]	837
2	Shanghai SE	21,389		18	National Stock Exchange of India	677
3	NYSE	19,991		19	Taiwan SE Corp.	638
4	Shenzhen SE	19,620		20	BM&F BOVESPA	498
5	BATS Global Markets – US	14,217		21	Saudi SE – Tadawul	443
6	Japan Exchange Group	6,157		22	Johannesburg SE	389
7	BATS Chi-x Europe	3,567		23	Borsa Istanbul	375
8	London SE Group	3,438		24	Stock Exchange of Thailand	297
9	Euronext	2,126		25	Singapore Exchange	203
10	Hong Kong Exchanges	2,126		26	Taipei Exchange	179
11	Korea Exchange[b]	1,954		27	Moscow Exchange	150
12	Deutsche Börse	1,579		28	Oslo Bors	139
13	TMX Group	1,185		29	Bursa Malaysia	130
14	BME Spanish Exchanges	1,048		30	Mexican Exchange	127
15	SIX Swiss Exchange	996		31	BSE India	122
16	Australian Securities Exchange[c]	898		32	Indonesia SE	105
				33	Warsaw SE	62
				34	Tel-Aviv SE	61

Number of listed companies[e]

End 2015

1	BSE India	5,836		20	Taipei Exchange	712
2	BME Spanish Exchanges	3,651		21	Stock Exchange of Thailand	639
3	TMX Group	3,559		22	Deutsche Börse	619
4	Japan Exchange Group	3,513		23	Indonesia SE	521
5	Nasdaq – US	2,859		24	Tel-Aviv SE	461
6	London SE Group	2,685		25	Borsa Istanbul	393
7	NYSE	2,424		26	Johannesburg SE	382
8	Australian Securities Exchange[c]	2,108		27	BM&F BOVESPA	359
9	Korea Exchange[b]	1,961		28	Tehran SE	318
10	Hong Kong Exchanges	1,866		29	Santiago SE	310
11	National Stock Exchange of India	1,794			Lima SE	310
12	Shenzhen SE	1,746		31	Ho Chi Minh City SE	307
13	Shanghai SE	1,081		32	Colombo SE	294
14	Euronext	1,068		33	SIX Swiss Exchange	270
15	Warsaw SE	905		34	Philippine SE	265
16	Bursa Malaysia	902		35	Moscow Exchange	254
17	Taiwan SE Corp.	896		36	Egyptian Exchange	252
18	NASDAQ OMX Nordic Exchange[d]	832		37	Athens SE	240
19	Singapore Exchange	769		38	Amman SE	228
				39	Oslo Bors	214
				40	Luxembourg SE	192

Note: Figures are not entirely comparable due to different reporting rules and calculations. a Includes electronic and negotiated deals. b Includes Kosdaq. c Includes investment funds. d Copenhagen, Helsinki, Iceland, Stockholm, Tallinn, Riga and Vilnius stock exchanges. e Domestic and foreign.

Public finance

Government debt
As % of GDP, 2015

1	Japan	229.2	16	Iceland	81.6
2	Greece	190.0	17	Netherlands	80.8
3	Italy	160.7	18	Germany	78.5
4	Portugal	148.9	19	Finland	73.3
5	Belgium	130.5	20	Poland	66.9
6	France	120.1	21	Israel	66.1
7	Ireland	120.0	22	Slovakia	59.6
8	Spain	118.9	23	Denmark	57.1
9	United Kingdom	116.4	24	Czech Republic	56.1
10	Euro area (15)	111.2	25	Sweden	53.9
11	United States	110.6	26	Switzerland	46.4
12	Austria	107.3	27	Australia	44.2
13	Slovenia	99.8	28	New Zealand	41.1
14	Hungary	99.6	29	Luxembourg	35.6
15	Canada	94.8	30	Norway	34.1

Government spending
As % of GDP, 2015

1	Finland	59.0	16	Iceland	43.8
2	France	57.1	17	United Kingdom	43.6
3	Denmark	56.8	18	Spain	42.8
4	Belgium	54.5	19	Czech Republic	42.6
5	Austria	51.7	20	Luxembourg	41.9
6	Italy	51.0	21	Poland	41.7
7	Sweden	50.5	22	Slovakia	41.5
8	Greece	50.2	23	Japan	41.2
9	Hungary	49.2	24	Israel	41.0
10	Euro area (15)	48.7	25	New Zealand	40.5
11	Portugal	47.8	26	Canada	40.1
12	Norway	47.7	27	Estonia	39.9
13	Slovenia	46.8	28	United States	37.9
14	Netherlands	44.9	29	Australia	36.4
15	Germany	43.9	30	Ireland	36.0

Tax revenue
As % of GDP, 2014

1	Denmark	50.9	14	Germany	36.1
2	France	45.2	15	Greece	35.9
3	Belgium	44.7	16	Portugal	34.4
4	Finland	43.9	17	Czech Republic	33.5
5	Italy	43.6	18	Spain	33.2
6	Austria	43.0	19	Estonia	32.9
7	Sweden	42.7	20	United Kingdom	32.6
8	Norway	39.1	21	New Zealand	32.4
9	Iceland	38.7	22	Poland[a]	31.9
10	Hungary	38.5	23	Israel	31.1
11	Luxembourg	37.8	24	Slovakia	31.0
12	Netherlands[a]	36.7	25	Canada	30.8
13	Slovenia	36.6	26	Japan[a]	30.3

Note: Includes only OECD countries.   a 2013

Democracy

Democracy index
Most democratic = 100, 2015

Most			Least		
1	Norway	88.1	1	Yemen	28.3
2	Switzerland	87.0	2	Syria	29.8
3	Sweden	86.6	3	Pakistan	38.2
4	Finland	86.0	4	Ivory Coast	38.9
5	Denmark	85.2	5	Togo	39.8
6	Netherlands	83.6	6	Egypt	40.2
7	Germany	82.0	7	Nigeria	40.6
8	New Zealand	81.8	8	China	40.8
9	Ireland	81.7	9	Guinea	41.2
10	Belgium	81.5	10	Mali	41.7
11	Austria	80.1	11	Bahrain	41.8
12	United Kingdom	80.0	12	Haiti	42.7
13	Australia	79.7	13	Burkina Faso	43.3
14	France	79.3	14	Mozambique	45.2
15	Canada	79.1	15	Morocco	45.3
16	United States	77.6	16	Russia	45.5
17	Portugal	76.1	17	Venezuela	45.7
	Slovenia	76.1	18	Niger	46.7
19	Spain	75.9	19	Kyrgyzstan	47.3
20	Japan	75.3	20	Zambia	48.1

Parliamentary seats
Lower or single house, seats per 100,000 population, April 2016

Most			Fewest		
1	Liechtenstein	66.6	1	India	0.04
2	Monaco	63.6	2	United States	0.13
3	Andorra	39.7	3	Pakistan	0.18
4	Iceland	19.1	4	Nigeria	0.20
5	Malta	16.7	5	Bangladesh	0.22
6	Montenegro	12.9		China	0.22
7	Equatorial Guinea	11.8		Indonesia	0.22
8	Barbados	10.6	8	Brazil	0.25
	Luxembourg	10.6	9	Philippines	0.29
10	Bahamas	9.8		Thailand	0.29

Women in parliament
Lower or single house, women as % of total seats, April 2016

1	Rwanda	63.8		Nicaragua	41.3
2	Bolivia	53.1	13	Spain	40.0
3	Cuba	48.9	14	Mozambique	39.6
4	Sweden	43.6		Norway	39.6
5	Senegal	42.7	16	Belgium	39.3
6	Mexico	42.4	17	Ethiopia	38.8
7	South Africa	42.1	18	Timor-Leste	38.5
8	Ecuador	41.6	19	Denmark	37.4
9	Finland	41.5	20	Netherlands	37.3
10	Iceland	41.3	21	Angola	36.8
	Namibia	41.3	22	Slovenia	36.7

Education

Primary enrolment
Number enrolled as % of relevant age group

Highest			Lowest		
1	Haiti	175	1	Eritrea	51
2	Madagascar	147	2	Sudan	69
	Malawi	147	3	Niger	71
4	Gabon	142	4	Mali	77
5	Rwanda	138	5	Syria	80
6	Timor-Leste	137	6	Senegal	81
7	Nepal	135	7	Equatorial Guinea	84
8	Sierra Leone	130		South Sudan	84
9	Angola	129	9	Guyana	85
10	Burundi	128	10	Gambia, The	86
11	Benin	126		Macedonia	86
12	Togo	125	12	Bermuda	87
13	Suriname	120		Burkina Faso	87
	Sweden	120		Tanzania	87
15	Algeria	119			

Highest secondary enrolment
Number enrolled as % of relevant age group

1	Belgium	163	12	New Zealand	117
2	Finland	143	13	Turkey	115
3	Australia	138	14	Norway	113
4	Netherlands	131	15	France	111
	Spain	131		Iceland	111
6	Denmark	130		Slovenia	111
7	Sweden	128	18	Canada	110
8	Ireland	126		Latvia	110
9	United Kingdom	124		Liechtenstein	110
10	Costa Rica	120		Uzbekistan	110
	Portugal	120			

Highest tertiary enrolment[a]
Number enrolled as % of relevant age group

1	Greece	110	11	Iceland	82
2	South Korea	95		Ukraine	82
3	Finland	91	13	Denmark	81
4	Belarus	89	14	Argentina	80
	United States	89		Austria	80
6	Australia	87		New Zealand	80
	Spain	87	17	Netherlands	79
8	Puerto Rico	85		Turkey	79
	Slovenia	85	19	Russia	78
10	Chile	84	20	Norway	76

Notes: Latest available year 2011–15. The gross enrolment ratios shown are the actual number enrolled as a percentage of the number of children in the official primary age group. They may exceed 100 when eg, children outside the primary age group are receiving primary education.

a Tertiary education includes all levels of post-secondary education including courses leading to awards not equivalent to a university degree, courses leading to a first university degree and postgraduate courses.

Least literate
% adult population

1	Niger	15.5		21	Rwanda	68.3
2	Guinea	25.3		22	India	69.3
3	Afghanistan	31.7		23	Uganda	70.2
4	Mali	33.6		24	Angola	70.8
5	Central African Rep.	36.8		25	Cameroon	71.3
6	Chad	38.2		26	Ghana	71.5
7	Ivory Coast	41.0		27	Eritrea	71.6
8	Senegal	42.8		28	Sudan	74.3
9	Sierra Leone	45.7		29	Congo-Kinshasa	75.0
10	Gambia, The	53.2		30	Egypt	75.1
11	Pakistan	56.8		31	Guatemala	77.0
12	Guinea-Bissau	57.8		32	Tanzania	79.0
13	Timor-Leste	58.3		33	Congo-Brazzaville	79.3
14	Nepal	59.6			Iraq	79.3
15	Bangladesh	59.7		35	Tunisia	79.7
16	Togo	60.4		36	Gabon	82.3
17	Malawi	61.3		37	Swaziland	83.1
18	Papua New Guinea	63.3		38	Iran	83.6
19	Morocco	67.1			Zimbabwe	83.6
20	Yemen	67.6		40	Syria	85.5

Education spending

As % of GDP, highest

As % of GDP, lowest

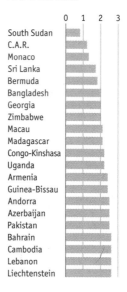

As % of GDP, highest	As % of GDP, lowest
Lithuania	South Sudan
Cuba	C.A.R.
Swaziland	Monaco
Denmark	Sri Lanka
Namibia	Bermuda
Sweden	Bangladesh
Moldova	Georgia
Norway	Zimbabwe
New Zealand	Macau
Finland	Madagascar
Bolivia	Congo-Kinshasa
Iceland	Uganda
Timor-Leste	Armenia
Malawi	Guinea-Bissau
Kyrgyzstan	Andorra
Malta	Azerbaijan
Niger	Pakistan
Barbados	Bahrain
Mozambique	Cambodia
Ukraine	Lebanon
Cyprus	Liechtenstein

Marriage and divorce

Highest marriage rates

Number of marriages per 1,000 population, 2014 or latest available year

1	Tajikistan	12.0	22	Lithuania	6.9
2	Lebanon	11.2		Moldova	6.9
3	Jordan	10.9	24	Georgia	6.8
4	Egypt	10.7		Macedonia	6.8
5	Uzbekistan	10.2		United States	6.8
6	Iran	10.1	27	Ukraine	6.7
7	Kazakhstan	9.9	28	Macau	6.6
8	West Bank & Gaza	9.7	29	Cyprus	6.4
9	China	9.6		Israel	6.4
10	Kyrgyzstan	9.4		South Korea	6.4
11	Azerbaijan	9.2	32	French Polynesia	6.3
	Belarus	9.2	33	Guyana	6.2
13	Guam	9.1		Montenegro	6.2
14	Russia	8.5	35	Malta	6.1
15	Albania	8.2	36	Armenia	6.0
16	Mauritius	7.9	37	Mongolia	5.8
	Turkey	7.9	38	Latvia	5.7
18	Hong Kong	7.7	39	Guatemala	5.6
19	Bermuda	7.6	40	Channel Islands[a]	5.5
20	Jamaica	7.5		Cuba	5.5
21	Singapore	7.3			

Lowest marriage rates

Number of marriages per 1,000 population, 2014 or latest available year

1	Qatar	1.8	23	Suriname	4.0
2	French Guiana	2.5	24	Czech Republic	4.1
3	Guadeloupe	2.8	25	Austria	4.3
	Uruguay	2.8		Estonia	4.3
5	Argentina	2.9		New Zealand	4.3
	Peru	2.9	28	Kuwait	4.4
7	Bulgaria	3.0	29	Croatia	4.5
	Slovenia	3.0		United Kingdom	4.5
9	Portugal	3.1	31	Dominican Rep.	4.6
10	Italy	3.2		Finland	4.6
	Luxembourg	3.2		Germany	4.6
	Martinique	3.2		Greece	4.6
13	Spain	3.3		Iceland	4.6
	Venezuela	3.3	36	Norway	4.7
15	New Caledonia	3.4		Poland	4.7
	Panama	3.4		Puerto Rico	4.7
17	France	3.5		Slovakia	4.7
18	Belgium	3.6	40	Bosnia & Herz.	4.8
19	Andorra	3.7		Ireland	4.8
	Chile	3.7	42	Denmark	4.9
	Hungary	3.7		Mexico	4.9
22	Netherlands	3.8		Switzerland	4.9

Note: The data are based on latest available figures (no earlier than 2010) and hence will be affected by the population age structure at the time. Marriage rates refer to registered marriages only and, therefore, reflect the customs surrounding registry and efficiency of administration.   a Jersey and Guernsey only.

Highest divorce rates

Number of divorces per 1,000 population, 2014 or latest available year

1	Guam	4.6	15	Czech Republic	2.7
2	Russia	4.5	16	Belgium	2.5
3	Belarus	3.8		Estonia	2.5
4	Ukraine	3.6		Finland	2.5
5	Latvia	3.5	19	Liechtenstein	2.4
6	Denmark	3.4	20	Costa Rica	2.3
	Lithuania	3.4		South Korea	2.3
8	Puerto Rico	3.3	22	Cyprus	2.2
9	Kazakhstan	3.0		Portugal	2.2
	Moldova	3.0	24	Australia	2.1
11	Cuba	2.9		Germany	2.1
	Jordan	2.9		Luxembourg	2.1
13	Sweden	2.8		Macau	2.1
	United States	2.8		Switzerland	2.1

Lowest divorce rates

Number of divorces per 1,000 population, 2014 or latest available year

1	Chile	0.1		Tajikistan	1.0
2	Guatemala	0.3	16	Panama	1.1
3	Bosnia & Herz.	0.4		Serbia	1.1
4	Peru	0.5		Slovenia	1.1
5	Ireland	0.6		Suriname	1.1
6	Qatar	0.7	20	Azerbaijan	1.2
7	Malta	0.8		Bahamas	1.2
	Montenegro	0.8		Greece	1.2
	Uzbekistan	0.8		New Caledonia	1.2
10	Italy	0.9	24	Albania	1.3
	Jamaica	0.9		Mongolia	1.3
	Mexico	0.9	26	Croatia	1.4
13	Armenia	1.0		Romania	1.4
	Macedonia	1.0	28	Bulgaria	1.5

Mean age of women at first marriage

Years, 2012 or latest available year[a]

Youngest			Oldest		
1	Niger	15.7	1	Sweden	32.9
2	Bangladesh	16.0	2	Denmark	32.1
	Chad	16.0		Iceland	32.1
4	Guinea	16.5	4	Ireland	31.2
5	Mali	16.7	5	Norway	31.0
6	Sierra Leone	17.1		Spain	31.0
7	Ethiopia	17.4	7	Netherlands	30.4
8	Mozambique	17.5	8	Finland	30.3
9	India	17.8		Germany	30.3
10	Burkina Faso	17.9	10	Italy	30.1
	Malawi	17.9	11	France	30.0
	Nepal	17.9	12	Luxembourg	29.9
13	Afghanistan	18.0		United Kingdom	29.9

a No earlier than 2000.

Households, living costs and giving

Number of households
Biggest, m, 2014

1	China	445.8		17	Iran	23.6
2	India	263.3		18	Egypt	22.7
3	United States	123.0		19	Philippines	22.3
4	Indonesia	64.5		20	Thailand	22.1
5	Brazil	61.2		21	Ethiopia	21.3
6	Russia	56.1		22	Turkey	20.8
7	Japan	52.9		23	Spain	18.6
8	Germany	41.3		24	South Korea	18.5
9	Nigeria	37.2		25	Ukraine	17.7
10	Bangladesh	36.5		26	South Africa	15.1
11	Mexico	32.2		27	Canada	13.9
12	France	29.1		28	Poland	13.6
13	Pakistan	27.5		29	Argentina	13.3
14	United Kingdom	27.0		30	Colombia	13.0
15	Italy	26.9		31	Congo-Kinshasa	11.1
16	Vietnam	26.4		32	Myanmar	10.9

Average household size, by number of people

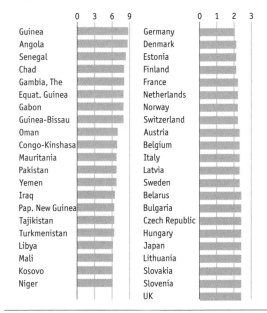

Biggest, 2014

	0	3	6	9
Guinea				
Angola				
Senegal				
Chad				
Gambia, The				
Equat. Guinea				
Gabon				
Guinea-Bissau				
Oman				
Congo-Kinshasa				
Mauritania				
Pakistan				
Yemen				
Iraq				
Pap. New Guinea				
Tajikistan				
Turkmenistan				
Libya				
Mali				
Kosovo				
Niger				

Smallest, 2014

	0	1	2	3
Germany				
Denmark				
Estonia				
Finland				
France				
Netherlands				
Norway				
Switzerland				
Austria				
Belgium				
Italy				
Latvia				
Sweden				
Belarus				
Bulgaria				
Czech Republic				
Hungary				
Japan				
Lithuania				
Slovakia				
Slovenia				
UK				

a The cost of living index shown is compiled by the Economist Intelligence Unit for use by companies in determining expatriate compensation: it is a comparison of the cost of maintaining a typical international lifestyle in the country rather than a comparison of the purchasing power of a citizen of the country. The index is based on typical urban prices an international executive and family will face abroad. The prices

Cost of living[a]

December 2015, US = 100

Highest			Lowest		
1	Singapore	116	1	Zambia	41
2	Hong Kong	114	2	Algeria	44
3	Switzerland	108		Kazakhstan	44
4	France	107		Pakistan	44
5	United Kingdom	101	5	India	45
6	United States	100	6	Syria	46
7	Denmark	99		Venezuela	46
	South Korea	99	8	Romania	47
9	Japan	97	9	Iran	48
10	Norway	96		Nepal	48
11	Israel	95		Ukraine	48
12	Finland	93	12	Nigeria	50
13	Austria	91		South Africa	50
14	Australia	90	14	Paraguay	51
15	Ireland	87	15	Brazil	53
16	Iceland	84		Russia	53
	Jordan	84	17	Bulgaria	54
18	China	83		Panama	54
19	Italy	82	19	Colombia	55
20	Belgium	81		Hungary	55
	Spain	81		Saudi Arabia	55
22	New Caledonia	80	22	Senegal	56
	New Zealand	80		Serbia	56
	Sweden	80			
25	Germany	78			
26	Canada	77			

World Giving Index[b]

Top givers, % of population, 2015

1	Myanmar	66	15	Guatemala	49
2	New Zealand	61		Kyrgyzstan	49
	United States	61		Norway	49
4	Canada	60	18	Thailand	48
5	Australia	59	19	Germany	47
6	United Kingdom	57		Jamaica	47
7	Ireland	56	21	Austria	46
	Netherlands	56		Indonesia	46
	Sri Lanka	56		Kuwait	46
10	Kenya	52	24	Hong Kong	45
	Malaysia	52		Liberia	45
12	Bahrain	51	26	Puerto Rico	44
	Malta	51		Sweden	44
14	United Arab Emirates	50		Uzbekistan	44

are for products of international comparable quality found in a supermarket or
department store. Prices found in local markets and bazaars are not used unless the
available merchandise is of the specified quality and the shopping area itself is safe
for executive and family members. New York City prices are used as the base, so
United States = 100.

b Three criteria are used to assess giving: in the previous month those surveyed either
gave money to charity, gave time to those in need or helped a stranger.

Transport: roads and cars

Longest road networks
Km, 2014 or latest

1	United States	6,646,149		26	Vietnam	224,979
2	India	5,411,636		27	Colombia	217,106
3	China	4,419,849		28	Malaysia	210,495
4	Brazil	1,691,473		29	Hungary	205,072
5	Russia	1,544,950		30	Nigeria	197,686
6	Canada	1,408,999		31	Philippines	197,412
7	Japan	1,222,835		32	Thailand	195,472
8	France	1,075,751		33	Peru	165,726
9	Australia	872,848		34	Egypt	163,070
10	South Africa	870,979		35	Ukraine	163,028
11	Spain	667,158		36	Belgium	155,307
12	Germany	643,275		37	Congo-Kinshasa	154,635
13	Indonesia	508,060		38	Netherlands	138,912
14	Italy	493,364		39	Czech Republic	130,091
15	Sweden	432,009		40	Austria	124,591
16	United Kingdom	421,128		41	Japan	122,835
17	Poland	416,558		42	Algeria	118,367
18	Turkey	391,643		43	Greece	116,960
19	Mexico	380,961		44	Ghana	109,515
20	Iran	302,415		45	South Korea	105,673
21	Saudi Arabia	272,490		46	Belarus	99,241
22	Pakistan	265,468		47	Zimbabwe	97,691
23	Bangladesh	265,270		48	Kazakhstan	96,421
24	Argentina	230,585		49	Venezuela	96,156
25	Romania	229,210		50	Ireland	96,017

Densest road networks
Km of road per km² land area, 2014 or latest

1	Monaco	38.1			United Kingdom	1.7
2	Macau	24.3		25	Czech Republic	1.6
3	Malta	9.8			India	1.6
4	Bermuda	8.3			Italy	1.6
5	Bahrain	6.0		28	Austria	1.5
6	Singapore	5.4		29	Cyprus	1.4
7	Belgium	5.1			Ireland	1.4
8	Barbados	3.7			Sri Lanka	1.4
9	Netherlands	3.3		32	Estonia	1.3
10	Japan	3.2			Lithuania	1.3
11	Puerto Rico	3.0			Poland	1.3
12	Liechtenstein	2.5			Spain	1.3
13	Hungary	2.2		36	Taiwan	1.2
14	France	2.0		37	Latvia	1.1
	Jamaica	2.0			Mauritius	1.1
	Luxembourg	2.0			South Korea	1.1
17	Guam	1.9		40	Portugal	1.0
	Hong Kong	1.9			Romania	1.0
	Slovenia	1.9			Sweden	1.0
20	Bangladesh	1.8		43	Greece	0.9
	Germany	1.8			Israel	0.9
22	Denmark	1.7			Qatar	0.9
	Switzerland	1.7			Slovakia	0.9

Most crowded road networks

Number of vehicles per km of road network, 2014 or latest

1	Japan	628.4	26	Liechtenstein	77.3
2	United Arab Emirates	479.0	27	Germany	74.1
3	Monaco	427.3	28	Armenia	73.3
4	Hong Kong	310.6	29	Tunisia	71.5
5	Kuwait	263.7	30	Dominican Rep.	68.1
6	Bahrain	252.3	31	Brunei	67.9
7	Singapore	239.5	32	Barbados	67.5
8	Macau	238.0		Switzerland	67.5
9	South Korea	190.4	34	Portugal	67.1
10	Taiwan	176.2	35	Netherlands	66.5
11	Israel	150.3	36	Croatia	61.5
12	Jordan	148.3	37	Malaysia	58.1
13	Puerto Rico	122.5	38	Argentina	58.0
14	Mauritius	111.8	39	Bermuda	57.9
15	Guam	108.8	40	Morocco	57.6
16	Guatemala	108.0	41	Poland	56.8
17	Malta	101.8	42	Ukraine	56.2
18	Qatar	97.7	43	Chile	55.4
19	Mexico	93.8	44	Greece	55.2
20	Syria	91.9	45	Moldova	53.9
21	United Kingdom	88.1	46	Slovakia	52.4
22	Bulgaria	85.6	47	Kazakhstan	50.0
23	Italy	85.0	48	Ecuador	49.5
24	Thailand	79.8	49	Bahamas	48.2
25	Luxembourg	79.5	50	Finland	48.1

Most road deaths

Fatalities per 100,000 population, 2013

1	Libya	73.4	24	Guinea	27.3
2	Thailand	36.2		Sierra Leone	27.3
3	Malawi	35.0	26	Senegal	27.2
4	Liberia	33.7	27	Angola	26.9
5	Congo-Kinshasa	33.2	28	Congo-Brazzaville	26.4
6	Tanzania	32.9		Niger	26.4
7	Central African Rep.	32.4	30	Jordan	26.3
8	Iran	32.1	31	Ghana	26.2
	Rwanda	32.1	32	Mali	25.6
10	Mozambique	31.6	33	Oman	25.4
11	Togo	31.1		Somalia	25.4
12	Burkina Faso	30.0	35	Ethiopia	25.3
13	Gambia, The	29.4	36	South Africa	25.1
14	Dominican Rep.	29.3	37	Zambia	24.7
15	Kenya	29.1	38	Mauritania	24.5
16	Madagascar	28.4		Vietnam	24.5
17	Lesotho	28.2	40	Tunisia	24.4
	Zimbabwe	28.2	41	Sudan	24.3
19	Benin	27.7	42	Ivory Coast	24.2
20	Cameroon	27.6		Kazakhstan	24.2
21	Guinea-Bissau	27.5		Swaziland	24.2
22	Saudi Arabia	27.4	45	Chad	24.1
	Uganda	27.4		Eritrea	24.1

Highest car ownership
Number of cars per 1,000 population, 2014

1	Puerto Rico	805	26	Czech Republic	461
2	Luxembourg	746	27	Greece	460
3	Iceland	720	28	Brunei	450
4	Malta	665	29	Kuwait	431
5	Bahrain	662	30	Portugal	421
6	New Zealand	648	31	Bulgaria	419
7	Lithuania	623	32	Denmark	417
8	Canada	612	33	Ireland	411
9	Italy	607	34	Cyprus	399
10	Finland	592	35	Guam	386
11	Australia	563	36	United States	375
12	Austria	552	37	Malaysia	365
13	Germany	537	38	Slovakia	355
14	Switzerland	535	39	Croatia	343
15	Poland	523	40	Latvia	329
16	United Kingdom	514	41	Libya	327
17	Slovenia	513	42	South Korea	318
18	Estonia	502	43	Israel	317
19	Norway	498	44	Belarus	316
20	Belgium	496	45	Bermuda	315
21	France	492	46	Hungary	314
22	Netherlands	488	47	Russia	304
23	Japan	478	48	Barbados	288
	Sweden	478	49	Qatar	283
25	Spain	468	50	Suriname	280

Lowest car ownership
Number of cars per 1,000 population, 2014

1	Ethiopia	1		Nicaragua	19
	Sudan	1		Togo	19
3	Burundi	2	26	Cuba	20
4	Bangladesh	3		Ghana	20
5	Haiti	4		Ivory Coast	20
	Malawi	4	29	Vietnam	21
	Uganda	4	30	Senegal	22
8	Honduras	5		Yemen	22
	Liberia	5	32	Bolivia	24
	Mauritania	5	33	Sri Lanka	26
	Tanzania	5	34	Philippines	31
12	Madagascar	8	35	Angola	32
13	Burkina Faso	9	36	Afghanistan	37
14	Mali	10	37	Guatemala	41
15	Cameroon	11	38	Iraq	45
	Mozambique	11		Peru	45
17	Pakistan	13	40	Egypt	47
18	Nigeria	16	41	Indonesia	50
	Zambia	16	42	Jamaica	52
20	El Salvador	17	43	Paraguay	54
	India	17		Zimbabwe	54
	Kenya	17	45	Ecuador	59
23	Benin	19	46	Colombia	62

Car production

Number produced, m, 2014

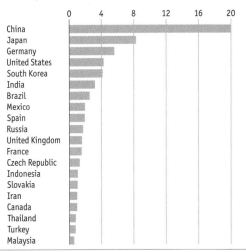

China	
Japan	
Germany	
United States	
South Korea	
India	
Brazil	
Mexico	
Spain	
Russia	
United Kingdom	
France	
Czech Republic	
Indonesia	
Slovakia	
Iran	
Canada	
Thailand	
Turkey	
Malaysia	

Cars sold

New car registrations, '000, 2014

1	China	19,708	27	Sweden	304
2	United States	7,749	28	Austria	303
3	Japan	4,700	29	Switzerland	302
4	Germany	3,037	30	Egypt	274
5	Brazil	2,795	31	Colombia	265
6	India	2,571	32	Chile	256
7	United Kingdom	2,476	33	Taiwan	235
8	Russia	2,333	34	Israel	228
9	France	1,796	35	United Arab Emirates	207
10	Italy	1,361	36	Czech Republic	192
11	South Korea	1,360	37	Denmark	189
12	Iran	1,107	38	Algeria	178
13	Spain	890	39	Kazakhstan	151
14	Indonesia	863	40	Norway	144
15	Canada	760	41	Portugal	143
16	Mexico	745	42	Peru	140
17	Saudi Arabia	633	43	Oman	139
18	Malaysia	588	44	Kuwait	126
19	Turkey	587	45	Pakistan	124
20	Australia	532	46	Morocco	110
21	Belgium	483	47	Finland	106
22	South Africa	439	48	Ukraine	97
23	Argentina	433	49	Ireland	96
24	Netherlands	388	50	New Zealand	90
25	Thailand	370		Philippines	90
26	Poland	328			

Transport: planes and trains

Most air travel
Passengers carried, m, 2014

1	United States	762.6		16	South Korea	59.1
2	China	390.9		17	Spain	53.0
3	United Kingdom	125.1		18	Malaysia	47.6
4	Japan	110.5		19	Thailand	44.0
5	Germany	107.6		20	Mexico	40.7
6	Ireland	101.0		21	Hong Kong	37.5
7	Brazil	100.4		22	Netherlands	33.9
8	Indonesia	94.5		23	Singapore	32.9
9	Turkey	92.6		24	Saudi Arabia	32.0
10	India	82.8		25	Philippines	30.9
11	United Arab Emirates	76.3		26	Switzerland	26.7
12	Canada	75.5		27	Italy	25.6
13	Russia	72.2		28	Colombia	25.1
14	Australia	67.7		29	Vietnam	24.7
15	France	63.4		30	Qatar	21.4

Busiest airports

Total passengers, m, 2015

1	Atlanta, Hartsfield	101.5
2	Beijing, Capital	89.9
3	Dubai, Intl.	78.0
4	Chicago, O'Hare	76.9
5	Tokyo, Haneda	75.3
6	London, Heathrow	75.0
7	Los Angeles, Intl.	74.7
8	Hong Kong, Intl.	68.3
9	Paris, Charles de Gaulle	65.8
10	Dallas, Ft Worth	64.1
11	Istanbul, Ataturk	61.8
12	Frankfurt, Main	61.0
13	Shanghai, Pudong Intl.	60.1
14	Amsterdam, Schiphol	58.3
15	New York, JFK	56.8

Total cargo, m tonnes, 2015

1	Hong Kong, Intl.	4.42
2	Memphis, Intl.	4.29
3	Shanghai, Pudong Intl.	3.27
4	Anchorage, Intl.	2.62
5	Seoul, Incheon	2.60
6	Dubai, Intl.	2.51
7	Louisville, Standiford Field	2.35
8	Tokyo, Narita	2.12
9	Frankfurt, Main	2.08
10	Taiwan, Taoyuan Intl.	2.03
11	Miami, Intl.	2.01
12	Los Angeles, Intl.	1.93
13	Beijing, Capital	1.89
	Singapore, Changi	1.89
15	Paris, Charles de Gaulle	1.86

Average daily aircraft movements, take-offs and landings, 2015

1	Atlanta, Hartsfield	2,418		13	Amsterdam, Schiphol	1,275
2	Chicago, O'Hare	2,398		14	Istanbul, Ataturk	1,274
3	Dallas, Ft Worth	1,866		15	Shanghai, Pudong Intl.	1,228
4	Los Angeles, Intl.	1,796		16	Toronto, Pearson Intl.	1,216
5	Beijing, Capital	1,617		17	Phoenix, Skyharbor Intl.	1,203
6	Denver, Intl.	1,483		18	Tokyo, Haneda	1,201
7	Charlotte/Douglas, Intl.	1,482			New York, JFK	1,201
8	Las Vegas, McCarran Intl.	1,453		20	San Francisco	1,178
9	Houston, George Bush Intercontinental	1,378		21	Mexico City, Intl.	1,169
				22	Hong Kong, Intl.	1,142
10	Paris, Charles de Gaulle	1,303		23	Newark	1,136
11	London, Heathrow	1,299		24	Miami	1,131
12	Frankfurt, Main	1,283		25	Philadelphia, Intl.	1,127

Longest railway networks
'000 km, 2014 or latest

#	Country		#	Country	
1	United States	228.2	21	Turkey	10.1
2	Russia	85.3	22	Sweden	9.7
3	China	67.0	23	Czech Republic	9.5
4	India	65.8	24	Iran	8.6
5	Canada	52.1	25	Hungary	7.9
6	Germany	33.4	26	Pakistan	7.8
7	Australia	32.8	27	Finland	5.9
8	France	30.0	28	Belarus	5.5
9	Brazil	29.8		Chile	5.5
10	Mexico	26.7	30	Thailand	5.3
11	Argentina	25.0	31	Egypt	5.2
12	Ukraine	21.5	32	Austria	5.1
13	South Africa	20.5	33	Indonesia	4.7
14	Japan	19.5	34	Sudan	4.3
15	Poland	18.9	35	Algeria	4.2
16	Italy	17.0		Norway	4.2
17	Spain	16.9		Uzbekistan	4.2
18	United Kingdom	14.8	38	Bulgaria	4.0
19	Kazakhstan	14.3	39	Serbia	3.8
20	Romania	10.8		Tunisia	3.8

Most rail passengers
Km per person per year, 2014 or latest

#	Country		#	Country	
1	Switzerland	2,255	13	Russia	904
2	Japan	2,047	14	Taiwan	844
3	Austria	1,363	15	Belarus	838
4	France	1,299	16	Luxembourg	746
5	Kazakhstan	1,114	17	Finland	717
6	Ukraine	1,096	18	Italy	651
7	United Kingdom	1,031	19	Czech Republic	650
8	Denmark	1,029	20	Sweden	639
9	Netherlands	1,013	21	Hungary	585
10	Belgium	977	22	Norway	581
11	Germany	959	23	China	579
12	India	914	24	Spain	531

Most rail freight
Million tonne-km per year, 2014 or latest

#	Country		#	Country	
1	United States	2,524,585	13	Belarus	44,997
2	China	2,308,669	14	Poland	32,017
3	Russia	2,298,564	15	France	32,012
4	India	665,810	16	Iran	24,461
5	Canada	352,535	17	Uzbekistan	22,686
6	Brazil	267,700	18	Japan	20,255
7	Ukraine	237,722	19	United Kingdom	19,230
8	Kazakhstan	235,845	20	Austria	15,661
9	South Africa	134,600	21	Latvia	15,257
10	Mexico	78,770	22	Lithuania	14,307
11	Germany	74,818	23	Argentina	12,111
12	Australia	59,649	24	Turkmenistan	11,992

Transport: shipping

Merchant fleets
Number of vessels, by country of domicile, January 2015

1	China	4,966	16	Vietnam	878
2	Greece	4,017	17	Taiwan	869
3	Japan	3,986	18	India	844
4	Germany	3,532	19	Italy	803
5	Singapore	2,356	20	United Arab Emirates	779
6	United States	1,972	21	Malaysia	608
7	Norway	1,857	22	France	457
8	Russia	1,739	23	Brazil	391
9	Indonesia	1,657	24	Canada	348
10	South Korea	1,618	25	Switzerland	338
11	Turkey	1,530	26	Sweden	335
12	Hong Kong	1,258	27	Bermuda	322
13	United Kingdom	1,227	28	Cyprus	320
14	Netherlands	1,220	29	Monaco	260
15	Denmark	930	30	Belgium	243

Shipbuilding
Deliveries[a], '000 dwt, 2015

1	China	39,487	11	Netherlands	115
2	South Korea	29,461	12	Norway	114
3	Japan	21,281	13	Indonesia	94
4	Philippines	2,511	14	Croatia	79
5	Vietnam	913	15	Germany	54
6	Taiwan	805	16	Russia	39
7	Brazil	592	17	Malaysia	36
8	Romania	575	18	India	31
9	United States	473	19	Bangladesh	24
10	Turkey	134	20	Italy	20

Busiest ports
Cargo volume, million TEU[b], 2014

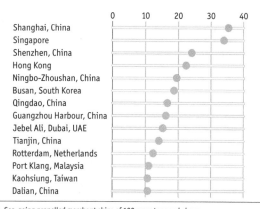

a Sea-going propelled merchant ships of 100 gross tons and above.
b Twenty-foot equivalent unit.

Crime and punishment

Murders

Homicides per 100,000 pop., 2013 or latest

1	Honduras	84.3
2	Venezuela	53.6
3	Virgin Islands (US)	52.6
4	Jamaica	42.9
5	El Salvador	39.8
6	Lesotho	38.0
7	Guatemala	34.6
8	South Africa	31.9
9	Colombia	31.8
10	Trinidad & Tobago	30.2
11	Bahamas	29.7
12	Brazil	26.5
	Puerto Rico	26.5
14	Dominican Rep.	22.0
15	Guyana	19.5
16	Mexico	18.9
17	Namibia	17.5
18	Swaziland	17.4
19	Panama	17.2
20	Botswana	15.4

Robberies

Per 100,000 pop., 2013 or latest

1	Belgium	1,616
2	Costa Rica	984
3	Mexico	596
4	Brazil	505
5	Uruguay	491
6	Nicaragua	488
7	Chile	468
8	Panama	264
9	Peru	263
10	Paraguay	261
11	Honduras	231
12	Trinidad & Tobago	221
13	Colombia	194
	France	194
15	Guyana	192
16	Spain	183
17	Portugal	156
18	Bolivia	137
19	Botswana	124
20	Barbados	123

Prisoners

Total prison pop., 2016 or latest

1	United States	2,217,000
2	China	1,649,804
3	Russia	646,319
4	Brazil	607,731
5	India	418,536
6	Thailand	315,969
7	Mexico	255,138
8	Iran	225,624
9	Turkey	179,611
10	Indonesia	173,713
11	South Africa	159,563
12	Vietnam	136,245
13	Colombia	120,736
14	Philippines	120,076
15	Ethiopia	111,050
16	United Kingdom	94,886
17	Pakistan	80,169
18	Peru	77,244
19	Morocco	76,000
20	Poland	71,250
21	Bangladesh	69,719
22	Ukraine	69,148
23	Argentina	69,060
24	France	66,678
25	Egypt	62,000
26	Germany	61,737
27	Taiwan	61,691

Per 100,000 pop., 2016 or latest

1	United States	698
2	Turkmenistan	583
3	Virgin Islands (US)	542
4	Cuba	510
5	El Salvador	509
6	Guam	469
7	Thailand	468
8	Russia	442
9	Rwanda	434
10	Panama	392
11	Bahamas	363
12	Bermuda	354
13	Costa Rica	352
14	Puerto Rico	350
15	Barbados	322
16	Belarus	306
17	Bahrain	301
	Brazil	301
19	South Africa	292
20	Uruguay	291
21	Swaziland	289
22	Iran	287
23	French Guiana	277
24	Georgia	274
25	Lithuania	268
26	Mongolia	266
27	Taiwan	263

War and peace

Defence spending
As % of GDP, 2015

1	Afghanistan	16.4		Ukraine	4.3
	Oman	16.4	13	Jordan	4.2
3	Saudi Arabia	13.0		Russia	4.2
4	Iraq	12.8	15	Armenia	3.9
5	South Sudan	10.5	16	Colombia	3.6
6	Algeria	6.2	17	Brunei	3.4
	Israel	6.2		Myanmar	3.4
8	Bahrain	5.0	19	Singapore	3.3
9	Namibia	4.5		United States	3.3
10	Angola	4.4	21	Morocco	3.2
11	Mali	4.3	22	Pakistan	2.8

Defence spending
$bn, 2015

				Per person, $, 2015		
1	United States	597.5		1	Oman	3,008
2	China	145.8		2	Saudi Arabia	2,949
3	Saudi Arabia	81.9		3	Israel	2,310
4	United Kingdom	56.2		4	United States	1,859
5	Russia[a]	51.6		5	Singapore	1,705
6	India	48.0		6	Bahrain	1,138
7	France	46.8		7	Norway	1,058
8	Japan	41.0		8	Australia	1,001
9	Germany	36.7		9	Brunei	922
10	South Korea	33.5		10	United Kingdom	878
11	Brazil	24.3		11	France	702
12	Australia	22.8		12	South Korea	681
13	Italy	21.5		13	Denmark	618
14	Iraq	21.1		14	Switzerland	595
15	Israel	18.6		15	Iraq	569

Armed forces
Million, 2016[b]

Regulars   Reserves

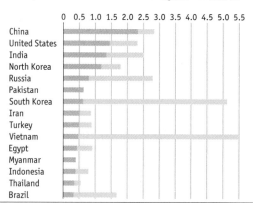

China
United States
India
North Korea
Russia
Pakistan
South Korea
Iran
Turkey
Vietnam
Egypt
Myanmar
Indonesia
Thailand
Brazil

a National defence budget only.   b Estimates.

Arms exporters

$m, 2015

1	United States	10,484
2	Russia	5,483
3	Germany	2,049
4	France	2,013
5	China	1,966
6	Spain	1,279
7	United Kingdom	1,214
8	Israel	710
9	Italy	570
10	Netherlands	444
11	Switzerland	369
12	Ukraine	323
13	Canada	312
14	Turkey	291
15	Sweden	186
16	Norway	155
17	Czech Republic	120
18	Australia	113
19	South Korea	105
20	United Arab Emirates	63

Arms importers

$m, 2015

1	Saudi Arabia	3,161
2	India	3,078
3	Australia	1,574
4	Egypt	1,475
5	United Arab Emirates	1,289
6	Iraq	1,215
7	China	1,214
8	Vietnam	870
9	Greece	762
10	Pakistan	735
11	Indonesia	683
12	Taiwan	681
13	Qatar	655
14	Bangladesh	653
15	Algeria	636
16	Israel	617
17	Italy	596
18	United States	565
19	Mexico	500
20	Turkey	448

Global Peace Index[a]

Most peaceful, 2016

1	Iceland	1.192
2	Denmark	1.246
3	Austria	1.278
4	New Zealand	1.287
5	Portugal	1.356
6	Czech Republic	1.360
7	Switzerland	1.370
8	Canada	1.388
9	Japan	1.395
10	Slovenia	1.408
11	Finland	1.429
12	Ireland	1.433
13	Sweden	1.461
14	Australia	1.465
15	Germany	1.486
16	Norway	1.500
17	Belgium	1.528
18	Hungary	1.534
19	Singapore	1.535
20	Netherlands	1.541
21	Poland	1.557
22	Mauritius	1.559
23	Slovakia	1.603
24	Spain	1.604

Least peaceful, 2016

1	Syria	3.806
2	South Sudan	3.593
3	Iraq	3.570
4	Afghanistan	3.538
5	Somalia	3.414
6	Yemen	3.399
7	Central African Rep.	3.354
8	Ukraine	3.287
9	Sudan	3.269
10	Libya	3.200
11	Pakistan	3.145
12	Congo-Kinshasa	3.112
13	Russia	3.079
14	North Korea	2.944
15	Nigeria	2.877
16	Colombia	2.764
17	Lebanon	2.752
18	Turkey	2.710
19	Israel	2.656
20	Venezuela	2.651
21	Egypt	2.574
22	India	2.566
23	Mexico	2.557
24	Philippines	2.511

a Ranks 163 countries using 23 indicators which gauge the level of safety and security in society, the extent of domestic or international conflict and the degree of militarisation.

Space

Space missions
Firsts and selected events

1957	Man-made satellite
	Dog in space, Laika
1961	Human in space, Yuri Gagarin
	Entire day in space, Gherman Titov
1963	Woman in space, Valentina Tereshkova
1964	Space crew, one pilot and two passengers
1965	Spacewalk, Alexei Leonov
	Computer guidance system
	Eight days in space achieved (needed to travel to Moon and back)
1966	Docking between spacecraft and target vehicle
	Autopilot re-entry and landing
1968	Live television broadcast from space
	Moon orbit
1969	Astronaut transfer from one craft to another in space
	Moon landing
1971	Space station, Salyut
	Drive on the Moon
1973	Space laboratory, Skylab
1978	Non-American, non-Soviet, Vladimir Remek (Czechoslovakia)
1982	Space shuttle, *Columbia* (first craft to carry four crew members)
1983	Five-crew mission
1984	Spacewalk, untethered
	Capture, repair and redeployment of satellite in space
	Seven-crew mission
1985	Classified US Defense Department mission
1986	Space shuttle explosion, *Challenger*
	Mir space station activated
1990	Hubble telescope deployed
2001	Dennis Tito, paying space tourist
2003	Space-shuttle explosion, *Columbia*. Shuttle programme suspended
	China manned space flight, Yang Liwei
2004	*SpaceShipOne*, successful private manned suborbital space flight
2010	SpaceX's privately-funded spacecraft made an orbital flight
2012	SpaceX craft docked with the International Space Station
2014	*Rosetta* probe landed on comet 67P after 12-year mission
2016	British astronaut completed marathon in space

Orbital launches

2015		Commercial	Non-commercial[a]	Total	2005–15
1	Russia	14	12	26	313
2	United States	4	16	20	196
3	China	12	7	19	141
4	Europe	5	6	11	81
5	India	3	2	5	30
6	Japan	1	3	4	32
7	Iran	1	0	1	7
8	Multinational[b]	0	0	0	22
9	Israel	0	0	0	3
	North Korea	0	0	0	3
	South Korea	0	0	0	3

a Government and non-profit launches.   b Sea Launch.

Environment

Biggest emitters of carbon dioxide
Million tonnes, 2012

1	China	8,106.4	31	Argentina	196.0
2	United States	5,270.4	32	Venezuela	184.8
3	India	1,830.9	33	Pakistan	146.9
4	Russia	1,781.7	34	Belgium	139.1
5	Japan	1,259.1	35	Algeria	133.9
6	Germany	788.3	36	Vietnam	131.7
7	South Korea	657.1	37	Iraq	130.7
8	Iran	603.6	38	Uzbekistan	123.2
9	Saudi Arabia	582.7	39	Kuwait	105.7
10	Canada	550.8	40	Qatar	99.2
11	Brazil	500.2	41	Czech Republic	91.2
12	United Kingdom	498.9	42	Hong Kong	88.6
13	South Africa	473.2	43	Greece	87.6
14	Indonesia	456.2	44	Nigeria	86.4
15	Mexico	453.8	45	Romania	86.1
16	Australia	420.6	46	Philippines	83.9
17	Italy	385.8	47	Chile	81.5
18	France	364.5	48	Israel	80.4
19	Spain	312.4	49	Colombia	74.9
20	Taiwan	307.1	50	Belarus	67.1
21	Turkey	296.9	51	North Korea	67.0
22	Thailand	290.7	52	Austria	66.7
23	Ukraine	290.4	53	Turkmenistan	65.0
24	Poland	289.5	54	Bangladesh	63.5
25	Netherlands	239.6	55	Oman	62.9
26	United Arab Emirates	234.1	56	Libya	54.6
27	Kazakhstan	224.2	57	Peru	53.6
28	Singapore	208.0	58	Trinidad & Tobago	51.3
29	Egypt	206.3	59	Portugal	51.2
30	Malaysia	198.8	60	Sweden	51.1

Largest amount of carbon dioxide emitted per person
Tonnes, 2011

1	Virgin Islands (US)	130.0	18	Netherlands	14.4
2	Netherlands Antilles	52.7	19	Belgium	13.4
3	United Arab Emirates	44.4		Taiwan	13.4
4	Qatar	44.1	21	South Korea	13.3
5	Trinidad & Tobago	42.5	22	Hong Kong	13.2
6	Singapore	39.2	23	Guam	12.7
7	Kuwait	38.7	24	New Caledonia	12.4
8	Montenegro	25.5	25	Kazakhstan	12.0
9	Bahrain	24.9		Russia	12.0
10	Luxembourg	23.1	27	Bahamas	11.6
11	Brunei	21.7	28	Iceland	11.5
12	Saudi Arabia	21.1	29	Turkmenistan	11.0
13	Australia	19.6	30	Greenland	10.7
14	Malta	18.4	31	Israel	10.0
15	Oman	17.7	32	Finland	9.8
16	United States	17.6	33	Germany	9.6
17	Canada	16.2		South Africa	9.6

Most polluted capital cities
Annual mean particulate matter concentration[a], micrograms per cubic metre
2013 or latest

1	Delhi, India	152.6	12	Sofia, Bulgaria	44.6
2	Doha, Qatar	93.4	13	Dakar, Senegal	40.0
3	Dhaka, Bangladesh	86.0	14	Hanoi, Vietnam	39.5
	Kabul, Afghanistan[b]	86.0	15	Ankara, Turkey	39.0
5	Cairo, Egypt	73.5	16	Lima, Peru	37.9
6	Ulaanbaatar, Mongolia	67.9	17	Belgrade, Serbia	34.1
7	Abu Dhabi, United		18	Guatemala City,	
	Arab Emirates	63.9		Guatemala	32.5
8	Beijing, China	55.6		Sarajevo, Bosnia & Herz.	32.5
9	Kathmandu, Nepal	50.0	20	Muscat, Oman	31.0
10	Accra, Ghana	49.3	21	Tehran, Iran	30.3
11	Amman, Jordan	48.1	22	Colombo, Sri Lanka	28.0

Lowest access to an improved water source
% of population, 2014

1	Papua New Guinea	40.0	15	Niger	58.1
2	Equatorial Guinea	47.8	16	South Sudan	58.7
3	Angola	48.6	17	West Bank & Gaza	60.6
4	Madagascar	50.6	18	Sierra Leone	61.6
5	Chad	50.8	19	Togo	62.4
6	Mozambique	50.9	20	Kenya	63.1
7	Congo-Kinshasa	52.1	21	Mongolia	64.2
8	Afghanistan	55.2	22	Zambia	64.6
9	Ethiopia	55.4	23	Nigeria	67.6
10	Sudan	55.5	24	Central African Rep.	68.4
	Tanzania	55.5	25	Timor-Leste	71.7
12	Haiti	57.5	26	Cambodia	73.4
13	Eritrea	57.7	27	Tajikistan	73.7
14	Mauritania	57.9	28	Swaziland	74.1

Lowest access to electricity
% of population, 2012

1	South Sudan	5.1	17	Lesotho	20.6
2	Chad	6.4	18	Mauritania	21.8
3	Burundi	6.5	19	Zambia	22.1
4	Liberia	9.8	20	Kenya	23.0
	Malawi	9.8	21	Mali	25.6
6	Central African Rep.	10.8	22	Guinea	26.2
7	Burkina Faso	13.1	23	Ethiopia	26.6
8	Sierra Leone	14.2	24	North Korea	29.6
9	Niger	14.4	25	Cambodia	31.1
10	Tanzania	15.3	26	Togo	31.5
11	Madagascar	15.4	27	Sudan	32.6
12	Congo-Kinshasa	16.4	28	Somalia	32.7
13	Rwanda	18.0	29	Gambia, The	34.5
14	Papua New Guinea	18.1	30	Eritrea	36.1
15	Uganda	18.2	31	Angola	37.0
16	Mozambique	20.2	32	Haiti	37.9

a Particulates less than 2.5 microns in diameter.   b Recorded at ISAF HQ.

Largest forests
Sq km, 2013

1	Russia	8,150,125
2	Brazil	4,955,060
3	Canada	3,471,622
4	United States	3,095,450
5	China	2,052,369
6	Congo-Kinshasa	1,532,008
7	Australia	1,241,350
8	Indonesia	923,788
9	Peru	743,082
10	India	703,252
11	Mexico	662,232
12	Colombia	585,552
13	Angola	581,056
14	Bolivia	553,420
15	Zambia	489,682
16	Venezuela	470,118
17	Tanzania	468,040
18	Mozambique	383,528
19	Papua New Guinea	335,646
20	Myanmar	301,338
21	Sweden	280,730
22	Argentina	277,056
23	Japan	249,612
24	Gabon	226,000
25	Congo-Brazzaville	223,648
26	Finland	222,180
27	Central African Rep.	222,012
28	Malaysia	221,666
29	Sudan	195,588
30	Cameroon	192,560

Most forest
% of land area, 2013

1	Suriname	98.3
2	Gabon	87.7
3	Guyana	84.1
4	Laos	79.6
5	Papua New Guinea	74.1
6	Finland	73.1
7	Brunei	72.1
8	Guinea-Bissau	70.8
9	Sweden	68.9
10	Japan	68.5
11	Congo-Kinshasa	67.6
12	Malaysia	67.5
13	Zambia	65.9
14	Congo-Brazzaville	65.5
15	South Korea	63.6
16	Panama	62.5
17	Slovenia	61.9
18	Montenegro	61.5
19	Brazil	59.3
20	Peru	58.1
21	Equatorial Guinea	56.7
22	Puerto Rico	55.2
23	Fiji	55.1
24	Cambodia	55.0
25	Latvia	54.0
26	Venezuela	53.3
27	Colombia	52.8
	Costa Rica	52.8
	Tanzania	52.8
30	Estonia	52.7

Deforestation
Biggest % decrease in forested land, 1990–2013

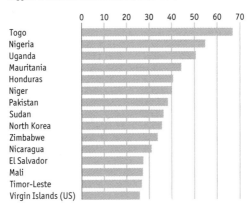

Species under threat
2015, number

Mammals

1	Indonesia	185
2	Madagascar	119
3	Mexico	101
4	India	93
5	Brazil	82
6	China	74
7	Malaysia	70
8	Australia	56
	Colombia	56
10	Peru	55
11	Thailand	54
	Vietnam	54
13	Ecuador	46
	Myanmar	46
15	Laos	45
16	Cameroon	43
17	Argentina	40
18	Papua New Guinea	39
	Philippines	39
20	Tanzania	38

Fish

1	United States	247
2	India	216
3	Mexico	179
4	Tanzania	175
5	Indonesia	150
6	China	131
	Turkey	131
8	Cameroon	119
9	Australia	111
10	South Africa	103
11	Thailand	99
12	Malawi	98
13	Congo-Kinshasa	93
14	Madagascar	87
15	Brazil	85
16	Greece	80
17	Philippines	77
	Spain	77
19	Vietnam	76

Birds

1	Brazil	165
2	Indonesia	131
3	Peru	120
4	Colombia	119
5	Ecuador	98
6	China	89

	Philippines	89
8	India	84
9	United States	77
10	New Zealand	67
11	Mexico	61
12	Bolivia	55

Biggest nationally protected land and marine areas[a]
As % of total territorial area, 2014

1	New Caledonia	54.3
2	Venezuela	53.9
3	Slovenia	53.6
4	Monaco	53.4
5	Liechtenstein	44.3
6	Brunei	44.1
7	Hong Kong	41.8
8	Bulgaria	40.5
9	Namibia	37.9
	Zambia	37.9
11	Croatia	37.7
12	Germany	37.4
13	Nicaragua	37.1
14	Slovakia	36.6
15	Congo-Brazzaville	35.2
16	Greece	34.9

17	Luxembourg	34.6
18	Morocco	33.6
19	New Zealand	32.5
20	Trinidad & Tobago	32.5
21	Tanzania	32.0
22	Guatemala	31.8
23	Peru	31.4
24	Saudi Arabia	31.3
25	Poland	30.0
26	Botswana	29.2
	Guinea	29.2
	Norway	29.2
29	Austria	28.4
	Brazil	28.4
	United Kingdom	28.4

a Scientific reserves with limited access, national parks, natural reserves and protected landscapes.

Environmental Performance Index[a]

Scores, 2016, 0=lowest, 100=highest

Best			Worst		
1	Finland	90.7	1	Somalia	27.7
2	Iceland	90.5	2	Eritrea	36.7
3	Sweden	90.4	3	Madagascar	37.1
4	Denmark	89.2	4	Afghanistan	37.5
5	Slovenia	89.0		Niger	37.5
6	Spain	88.9	6	Chad	37.8
7	Estonia	88.6	7	Mali	41.5
	Portugal	88.6	8	Bangladesh	41.8
9	Malta	88.5		Mozambique	41.8
10	France	88.2	10	Congo-Kinshasa	42.1
11	New Zealand	88.0	11	Sudan	42.3
12	United Kingdom	87.4	12	Haiti	43.3
13	Australia	87.2	13	Burundi	43.4
14	Croatia	87.0		Liberia	43.4
	Singapore	87.0	15	Benin	43.7
16	Norway	86.9		Burkina Faso	43.7
	Switzerland	86.9	17	Ethiopia	45.8
18	Austria	86.6	18	Sierra Leone	46.0
	Ireland	86.6	19	Togo	46.1
	Luxembourg	86.6	20	Mauritania	46.3
21	Greece	85.8	21	Central African Rep.	46.5
22	Latvia	85.7	22	Lesotho	47.2
23	Lithuania	85.5	23	Papua New Guinea	48.0
24	Slovakia	85.4	24	Guinea-Bissau	48.2

Worst natural catastrophes

Number of victims, 1970–2015

1	Bangladesh, 1970	Storms and floods	300,000
2	China, 1976	Earthquake	255,000
3	Haiti, 2010	Earthquake	222,570
4	Indonesia, Thailand and others, 2004	Earthquake, tsunami	220,000
5	Myanmar, Bay of Bengal, 2008	Tropical cyclone	138,300
6	Bangladesh, 1991	Tropical cyclone	138,000
7	China, 2008	Earthquake	87,449
8	Pakistan, India, Afghanistan, 2005	Earthquake	74,310
9	Peru, 1970	Earthquake	66,000
10	Russia, Czech Republic, 2010	Heatwave	55,630
11	Iran, 1990	Earthquake	40,000
12	France, Italy, Germany and others, 2003	Heatwave	35,000
13	Iran, 2003	Earthquake	26,271
14	Armenia, 1988	Earthquake	25,000
	Iran, 1978	Earthquake	25,000
16	Colombia, 1985	Volcanic eruption	23,000
17	Guatemala, 1976	Earthquake	22,300
18	India, Pakistan, 2001	Earthquake	19,737
19	Turkey, 1999	Earthquake	19,118
20	Japan, 2011	Earthquake, tsunami	18,520

a Compiled from more than 20 environmental indicators including pollution, policy on
climate change and biodiversity.

Life expectancy

Highest life expectancy
Years, 2015–20

1	Monaco[a]	89.5	25	Portugal	81.7
2	Hong Kong	84.5	26	Greece	81.6
3	Japan	84.1	27	Finland	81.5
4	Italy	83.8		Germany	81.5
5	Singapore	83.7		Ireland	81.5
6	Switzerland	83.6	30	Belgium	81.4
7	Spain	83.2		Macau	81.4
8	Iceland	83.1	32	United Kingdom	81.3
9	Australia	83.0	33	Channel Islands	81.2
	Israel	83.0		Virgin Islands (US)	81.2
11	France	82.9	35	Bermuda[a]	81.2
12	South Korea	82.8		Malta	81.2
	Sweden	82.8	37	Slovenia	81.0
14	Andorra[a]	82.7	38	Cyprus	80.8
	Chile	82.7		Réunion	80.8
16	Canada	82.6	40	Denmark	80.7
	Martinique	82.6	41	French Guiana	80.3
18	New Zealand	82.4		Lebanon	80.3
19	Luxembourg	82.3	43	Puerto Rico	80.2
20	Norway	82.1	44	Costa Rica	80.1
21	Austria	82.1	45	Cuba	80.0
	Netherlands	82.1		Guam	80.0
23	Guadeloupe	82.0		Taiwan[a]	80.0
24	Liechtenstein[a]	81.8	48	United States	79.6

Highest male life expectancy
Years, 2015–20

1	Monaco[a]	85.6		Japan	80.8
2	Hong Kong	81.7		New Zealand	80.8
	Iceland	81.7	12	Andorra[a]	80.6
4	Switzerland	81.6		Singapore	80.6
5	Israel	81.3	14	Spain	80.5
	Italy	81.3	15	Netherlands	80.3
7	Australia	81.1	16	Luxembourg	80.2
	Sweden	81.1		Norway	80.2
9	Canada	80.8	18	France	80.0

Highest female life expectancy
Years, 2015–20

1	Monaco[a]	93.6		Switzerland	85.5
2	Hong Kong	87.4	11	Chile	85.3
3	Japan	87.3	12	Andorra[a]	85.0
4	Singapore	86.7	13	Australia	85.0
5	Italy	86.0		Guadeloupe	85.0
6	Spain	85.8	15	Israel	84.6
7	South Korea	85.7	16	Iceland	84.5
8	France	85.6		Liechtenstein[a]	84.5
9	Martinique	85.5			

a 2015 estimate.

Lowest life expectancy

Years, 2015–20

1	Swaziland	48.7	26	Ghana	62.0
2	Lesotho	50.4		Liberia	62.0
3	Sierra Leone	52.1	28	Zambia	62.3
4	Chad	52.5	29	Zimbabwe	62.4
5	Ivory Coast	52.8	30	Niger	62.8
6	Central African Rep.	53.3	31	Papua New Guinea	63.2
7	Angola	53.7	32	Kenya	63.3
	Nigeria	53.7	33	Mauritania	63.6
9	Guinea-Bissau	56.2	34	Congo-Brazzaville	63.9
	Mozambique	56.2		Haiti	63.9
11	Somalia	56.5	36	Sudan	64.2
12	Cameroon	57.0	37	Yemen	64.5
13	South Sudan	57.1	38	Botswana	64.6
14	South Africa	57.7	39	Eritrea	65.1
15	Burundi	58.1	40	Namibia	65.3
16	Equatorial Guinea	58.6	41	Ethiopia	65.8
17	Mali	59.7		Malawi	65.8
18	Burkina Faso	59.8	43	Gabon	66.0
19	Congo-Kinshasa	59.9		Rwanda	66.0
20	Guinea	60.2	45	Turkmenistan	66.1
21	Benin	60.3	46	Madagascar	66.4
22	Uganda	61.0		Tanzania	66.4
23	Gambia, The	61.1	48	Myanmar	66.5
	Togo	61.1	49	Guyana	66.8
25	Afghanistan	61.5		Pakistan	66.8

Lowest male life expectancy

Years, 2015–20

1	Swaziland	49.5	11	Mozambique	55.0
2	Lesotho	50.3	12	South Africa	55.7
3	Central African Rep.	51.1	13	Cameroon	55.9
4	Chad	51.4	14	Burundi	56.0
5	Sierra Leone	51.5	15	South Sudan	56.1
6	Ivory Coast	52.0	16	Equatorial Guinea	57.3
7	Angola	52.2	17	Congo-Kinshasa	58.4
8	Nigeria	53.3	18	Burkina Faso	58.5
9	Guinea-Bissau	54.4	19	Benin	58.8
10	Somalia	54.9	20	Uganda	58.9

Lowest female life expectancy

Years, 2015–20

1	Swaziland	47.7	10	Guinea-Bissau	58.0
2	Lesotho	50.2	11	South Sudan	58.1
3	Sierra Leone	52.7	12	Cameroon	58.2
4	Chad	53.6		Somalia	58.2
5	Ivory Coast	53.8	14	South Africa	59.3
6	Nigeria	54.1	15	Mali	59.6
7	Angola	55.2	16	Equatorial Guinea	60.0
8	Central African Rep.	55.5	17	Burundi	60.2
9	Mozambique	57.3	18	Guinea	60.7

Death rates and infant mortality

Highest death rates
Number of deaths per 1,000 population, 2015–20

#	Country	Rate	#	Country	Rate
1	Lithuania	16.2	49	Austria	9.5
2	Ukraine	15.7	50	North Korea	9.4
3	Bulgaria	15.6		Uruguay	9.4
4	Latvia	15.4	52	Mali	9.3
5	Swaziland	14.9		Malta	9.3
6	Lesotho	14.7	54	Guinea	9.2
7	Belarus	14.6		Monaco[a]	9.2
8	Russia	14.3	56	Channel Islands	9.1
9	Romania	13.7		France	9.1
10	Hungary	13.5		Spain	9.1
11	Chad	13.3		United Kingdom	9.1
12	Central African Rep.	13.1	60	Benin	9.0
	Serbia	13.1		Kazakhstan	9.0
14	Croatia	12.8		Martinique	9.0
	Ivory Coast	12.8		Sweden	9.0
	Sierra Leone	12.8	64	Burkina Faso	8.9
17	Angola	12.7	65	Netherlands	8.8
	Estonia	12.7	66	Ghana	8.5
19	South Africa	12.6		Guyana	8.5
20	Nigeria	12.2		Haiti	8.5
21	Moldova	11.7		Uganda	8.5
22	Georgia	11.5	70	Myanmar	8.4
23	Guinea-Bissau	11.4		Thailand	8.4
24	Germany	11.3		United States	8.4
	Greece	11.3	73	Niger	8.3
	Somalia	11.3	74	Bermuda[a]	8.2
27	Bosnia & Herz.	11.1		Cuba	8.2
28	Barbados	10.9		Gambia, The	8.2
	Japan	10.9		Togo	8.2
	South Sudan	10.9	78	Liberia	8.1
31	Mozambique	10.8		Virgin Islands (US)	8.1
32	Portugal	10.7	80	Mauritius	8.0
33	Cameroon	10.6		Puerto Rico	8.0
	Czech Republic	10.6		Switzerland	8.0
35	Burundi	10.5		Zambia	8.0
36	Poland	10.4	84	Gabon	7.9
37	Equatorial Guinea	10.3		Norway	7.9
	Montenegro	10.3	86	Congo-Brazzaville	7.8
39	Italy	10.2		Turkmenistan	7.8
	Slovakia	10.2		Zimbabwe	7.8
41	Slovenia	10.0	89	Albania	7.7
42	Finland	9.9		Botswana	7.7
43	Trinidad & Tobago	9.8		Mauritania	7.7
44	Belgium	9.7	92	Afghanistan	7.6
	Macedonia	9.7		Azerbaijan	7.6
46	Armenia	9.6		Kenya	7.6
	Congo-Kinshasa	9.6		Papua New Guinea	7.6
	Denmark	9.6		Suriname	7.6

Note: Both death and, in particular, infant mortality rates can be underestimated in certain countries where not all deaths are officially recorded.   a 2015 estimate.

Highest infant mortality
Number of deaths per 1,000 live births, 2015–20

#	Country	Rate		#	Country	Rate
1	Angola	88		23	Liberia	52
2	Chad	87			Malawi	52
3	Central African Rep.	84		25	Guinea	50
4	Guinea-Bissau	82			Lesotho	50
5	Sierra Leone	81			Niger	50
6	Burundi	71		28	Yemen	49
7	Mali	70		29	Kenya	48
	Somalia	70			Sudan	48
9	Nigeria	68		31	Ghana	47
	South Sudan	68			Zambia	47
11	Congo-Kinshasa	66		33	Papua New Guinea	45
12	Cameroon	65		34	Congo-Brazzaville	44
13	Afghanistan	64		35	Ethiopia	43
14	Benin	63			Gambia, The	43
	Ivory Coast	63			Myanmar	43
	Mauritania	63			Rwanda	43
	Pakistan	63			Turkmenistan	43
18	Equatorial Guinea	62		40	Haiti	42
19	Burkina Faso	58			Togo	42
	Swaziland	58		42	Uzbekistan	41
21	Mozambique	57		43	Zimbabwe	39
22	Uganda	56				

Lowest death rates
No. deaths per 1,000 pop., 2015–20

#	Country	Rate
1	Qatar	1.5
2	United Arab Emirates	1.8
3	Bahrain	2.5
4	Kuwait	2.6
5	Oman	2.7
6	French Guiana	3.0
7	Brunei	3.2
8	Saudi Arabia	3.5
	West Bank & Gaza	3.5
10	Jordan	3.8
11	Lebanon	4.5
12	Iran	4.6
13	Nicaragua	4.8
14	Guam	4.9
	Macau	4.9
	Mexico	4.9
17	Costa Rica	5.0
	Honduras	5.0
	Iraq	5.0
20	Algeria	5.1
	Ecuador	5.1
	Panama	5.1
	Singapore	5.1

Lowest infant mortality
No. deaths per 1,000 live births, 2015–20

#	Country	Rate
1	Luxembourg	1
	Singapore	1
3	Czech Republic	2
	Finland	2
	Greece	2
	Hong Kong	2
	Iceland	2
	Ireland	2
	Italy	2
	Japan	2
	Monaco[a]	2
	Norway	2
	South Korea	2
	Sweden	2

Death and disease

Diabetes

Prevalence in pop. aged 20–79, %
2015 age-standardised estimate[a]

1	Mauritius	22.3
2	Kuwait	20.0
	Qatar	20.0
	Saudi Arabia	20.0
5	Bahrain	19.6
	New Caledonia	19.6
7	French Polynesia	19.4
8	United Arab Emirates	19.3
9	Guam	18.7
10	Malaysia	17.9
11	Egypt	16.7
12	Mexico	15.8
	Réunion	15.8
14	Papua New Guinea	15.3
15	Oman	14.8
16	Fiji	13.8

Cardiovascular disease

No. of deaths per 100,000 pop.,
2012 age-standardised estimate[a]

1	Turkmenistan	712.1
2	Kazakhstan	635.5
3	Mongolia	586.7
4	Uzbekistan	577.7
5	Kyrgyzstan	549.4
6	Guyana	544.8
7	Ukraine	536.1
8	Russia	531.0
9	Afghanistan	511.5
10	Tajikistan	510.3
11	Moldova	507.7
12	Armenia	473.9
13	Belarus	464.2
14	Egypt	445.1
15	Azerbaijan	442.2
16	Albania	436.2

Cancer

Deaths per 100,000 population,
2012 age-standardised estimate[a]

1	Mongolia	161.0
2	Hungary	152.1
3	Armenia	150.3
4	Serbia	147.8
5	Uruguay	144.8
6	Zimbabwe	142.7
7	Macedonia	141.6
8	Kazakhstan	140.2
9	Montenegro	139.0
10	Croatia	136.7
11	Kenya	135.3
12	French Polynesia	134.4
13	Uganda	134.2
14	Poland	131.0
15	Timor-Leste	129.7
16	Lithuania	129.0
17	Latvia	128.8
	Turkey	128.8
19	New Caledonia	127.3
20	Romania	127.1
21	Slovakia	125.8
22	North Korea	125.5
23	Slovenia	125.4
24	Papua New Guinea	125.1

Tuberculosis

Incidence per 100,000 pop., 2013

1	Timor-Leste	820
2	South Africa	696
3	Lesotho	671
4	Cambodia	668
5	Indonesia	647
6	Namibia	627
7	Gabon	615
8	Swaziland	605
9	Mozambique	554
10	North Korea	552
11	Congo-Kinshasa	532
12	Papua New Guinea	529
13	Tanzania	528
14	Liberia	510
15	Somalia	491

Ebola

Deaths since 2014 outbreak[b]

1	Liberia	4,809
2	Sierra Leone	3,956
3	Guinea	2,543
4	Nigeria	8
5	Mali	6
6	United States	1

a Assumes that every country and region has the same age profile (the age profile of
the world population has been used).   b To start of April 2016.
Note: Statistics are not available for all countries. The number of cases diagnosed and
reported depends on the quality of medical practice and administration and can be
under-reported in a number of countries.

Measles immunisation
Lowest % of children aged 12–23 months, 2014

1	South Sudan	22
2	Equatorial Guinea	44
3	Somalia	46
4	Central African Rep.	49
5	Nigeria	51
6	Guinea	52
7	Haiti	53
8	Chad	54
	Syria	54
10	Iraq	57
11	Liberia	58
12	Gabon	61
13	Benin	63
	Ivory Coast	63
	Pakistan	63
16	Madagascar	64
17	Papua New Guinea	65
18	Afghanistan	66

DPT[a] immunisation
Lowest % of children aged 12–23 months, 2013

1	Equatorial Guinea	24
2	South Sudan	39
3	Somalia	42
4	Syria	43
5	Chad	46
6	Central African Rep.	47
7	Haiti	48
8	Liberia	50
9	Guinea	51
10	Papua New Guinea	62
11	Iraq	64
12	Nigeria	66
13	Ivory Coast	67
14	Niger	68
15	Benin	70
	Gabon	70
	South Africa	70

HIV/AIDS
Prevalence per 100,000 population, 2013

1	Lesotho	17,564
2	Swaziland	16,332
3	Botswana	15,817
4	South Africa	11,888
5	Namibia	10,652
6	Zimbabwe	9,826
7	Zambia	7,638
8	Malawi	6,246
9	Mozambique	6,066
10	Uganda	4,156
11	Kenya	3,606
12	Tanzania	2,843
13	Cameroon	2,713
14	Central African Rep.	2,574
15	Gabon	2,434
16	Guinea-Bissau	2,429
17	Bahamas	2,034
18	Nigeria	1,860
19	Ivory Coast	1,829
20	Togo	1,661
21	Rwanda	1,659
22	Chad	1,601
23	Congo-Brazzaville	1,548
24	South Sudan	1,355
25	Haiti	1,346

AIDS
Deaths per 100,000 population, 2013

1	Lesotho	778
2	Zimbabwe	451
3	South Africa	370
4	Swaziland	364
5	Mozambique	319
6	Malawi	292
7	Botswana	286
8	Namibia	286
9	Central African Rep.	234
10	Cameroon	196
11	Zambia	186
12	Uganda	168
13	Tanzania	159
14	Bahamas	144
15	Ivory Coast	138
16	Guinea-Bissau	134
17	Kenya	132
18	Gabon	124
19	Congo-Brazzaville	121
	Nigeria	121
21	Chad	114
22	South Sudan	112
23	Togo	97
24	Mauritius	69

a Diphtheria, pertussis and tetanus.

Health

Highest health spending
As % of GDP, 2014

1	United States	17.1
2	Haiti	13.2
3	Sweden	11.9
4	Switzerland	11.7
5	France	11.5
6	Germany	11.3
7	Austria	11.2
8	Cuba	11.1
	Sierra Leone	11.1
10	New Zealand	11.0
11	Netherlands	10.9
12	Denmark	10.8
13	Belgium	10.6
	Lesotho	10.6
15	Canada	10.4
	Serbia	10.4
17	Moldova	10.3
18	Japan	10.2
19	Liberia	10.0
20	Paraguay	9.8
21	Finland	9.7
	Malta	9.7
	Norway	9.7
24	Bosnia & Herz.	9.6
	Malawi	9.6

Lowest health spending
As % of GDP, 2014

1	Timor-Leste	1.5
2	Laos	1.9
3	Turkmenistan	2.1
4	Qatar	2.2
5	Myanmar	2.3
6	Brunei	2.6
	Congo-Kinshasa	2.6
	Pakistan	2.6
9	South Sudan	2.7
10	Bangladesh	2.8
	Indonesia	2.8
12	Kuwait	3.0
	Madagascar	3.0
14	Angola	3.3
	Eritrea	3.3
	Syria	3.3
17	Gabon	3.4
18	Sri Lanka	3.5
19	Bhutan	3.6
	Chad	3.6
	Ghana	3.6
	Oman	3.6
	United Arab Emirates	3.6
24	Nigeria	3.7
25	Equatorial Guinea	3.8
	Mauritania	3.8

Highest pop. per doctor
2014 or latest[a]

1	Liberia	71,429
2	Malawi	52,632
	Niger	52,632
4	Ethiopia	45,455
	Sierra Leone	45,455
6	Tanzania	32,258
7	Somalia	28,571
8	Gambia, The	26,316
9	Mozambique	25,000
10	Guinea-Bissau	22,222
11	Burkina Faso	21,277
12	Togo	18,868
13	Rwanda	17,857
14	Papua New Guinea	17,241
15	Benin	16,949
	Senegal	16,949
17	Mauritania	14,627
18	Timor-Leste	13,699
19	Mali	12,048
	Zimbabwe	12,048

Lowest pop. per doctor
2014 or latest[a]

1	Qatar	129
2	Monaco	140
3	Cuba	149
4	Greece	162
5	Spain	202
6	Belgium	205
7	Austria	207
8	Russia	232
9	Georgia	234
	Norway	234
11	Lithuania	243
12	Portugal	244
13	Switzerland	247
14	Andorra	250
15	Belarus	255
	Sweden	255
17	Germany	257
18	Argentina	259
	Bulgaria	259
20	Italy	266

a 2010–14

Obesity[a]

% of adult population
18 years or over, 2014

● Overall ● Men ● Women

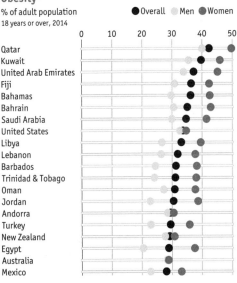

| | 0 | 10 | 20 | 30 | 40 | 50 |

Qatar
Kuwait
United Arab Emirates
Fiji
Bahamas
Bahrain
Saudi Arabia
United States
Libya
Lebanon
Barbados
Trinidad & Tobago
Oman
Jordan
Andorra
Turkey
New Zealand
Egypt
Australia
Mexico

Food deficit

Average kilocalories needed[b] per person per day, 2015 or latest

Highest deficit			Lowest deficit	
1	Haiti	510	1	Turkey	1
2	Zambia	415	2	Tunisia	4
3	North Korea	344	3	South Korea	5
4	Namibia	315	4	Argentina	6
5	Central African Rep.	302	5	Cuba	10
6	Chad	288	6	Brazil	11
7	Liberia	269		Saudi Arabia	11
8	Tajikistan	268	8	Egypt	12
9	Zimbabwe	259		Venezuela	12
10	Ethiopia	250	10	Jordan	13
11	Rwanda	247	11	Azerbaijan	15
12	Tanzania	241		Brunei	15
13	Madagascar	223	13	South Africa	16
14	Sri Lanka	209	14	Kuwait	17
15	Timor-Leste	198	15	Gabon	20
16	Mozambique	195		Kazakhstan	20
17	Botswana	191		Malaysia	20
18	Iraq	190			
19	Congo-Brazzaville	188			
20	Swaziland	186			

a Defined as body mass index of 30 or more – see page 248.
b To lift the undernourished from their status.

Telephones and the internet

Mobile telephones
Subscriptions per 100 population, 2014

1	Macau	322.6	24	Poland	148.9
2	Hong Kong	233.6	25	Malaysia	148.8
3	Kuwait	218.4	26	Jordan	147.8
4	Saudi Arabia	179.6	27	Trinidad & Tobago	147.3
5	United Arab Emirates	178.1	28	Vietnam	147.1
6	Bahrain	173.3	29	Lithuania	147.0
7	Kazakhstan	172.2	30	Singapore	146.9
8	Gabon	171.4	31	Qatar	145.8
9	Suriname	170.6	32	Thailand	144.4
10	Botswana	167.3	33	Ukraine	144.1
11	Montenegro	163.0	34	El Salvador	144.0
12	Libya	161.1	35	Costa Rica	143.8
13	Uruguay	160.8	36	Finland	139.7
14	Estonia	160.7	37	Brazil	139.0
15	Argentina	158.8	38	Bulgaria	137.7
16	Panama	158.1	39	Switzerland	136.7
17	Oman	157.8	40	Turkmenistan	135.8
18	Russia	155.1	41	Kyrgyzstan	134.5
19	Italy	154.2	42	Chile	133.3
20	Austria	151.9	43	Cambodia	132.7
21	Luxembourg	149.5	44	Mauritius	132.2
22	South Africa	149.2	45	Morocco	131.7
23	Mali	149.1	46	Australia	131.2

Digital adoption index[a]
2016, 1=best possible score

● Overall ○ People ● Business ● Government

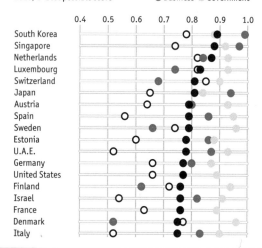

a Measures technology adoption in three areas of the economy: business, people and government. It includes indicators such as 3G coverage, secure servers, internet access at home and online public services.

Internet users
Per 100 population, 2014

1	Iceland	98.2	26	Taiwan	84.0
2	Bermuda	96.8	27	France	83.8
3	Norway	96.3	28	Singapore	82.0
4	Denmark	96.0	29	Austria	81.0
5	Andorra	95.9	30	Slovakia	80.0
6	Liechtenstein	95.2	31	Czech Republic	79.7
7	Luxembourg	94.7		Ireland	79.7
8	Netherlands	93.2	33	Puerto Rico	78.8
9	Sweden	92.5	34	Kuwait	78.7
10	Finland	92.4	35	Bahamas	76.9
	Monaco	92.4	36	Barbados	76.7
12	United Kingdom	91.6	37	Spain	76.2
13	Qatar	91.5	38	Hungary	76.1
14	Bahrain	91.0	39	Latvia	75.8
15	Japan	90.6	40	Lebanon	74.7
16	United Arab Emirates	90.4	41	Hong Kong	74.6
17	United States	87.4	42	Malta	73.2
18	Canada	87.1	43	Chile	72.4
19	Switzerland	87.0	44	Lithuania	72.1
20	Germany	86.2	45	Slovenia	71.6
21	New Zealand	85.5	46	Israel	71.5
22	Belgium	85.0	47	Russia	70.5
23	Australia	84.6	48	Oman	70.2
24	South Korea	84.3	49	New Caledonia	70.0
25	Estonia	84.2	50	Macau	69.8

Broadband
Fixed-broadband subscriptions per 100 population, 2014

1	Bermuda	53.1	23	New Zealand	31.0
2	Monaco	46.8	24	Japan	29.3
3	Switzerland	42.5	25	Estonia	28.9
4	Liechtenstein	42.0	26	Belarus	28.8
5	Denmark	41.3	27	Greece	28.4
6	Netherlands	40.8	28	Macau	28.1
7	France	40.2	29	Czech Republic	27.9
8	Norway	38.8	30	Australia	27.7
	South Korea	38.8		Austria	27.7
10	United Kingdom	37.4	32	Hungary	27.4
11	Belgium	36.0	33	Spain	27.3
12	Andorra	35.9	34	Barbados	27.2
	Iceland	35.9		Israel	27.2
14	Germany	35.8	36	Ireland	26.9
15	Canada	35.4	37	Lithuania	26.7
16	Malta	35.2		Singapore	26.7
17	Luxembourg	34.8	39	Slovenia	26.6
18	Sweden	34.1	40	Portugal	25.7
19	Finland	32.3	41	Latvia	24.7
20	Taiwan	31.9	42	Uruguay	24.6
21	Hong Kong	31.4	43	Italy	23.5
22	United States	31.1	44	Saudi Arabia	23.4

Arts and entertainment

Music sales

Total including downloads, $m, 2015

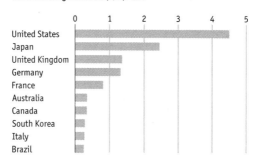

United States	
Japan	
United Kingdom	
Germany	
France	
Australia	
Canada	
South Korea	
Italy	
Brazil	

$ per person, 2015

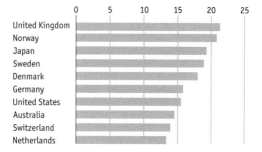

United Kingdom	
Norway	
Japan	
Sweden	
Denmark	
Germany	
United States	
Australia	
Switzerland	
Netherlands	

Book publishing
New titles per million population, 2014

1	United Kingdom	3,470	16	South Korea[b]	795
2	Brazil	2,482	17	Finland[a]	793
3	Slovenia[a]	1,831	18	Austria[a]	757
	Taiwan[a]	1,831	19	Russia[a]	699
5	Spain	1,667	20	Turkey	670
6	Georgia[a]	1,547	21	Malaysia[b]	639
7	Netherlands	1,535	22	Argentina[a]	614
8	France	1,522	23	Japan	602
9	Czech Republic[a]	1,509	24	New Zealand[b]	479
10	Norway	1,275	25	Belgium	401
11	Australia[a]	1,176	26	Poland[a]	353
12	Germany	1,054	27	China	325
13	Italy	1,046	28	Colombia[a]	229
14	United States[a]	959	29	Mexico[a]	200
15	Hungary[a]	920	30	Indonesia[a]	119

a 2013   b 2012

Cinema attendances

Total visits, m, 2014

1	India	2,117.6
2	United States	1,270.0
3	China	830.0
4	Mexico	257.0
5	South Korea	215.1
6	France	208.8
7	Russia	176.8
8	Japan	161.1
9	United Kingdom	157.5
10	Brazil	153.0
11	Germany	121.7
12	Italy	109.0
13	Spain	88.0
14	Australia	78.6
15	Malaysia	69.0
16	Turkey	61.9
17	Argentina	48.8
18	Colombia	46.9
19	Philippines	40.6
20	Poland	40.5
21	Peru	37.1
22	Netherlands	30.8
23	Thailand	28.9
24	Hong Kong	27.6
25	Venezuela	29.1
26	Chile	21.5
27	Singapore	21.6
28	South Africa	20.9
29	Belgium	20.5

Visits per person, 2014

1	South Korea	4.3
2	Iceland	4.2
3	Singapore	3.9
4	United States	4.0
5	Hong Kong	3.8
6	Australia	3.3
	France	3.3
	New Zealand	3.3
9	Bahrain	3.2
10	Ireland	3.1
11	United Kingdom	2.4
12	Malaysia	2.3
13	Denmark	2.2
	Luxembourg	2.2
	Norway	2.2
16	Estonia	2.0
	Mexico	2.0
18	Israel	1.9
	Spain	1.9
	United Arab Emirates	1.9
21	Belgium	1.8
	Italy	1.8
	Netherlands	1.8
24	Austria	1.7
	India	1.7
	Malta	1.7
	Sweden	1.7
	Switzerland	1.7

Top Oscar winners

		Awards	Nominations
1	*Ben-Hur* (1959)	11	12
	Titanic (1997)	11	14
	The Lord of the Rings: The Return of the King (2003)	11	11
4	*West Side Story* (1961)	10	11
5	*Gigi* (1958)	9	9
	The Last Emperor (1987)	9	9
	The English Patient (1996)	9	12
8	*Gone With the Wind* (1939)	8	13
	From Here to Eternity (1953)	8	13
	On the Waterfront (1954)	8	12
	My Fair Lady (1964)	8	12
	Cabaret[a] (1972)	8	10
	Gandhi (1982)	8	11
	Amadeus (1984)	8	11
	Slumdog Millionaire (2008)	8	10

a Did not win best picture award.

The press

Daily newspapers
Copies per '000 population, 2014

1	Luxembourg	709		16	Denmark	194
2	Hong Kong	522		17	United Kingdom	189
3	Ecuador	450		18	Canada	150
4	Iceland	424			Taiwan	150
5	Japan	358		20	Israel	139
6	Austria	342		21	France	138
7	Switzerland	340		22	Estonia	137
8	Sweden	321		23	Belgium	135
9	Norway	301		24	United States	132
10	Finland	285		25	Hungary	122
11	Singapore	246		26	Thailand	117
12	South Korea	215		27	United Arab Emirates	116
13	Netherlands	212		28	Czech Republic	113
14	India	209			New Zealand	113
15	Germany	197		30	Slovenia	109

Press freedom[a]
Scores, 1 = best, 100 = worst, 2015

Most free			Least free		
1	Finland	7.5	1	Eritrea	84.9
2	Norway	7.8	2	North Korea	83.3
3	Denmark	8.2	3	Turkmenistan	80.8
4	Netherlands	9.2	4	Syria	77.3
5	Sweden	9.5	5	China	73.6
6	New Zealand	10.1	6	Vietnam	72.6
7	Austria	10.9	7	Iran	72.3
8	Canada	11.0		Somalia	72.3
9	Estonia	11.2		Sudan	72.3
	Ireland	11.2	10	Laos	71.3
	Jamaica	11.2	11	Cuba	70.2
12	Germany	11.5	12	Yemen	66.4
13	Czech Republic	11.6	13	Equatorial Guinea	66.2
14	Slovakia	11.7	14	Uzbekistan	61.1
15	Belgium	12.0	15	Sri Lanka	60.3
16	Costa Rica	12.3	16	Saudi Arabia	59.4
17	Namibia	12.5	17	Bahrain	58.7
18	Poland	12.7	18	Azerbaijan	58.4
19	Luxembourg	13.6	19	Rwanda	56.6
20	Iceland	13.9	20	Kazakhstan	53.5
	Switzerland	13.9	21	Pakistan	50.5
22	Ghana	15.5	22	Egypt	50.2
23	Uruguay	15.9	23	Belarus	48.0
24	Cyprus	16.5	24	Iraq	47.8
25	Australia	17.0	25	Swaziland	47.3
26	Portugal	17.1	26	Libya	46.0
27	Liechtenstein	17.7	27	Singapore	45.9
28	Latvia	18.1	28	Russia	45.0
29	Suriname	18.2	29	Gambia, The	44.5

a Based on data for deaths and violence against journalists, and attacks on organisations, plus 87 questions on media topics.

Nobel prize winners: 1901–2015

Peace (two or more)

1	United States	19
2	United Kingdom	12
3	France	9
4	Sweden	5
5	Belgium	4
	Germany	4
7	Austria	3
	Norway	3
	South Africa	3
	Switzerland	3
11	Argentina	2
	Egypt	2
	India	2
	Israel	2
	Russia	2

Medicine (three or more)

1	United States	56
2	United Kingdom	25
3	Germany	15
4	France	8
5	Sweden	7
6	Switzerland	6
7	Austria	5
	Denmark	5
9	Australia	3
	Belgium	3
	Italy	3

Literature (three or more)

1	France	16
2	United States	12
3	United Kingdom	11
4	Germany	8
5	Sweden	7
6	Italy	5
	Spain	5
8	Norway	3
	Poland	3
	Russia	3

Economics[a]

1	United States	38
2	United Kingdom	9
3	France	2
	Norway	2
	Sweden	2
6	Denmark	1
	Germany	1
	Israel	1
	Netherlands	1
	Russia	1

Physics

1	United States	53
2	United Kingdom	21
3	Germany	19
4	France	10
5	Japan	6
	Netherlands	6
	Russia	6
8	Sweden	4
	Switzerland	4
10	Austria	3
	Canada	3
	Italy	3
13	Denmark	2
14	Australia	1
	Belgium	1
	China	1
	India	1
	Ireland	1
	Pakistan	1
	Poland	1

Chemistry

1	United States	49
2	United Kingdom	23
3	Germany	16
4	France	7
5	Switzerland	6
6	Japan	5
	Sweden	5
8	Canada	4
9	Israel	3
10	Argentina	1
	Austria	1
	Belgium	1
	Czech Republic	1
	Denmark	1
	Finland	1
	Italy	1
	Netherlands	1
	Norway	1
	Russia	1

a Since 1969.
Notes: Prizes by country of residence at time awarded. When prizes have been shared in the same field, one credit given to each country.

Sports champions and cheats

World Cup winners and finalists

Men's football (since 1930)	Winner	Runner-up
1 Brazil	5	2
2 Germany	4	4
3 Italy	4	2
4 Argentina	2	3
5 Uruguay	2	0
6 France	1	1
7 England	1	0
Spain	1	0
9 Netherlands	0	3
10 Czechoslovakia[a]	0	2
Hungary	0	2
12 Sweden	0	1

Women's football (since 1991)	Winner	Runner-up
1 United States	3	1
2 Germany	2	1
3 Norway	1	1
4 Japan	1	0
5 Brazil	0	1
Sweden	0	1
China	0	1

Men's cricket (since 1975)	Winner	Runner-up
1 Australia	5	2
2 India	2	1
West Indies	2	1
4 Sri Lanka	1	2
5 Pakistan	1	1
6 England	0	3
7 New Zealand	0	1

Women's cricket (since 1973)	Winner	Runner-up
1 Australia	6	2
2 England	3	3
3 New Zealand	1	3
4 India	0	1
West Indies	0	1

Men's rugby (since 1989)	Winner	Runner-up
1 New Zealand	3	1
2 Australia	2	1
3 South Africa	2	0
4 England	1	2
5 France	0	3

Women's rugby (since 1991)	Winner	Runner-up
1 New Zealand	4	0
2 England	2	4
3 United States	1	2
4 Canada	0	1

Note: Data as of May 2016.   a Until 1993.

Olympic games

Summer: 1896–2012	Gold	Silver	Bronze
1 United States	971	755	670
2 Soviet Union/Unified Team (1952–92)[a]	440	357	325
3 Great Britain	238	273	273
4 France	206	225	250
5 Germany	202	237	252
6 China	201	144	128
7 Italy	199	166	185
8 Hungary	167	144	165
9 Estonia	153	129	127
10 East Germany (1968–88)	143	157	179
11 Sweden	143	164	176
12 Russia	133	126	147
13 Japan	130	126	142
14 Finland	101	84	117
15 Romania	88	94	119

Winter: 1924–2014	Gold	Silver	Bronze
1 Norway	118	111	100
2 United States	96	102	83
3 Germany	86	84	58
4 Soviet Union/Unified Team (1952–92)[a]	87	63	67
5 Canada	62	55	53
6 Austria	59	78	81
7 Sweden	50	40	54
8 Switzerland	50	40	48
9 Russia	49	40	35
10 Finland	42	62	57
11 East Germany (1968–88)	39	36	35
12 Italy	37	34	43
13 Netherlands	37	38	35
14 France	31	31	45
15 South Korea	26	17	10

Doping

Anti-doping rule violations, 2014

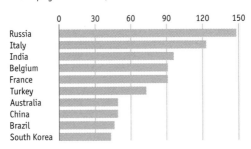

a Former Soviet states of Armenia, Belarus, Kazakhstan, Russia, Ukraine and Uzbekistan.

Vices

Beer drinkers
Retail sales, litres per person, 2014

1	Czech Republic	147.0
2	Germany	113.7
3	Austria	107.3
4	Estonia	103.0
5	Poland	99.7
6	Bahamas	96.8
7	Botswana	96.3
8	Lithuania	94.3
9	Romania	93.4
10	Ireland	92.2
11	Finland	80.7
12	Belgium	79.6
13	Australia	78.8
14	Virgin Islands (US)	78.5
15	Slovenia	78.4
16	Latvia	77.9
17	United States	76.6
18	Hungary	74.8
19	Croatia	74.7
20	Slovakia	74.4
21	Bulgaria	74.3
22	United Kingdom	74.1
23	Spain	72.1
24	Kosovo	69.7

Smokers
Av. ann. consumption of cigarettes per person per day, 2015

1	Belarus	7.1
2	Lebanon	6.9
3	Russia	5.9
4	Serbia	5.6
5	China	5.2
6	Slovenia	5.1
7	Moldova	5.0
8	Czech Republic	4.9
	Macedonia	4.9
	South Korea	4.9
11	Georgia	4.6
12	Bulgaria	4.4
13	Ukraine	4.3
	Taiwan	4.3
15	Austria	4.2
	Bosnia & Herz.	4.2
17	Greece	4.1
18	Albania	3.9
	Japan	3.9
20	Azerbaijan	3.8
21	Estonia	3.7
22	Armenia	3.6
	Belgium	3.6
24	Slovakia	3.5

Gambling losses[a]
Total, $bn, 2015

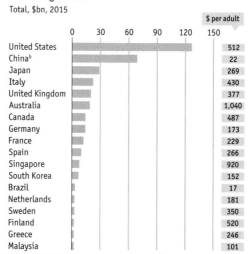

	Total, $bn, 2015	$ per adult
United States		512
China[b]		22
Japan		269
Italy		430
United Kingdom		377
Australia		1,040
Canada		487
Germany		173
France		229
Spain		266
Singapore		920
South Korea		152
Brazil		17
Netherlands		181
Sweden		350
Finland		520
Greece		246
Malaysia		101

a Data according to H2 Gambling Capital – March 2016.
b Includes Macau and Hong Kong.

Tourism

Most tourist arrivals
Number of arrivals, '000, 2014

1	France	83,767	21	Netherlands	13,925
2	United States	75,011	22	Japan	13,413
3	Spain	64,995	23	Ukraine	12,712
4	China	55,622	24	Hungary	12,140
5	Italy	48,576	25	Singapore	11,864
6	Turkey	39,811	26	Croatia	11,623
7	Germany	32,999	27	Czech Republic	10,617
8	United Kingdom	32,613	28	Bahrain	10,452
9	Russia	32,421	29	Morocco	10,283
10	Mexico	29,346	30	Denmark	10,267
11	Hong Kong	27,770	31	Taiwan	9,910
12	Malaysia	27,437	32	Egypt	9,628
13	Austria	25,291	33	South Africa	9,549
14	Thailand	24,810	34	Indonesia	9,435
15	Greece	22,033	35	Switzerland	9,158
16	Saudi Arabia	18,259	36	Portugal	9,092
17	Canada	16,537	37	Ireland	8,813
18	Poland	16,000	38	Romania	8,442
19	Macau	14,566	39	Belgium	7,887
20	South Korea	14,202	40	Vietnam	7,874

Biggest tourist spenders
$m, 2014

1	China	164.9	13	South Korea	25.9
2	United States	145.7	14	Saudi Arabia	25.1
3	Germany	106.6	15	Singapore	23.9
4	United Kingdom	79.9	16	Hong Kong	22.0
5	France	59.4	17	Netherlands	21.4
6	Russia	55.4	18	Switzerland	20.2
7	Canada	33.8	19	Norway	19.3
8	Australia	31.9	20	Sweden	18.5
9	Brazil	30.0	21	Spain	18.0
10	Italy	28.9	22	United Arab Emirates	17.7
11	Japan	28.6	23	India	17.5
12	Belgium	26.4	24	Qatar	12.9

Largest tourist receipts
$m, 2014

1	United States	177.2	13	Malaysia	21.8
2	Spain	65.2	14	Austria	20.6
3	China	56.9	15	India	19.7
4	France	55.4	16	Singapore	19.2
5	Macau	50.8	17	Japan	18.9
6	Italy	45.5	18	South Korea	18.1
7	United Kingdom	45.3	19	Greece	17.8
8	Germany	43.3	20	Canada	17.4
9	Hong Kong	38.4		Switzerland	17.4
	Thailand	38.4	22	Mexico	16.3
11	Australia	32.0	23	Netherlands	14.7
12	Turkey	29.6	24	Taiwan	14.6

Country profiles

110	Algeria
112	Argentina
114	Australia
116	Austria
118	Bangladesh
120	Belgium
122	Brazil
124	Bulgaria
126	Cameroon
128	Canada
130	Chile
132	China
134	Colombia
136	Czech Republic
138	Denmark
140	Egypt
142	Finland
144	France
146	Germany
148	Greece
150	Hong Kong
152	Hungary
154	India
156	Indonesia
158	Iran
160	Ireland
162	Israel
164	Italy
166	Ivory Coast
168	Japan
170	Kenya
172	Malaysia
174	Mexico

176	Morocco
178	Netherlands
180	New Zealand
182	Nigeria
184	Norway
186	Pakistan
188	Peru
190	Philippines
192	Poland
194	Portugal
196	Romania
198	Russia
200	Saudi Arabia
202	Singapore
204	Slovakia
206	Slovenia
208	South Africa
210	South Korea
212	Spain
214	Sweden
216	Switzerland
218	Taiwan
220	Thailand
222	Turkey
224	Ukraine
226	United Arab Emirates
228	United Kingdom
230	United States
232	Venezuela
234	Vietnam
236	Zimbabwe
238	Euro area
240	World

ALGERIA

Area	2,381,741 sq km	Capital	Algiers
Arable as % of total land	3.1	Currency	Algerian dinar (AD)

People

Population, m	39.9	Life expectancy: men	73.4 yrs
Pop. per sq km	16.3	women	78.0 yrs
Average annual growth		Adult literacy	...
in pop. 2015–20, %	1.6	Fertility rate (per woman)	2.6
Pop. aged 0–19, %	36.1	Urban population, %	70.7
Pop. aged 65 and over, %	5.9		per 1,000 pop.
No. of men per 100 women	101.3	Crude birth rate	21.5
Human Development Index	73.6	Crude death rate	5.1

The economy

GDP	AD17,205bn	GDP per head	$5,484
GDP	$214bn	GDP per head in purchasing	
Av. ann. growth in real		power parity (USA=100)	25.7
GDP 2009–14	3.1%	Economic freedom index	50.1

Origins of GDP		**Components of GDP**	
	% of total		% of total
Agriculture	11	Private consumption	36
Industry, of which:	46	Public consumption	19
manufacturing	...	Investment	46
Services	43	Exports	31
		Imports	-32

Structure of employment

	% of total		% of labour force
Agriculture	10.8	Unemployed 2014	9.5
Industry	30.9	Av. ann. rate 2005–14	11.3
Services	58.4		

Energy

	m TOE		
Total output	137.7	Net energy imports as %	
Total consumption	47.6	of energy use	-189
Consumption per head			
kg oil equivalent	1,246		

Inflation and finance

Consumer price		av. ann. increase 2010–15	
inflation 2015	4.8%	Narrow money (M1)	10.0%
Av. ann. inflation 2010–15	4.9%	Broad money	10.6%
Treasury bill rate, Dec. 2015	0.62%		

Exchange rates

	end 2015		December 2015
AD per $	107.1	Effective rates	2010 = 100
AD per SDR	148.5	– nominal	86.30
AD per €	117.1	– real	98.48

Trade

Principal exports		Principal imports	
	$bn fob		*$bn cif*
Hydrocarbons	58.4	Capital goods	18.1
Semi-finished goods	1.2	Semi-finished goods	12.3
Raw materials	0.1	Foodstuffs	10.6
		Consumer goods	9.9
Total incl. others	**60.0**	Total incl. others	**58.3**

Main export destinations		Main origins of imports	
	% of total		*% of total*
Spain	16.2	China	14.1
Italy	14.0	France	10.9
France	11.2	Italy	8.5
United Kingdom	9.1	Spain	8.5

Balance of payments, reserves and debt, $bn

Visible exports fob	59.7	Change in reserves	-15.9
Visible imports fob	-59.4	Level of reserves	
Trade balance	0.2	end Dec.	185.5
Invisibles inflows	6.7	No. months of import cover	28.1
Invisibles outflows	-19.9	Official gold holdings, m oz	5.6
Net transfers	3.3	Foreign debt	5.5
Current account balance	-9.7	– as % of GDP	2.6
– as % of GDP	-4.5	– as % of total exports	8.1
Capital balance	3.8	Debt service ratio	0.4
Overall balance	-5.9		

Health and education

Health spending, % of GDP	7.2	Education spending, % of GDP	...
Doctors per 1,000 pop.	1.2	Enrolment, %: primary	119
Hospital beds per 1,000 pop.	...	secondary	100
Improved-water source access,		tertiary	35
% of pop.	83.6		

Society

No. of households, m	7.1	Cost of living, Dec. 2015	
Av. no. per household	5.5	New York = 100	44
Marriages per 1,000 pop.	...	Cars per 1,000 pop.	87
Divorces per 1,000 pop.	...	Colour TV households, % with:	
Religion, % of pop.		cable	...
Muslim	97.9	satellite	93.1
Non-religious	1.8	Telephone lines per 100 pop.	7.8
Christian	0.2	Mobile telephone subscribers	
Hindu	<0.1	per 100 pop.	92.9
Jewish	<0.1	Broadband subs per 100 pop.	4.0
Other	<0.1	Internet users, % of pop.	18.1

ARGENTINA

Area	2,780,400 sq km	Capital	Buenos Aires
Arable as % of total land	14.5	Currency	Peso (P)

People

Population, m	41.8	Life expectancy: men	73.2 yrs
Pop. per sq km	15.0	women	80.6 yrs
Average annual growth		Adult literacy	98.0
in pop. 2015–20, %	0.9	Fertility rate (per woman)	2.3
Pop. aged 0–19, %	33.1	Urban population, %	91.8
Pop. aged 65 and over, %	10.9		per 1,000 pop.
No. of men per 100 women	95.8	Crude birth rate	16.9
Human Development Index	83.6	Crude death rate	7.5

The economy

GDP	P4,425bn	GDP per head	$12,674
GDP	$545bn	GDP per head in purchasing	
Av. ann. growth in real		power parity (USA=100)	40.7
GDP 2009–14	4.3%	Economic freedom index	43.8

Origins of GDP		**Components of GDP**	
	% of total		% of total
Agriculture	8	Private consumption	64
Industry, of which:	29	Public consumption	16
manufacturing	14	Investment	20
Services	63	Exports	15
		Imports	-14

Structure of employment

	% of total		% of labour force
Agriculture	0.5	Unemployed 2014	8.2
Industry	24.0	Av. ann. rate 2005–14	8.3
Services	74.7		

Energy

	m TOE		
Total output	71.4	Net energy imports as %	
Total consumption	80.6	of energy use	11
Consumption per head			
kg oil equivalent	1,895		

Inflation and finance

Consumer price		av. ann. increase 2010–15	
inflation 2015	10.6%	Narrow money (M1)	22.8%
Av. ann. inflation 2010–15	10.3%	Broad money	29.4%
Money market rate, Dec. 2015	25.89%		

Exchange rates

	end 2015		December 2015
P per $	13.10	Effective rates	2010 = 100
P per SDR	18.15	– nominal	...
P per €	14.32	– real	...

Trade

Principal exports		Principal imports	
	$bn fob		*$bn cif*
Processed agricultural products	27.9	Intermediate goods	18.9
Manufactured goods	24.2	Capital goods	12.6
Primary products	14.8	Fuels	10.9
Fuels & energy	4.9	Consumer goods	6.7
Total	**71.9**	**Total incl. others**	**65.2**

Main export destinations		Main origins of imports	
	% of total		*% of total*
Brazil	19.3	Brazil	22.0
China	6.2	United States	16.2
Chile	5.4	China	13.9
United States	3.9	Germany	5.4

Balance of payments, reserves and debt, $bn

Visible exports fob	68.3	Change in reserves	0.6
Visible imports fob	-62.4	Level of reserves	
Trade balance	5.9	end Dec.	31.1
Invisibles inflows	16.3	No. months of import cover	4.0
Invisibles outflows	-30.1	Official gold holdings, m oz	2.0
Net transfers	-0.2	Foreign debt	139.6
Current account balance	-8.1	– as % of GDP	25.5
– as % of GDP	-1.5	– as % of total exports	156.8
Capital balance	7.2	Debt service ratio	15.8
Overall balance	-0.8		

Health and education

Health spending, % of GDP	4.8	Education spending, % of GDP	5.3
Doctors per 1,000 pop.	3.9	Enrolment, %: primary	111
Hospital beds per 1,000 pop.	4.7	secondary	106
Improved-water source access,		tertiary	80
% of pop.	99.1		

Society

No. of households, m	13.3	Cost of living, Dec. 2015	
Av. no. per household	3.2	New York = 100	73
Marriages per 1,000 pop.	2.9	Cars per 1,000 pop.	243
Divorces per 1,000 pop.	...	Colour TV households, % with:	
Religion, % of pop.		cable	64.8
Christian	85.2	satellite	14.4
Non-religious	12.2	Telephone lines per 100 pop.	23.0
Other	1.1	Mobile telephone subscribers	
Muslim	1.0	per 100 pop.	158.8
Jewish	0.5	Broadband subs per 100 pop.	15.6
Hindu	<0.1	Internet users, % of pop.	64.7

AUSTRALIA

Area	7,692,024 sq km	Capital	Canberra
Arable as % of total land	6.0	Currency	Australian dollar (A$)

People

Population, m	23.6	Life expectancy: men	81.1 yrs
Pop. per sq km	3.1	women	85.0 yrs
Average annual growth		Adult literacy	...
in pop. 2015–20, %	1.3	Fertility rate (per woman)	1.9
Pop. aged 0–19, %	24.9	Urban population, %	89.4
Pop. aged 65 and over, %	15.0		per 1,000 pop.
No. of men per 100 women	99.9	Crude birth rate	13.0
Human Development Index	93.5	Crude death rate	6.7

The economy

GDP	A$1,600bn	GDP per head	$61,042
GDP	$1,442bn	GDP per head in purchasing	
Av. ann. growth in real		power parity (USA=100)	85.7
GDP 2009–14	2.7%	Economic freedom index	80.3

Origins of GDP		**Components of GDP**	
	% of total		% of total
Agriculture	2	Private consumption	55
Industry, of which:	27	Public consumption	18
manufacturing	7	Investment	27
Services	71	Exports	21
		Imports	-21

Structure of employment

	% of total		% of labour force
Agriculture	2.6	Unemployed 2014	6.0
Industry	20.8	Av. ann. rate 2005–14	5.1
Services	69.5		

Energy

	m TOE		
Total output	343.9	Net energy imports as %	
Total consumption	129.1	of energy use	-166
Consumption per head			
kg oil equivalent	5,586		

Inflation and finance

Consumer price		av. ann. increase 2010–15	
inflation 2015	1.5%	Narrow money (M1)	4.2%
Av. ann. inflation 2010–15	2.3%	Broad money	7.0%
Money market rate, Dec. 2015	2.00%		

Exchange rates

	end 2015		December 2015
A$ per $	1.37	Effective rates	2010 = 100
A$ per SDR	1.90	– nominal	90.84
A$ per €	1.50	– real	92.23

Trade

Principal exports		Principal imports	
	$bn fob		*$bn cif*
Crude materials	88.0	Machinery & transport equip.	85.2
Fuels	63.7	Manufactured goods	36.1
Food	28.0	Mineral fuels	31.4
Manufactured goods	13.9	Miscellaneous manufactured articles	26.0
Total incl. others	**240.0**	**Total incl. others**	**227.7**

Main export destinations		Main origins of imports	
	% of total		*% of total*
China	33.8	China	22.6
Japan	18.0	United States	11.7
South Korea	7.4	Japan	7.5
United States	4.2	Singapore	5.5

Balance of payments, reserves and aid, $bn

Visible exports fob	240.7	Overall balance	3.6
Visible imports fob	-240.4	Change in reserves	0.7
Trade balance	0.4	Level of reserves	
Invisibles inflows	101.0	end Dec.	53.5
Invisibles outflows	-143.5	No. months of import cover	1.7
Net transfers	-2.0	Official gold holdings, m oz	2.6
Current account balance	-44.1	Aid given	4.4
– as % of GDP	-3.0	– as % of GDP	0.3
Capital balance	45.0		

Health and education

Health spending, % of GDP	9.4	Education spending, % of GDP	4.9
Doctors per 1,000 pop.	3.3	Enrolment, %: primary	107
Hospital beds per 1,000 pop.	3.9	secondary	138
Improved-water source access, % of pop.	100	tertiary	87

Society

No. of households, m	8.6	Cost of living, Dec. 2015	
Av. no. per household	2.7	New York = 100	90
Marriages per 1,000 pop.	5.1	Cars per 1,000 pop.	563
Divorces per 1,000 pop.	2.1	Colour TV households, % with:	
Religion, % of pop.		cable	24.9
Christian	67.3	satellite	33.7
Non-religious	24.2	Telephone lines per 100 pop.	38.9
Other	4.2	Mobile telephone subscribers	
Muslim	2.4	per 100 pop.	131.2
Hindu	1.4	Broadband subs per 100 pop.	27.7
Jewish	0.5	Internet users, % of pop.	84.6

AUSTRIA

Area	83,871 sq km	Capital	Vienna
Arable as % of total land	16.4	Currency	Euro (€)

People

Population, m	8.5	Life expectancy: men	79.7 yrs
Pop. per sq km	101.3	women	84.4 yrs
Average annual growth		Adult literacy	...
in pop. 2015–20, %	0.3	Fertility rate (per woman)	1.5
Pop. aged 0–19, %	19.6	Urban population, %	66.0
Pop. aged 65 and over, %	18.8		per 1,000 pop.
No. of men per 100 women	96.5	Crude birth rate	9.7
Human Development Index	88.5	Crude death rate	9.5

The economy

GDP	€329bn	GDP per head	$51,378
GDP	$438bn	GDP per head in purchasing	
Av. ann. growth in real		power parity (USA=100)	85.8
GDP 2009–14	1.2%	Economic freedom index	71.7

Origins of GDP		**Components of GDP**	
	% of total		% of total
Agriculture	1	Private consumption	54
Industry, of which:	28	Public consumption	20
manufacturing	18	Investment	23
Services	71	Exports	53
		Imports	-49

Structure of employment

	% of total		% of labour force
Agriculture	4.3	Unemployed 2014	5.0
Industry	26.1	Av. ann. rate 2005–14	4.6
Services	69.7		

Energy

	m TOE		
Total output	12.1	Net energy imports as %	
Total consumption	33.2	of energy use	64
Consumption per head			
kg oil equivalent	3,918		

Inflation and finance

Consumer price		av. ann. increase 2010–15	
inflation 2015	1.5%	Euro area:	
Av. ann. inflation 2010–15	0.8%	Narrow money (M1)	6.7%
Deposit rate, h'holds, Dec. 2015	0.37%	Broad money	3.1%

Exchange rates

	end 2015		December 2015
€ per $	0.92	Effective rates	2010 = 100
€ per SDR	1.27	– nominal	98.13
		– real	100.13

Trade

Principal exports		Principal imports	
	$bn fob		*$bn cif*
Machinery & transport equip.	70.5	Machinery & transport equip.	62.6
Chemicals & related products	24.2	Chemicals & related products	24.0
Food, drink & tobacco	12.9	Mineral fuels & lubricants	17.3
Raw materials	5.5	Food, drink & tobacco	13.4
Total incl. others	**178.3**	Total incl. others	**182.1**

Main export destinations		Main origins of imports	
	% of total		*% of total*
Germany	29.2	Germany	41.3
Italy	6.3	Italy	6.4
United States	5.6	Switzerland	5.6
Switzerland	5.5	Czech Republic	4.2
EU28	69.9	EU28	76.8

Balance of payments, reserves and aid, $bn

Visible exports fob	166.0	Overall balance	2.9
Visible imports fob	-164.0	Change in reserves	0.4
Trade balance	2.0	Level of reserves	
Invisibles inflows	105.9	end Dec.	23.7
Invisibles outflows	-95.2	No. months of import cover	1.1
Net transfers	-4.4	Official gold holdings, m oz	9.0
Current account balance	8.3	Aid given	1.2
– as % of GDP	1.9	– as % of GDP	0.3
Capital balance	0.3		

Health and education

Health spending, % of GDP	11.2	Education spending, % of GDP	5.5
Doctors per 1,000 pop.	4.8	Enrolment, %: primary	102
Hospital beds per 1,000 pop.	7.6	secondary	99
Improved-water source access,		tertiary	80
% of pop.	100		

Society

No. of households, m	3.7	Cost of living, Dec. 2015	
Av. no. per household	2.3	New York = 100	91
Marriages per 1,000 pop.	4.3	Cars per 1,000 pop.	552
Divorces per 1,000 pop.	1.9	Colour TV households, % with:	
Religion, % of pop.		cable	38.6
Christian	80.4	satellite	54.3
Non-religious	13.5	Telephone lines per 100 pop.	38.2
Muslim	5.4	Mobile telephone subscribers	
Other	0.5	per 100 pop.	151.9
Jewish	0.2	Broadband subs per 100 pop.	27.7
Hindu	<0.1	Internet users, % of pop.	81.0

BANGLADESH

Area	147,570 sq km	Capital	Dhaka
Arable as % of total land	59.0	Currency	Taka (Tk)

People

Population, m	158.5	Life expectancy: men	71.6 yrs
Pop. per sq km	1,074.1	women	74.3 yrs
Average annual growth		Adult literacy	59.7
in pop. 2015–20, %	1.1	Fertility rate (per woman)	2.1
Pop. aged 0–19, %	39.5	Urban population, %	34.3
Pop. aged 65 and over, %	5.0		per 1,000 pop.
No. of men per 100 women	102.0	Crude birth rate	18.6
Human Development Index	57.0	Crude death rate	5.3

The economy

GDP	Tk14,286bn	GDP per head	$1,156
GDP	$184bn	GDP per head in purchasing	
Av. ann. growth in real		power parity (USA=100)	6.2
GDP 2009–14	6.2%	Economic freedom index	53.3

Origins of GDP		**Components of GDP**	
	% of total		% of total
Agriculture	16	Private consumption	73
Industry, of which:	28	Public consumption	5
manufacturing	17	Investment	29
Services	56	Exports	19
		Imports	-26

Structure of employment

	% of total		% of labour force
Agriculture	47.5	Unemployed 2014	4.3
Industry	17.7	Av. ann. rate 2005–14	4.5
Services	35.3		

Energy

	m TOE		
Total output	28.7	Net energy imports as %	
Total consumption	33.9	of energy use	15
Consumption per head			
kg oil equivalent	216		

Inflation and finance

		av. ann. increase 2010–15	
Consumer price			
inflation 2015	6.4%	Narrow money (M1)	11.0%
Av. ann. inflation 2010–15	7.7%	Broad money	15.8%
Deposit rate, Dec. 2015	6.54%		

Exchange rates

	end 2015		December 2015
Tk per $	78.50	Effective rates	2010 = 100
Tk per SDR	108.78	– nominal	...
Tk per €	85.83	– real	...

Trade

Principal exports		Principal imports	
	$bn fob		*$bn cif*
Clothing	19.5	Fuels	5.3
Jute goods	0.7	Textiles & yarns	3.5
Fish & fish products	0.5	Iron & steel	2.7
Leather	0.5	Capital machinery	2.4
Total incl. others	**28.4**	Total incl. others	**41.6**

Main export destinations		Main origins of imports	
	% of total		*% of total*
United States	14.3	China	18.8
Germany	13.6	India	14.8
United Kingdom	7.9	Singapore	5.8
France	5.2	Japan	3.4

Balance of payments, reserves and debt, $bn

Visible exports fob	29.9	Change in reserves	4.2
Visible imports fob	-40.1	Level of reserves	
Trade balance	-10.2	end Dec.	22.3
Invisibles inflows	3.3	No. months of import cover	5.3
Invisibles outflows	-10.4	Official gold holdings, m oz	0.4
Net transfers	15.6	Foreign debt	34.9
Current account balance	-1.7	– as % of GDP	20.2
– as % of GDP	-1.0	– as % of total exports	72.5
Capital balance	4.8	Debt service ratio	3.6
Overall balance	4.6		

Health and education

Health spending, % of GDP	2.8	Education spending, % of GDP	2.0
Doctors per 1,000 pop.	0.4	Enrolment, %: primary	112
Hospital beds per 1,000 pop.	0.6	secondary	58
Improved-water source access,		tertiary	13
% of pop.	86.9		

Society

No. of households, m	36.5	Cost of living, Dec. 2015	
Av. no. per household	4.3	New York = 100	70
Marriages per 1,000 pop.	...	Cars per 1,000 pop.	3.0
Divorces per 1,000 pop.	...	Colour TV households, % with:	
Religion, % of pop. of pop.		cable	...
Muslim	89.8	satellite	...
Hindu	9.1	Telephone lines per 100 pop.	0.6
Other	0.9	Mobile telephone subscribers	
Christian	0.2	per 100 pop.	80.0
Jewish	<0.1	Broadband subs per 100 pop.	2.0
Non-religious	<0.1	Internet users, % of pop.	9.6

BELGIUM

Area	30,528 sq km	Capital	Brussels
Arable as % of total land	26.9	Currency	Euro (€)

People

Population, m	11.1	Life expectancy: men	79.1 yrs
Pop. per sq km	363.6	women	83.7 yrs
Average annual growth		Adult literacy	...
in pop. 2015–20, %	0.6	Fertility rate (per woman)	1.8
Pop. aged 0–19, %	22.4	Urban population, %	97.9
Pop. aged 65 and over, %	18.2		per 1,000 pop.
No. of men per 100 women	96.8	Crude birth rate	11.4
Human Development Index	89.0	Crude death rate	9.7

The economy

GDP	€401bn	GDP per head	$47,424
GDP	$532bn	GDP per head in purchasing	
Av. ann. growth in real		power parity (USA=100)	79.2
GDP 2009–14	1.1%	Economic freedom index	68.4

Origins of GDP		Components of GDP	
	% of total		% of total
Agriculture	1	Private consumption	52
Industry, of which:	22	Public consumption	24
manufacturing	14	Investment	23
Services	77	Exports	84
		Imports	-83

Structure of employment

	% of total		% of labour force
Agriculture	1.1	Unemployed 2014	8.5
Industry	21.7	Av. ann. rate 2005–14	7.9
Services	77.1		

Energy

	m TOE		
Total output	14.9	Net energy imports as %	
Total consumption	56.4	of energy use	74
Consumption per head			
kg oil equivalent	5,039		

Inflation and finance

		av. ann. increase 2010–15	
Consumer price			
inflation 2015	0.6%	Euro area:	
Av. ann. inflation 2010–15	1.7%	Narrow money (M1)	6.7%
Treasury bill rate, Dec. 2015	-0.44%	Broad money	3.1%

Exchange rates

	end 2015		December 2015
€ per $	0.92	Effective rates	2010 = 100
€ per SDR	1.27	– nominal	96.59
		– real	95.69

Trade

Principal exports	$bn fob	Principal imports	$bn cif
Chemicals & related products	138.3	Chemicals & related products	108.7
Machinery & transport equip.	96.6	Machinery & transport equip.	101.7
Mineral fuels & lubricants	53.8	Mineral fuels & lubricants	74.3
Food, drink & tobacco	42.3	Food, drink & tobacco	36.9
Total incl. others	**473.7**	Total incl. others	**454.8**

Main export destinations	% of total	Main origins of imports	% of total
Germany	16.7	Netherlands	19.9
France	15.7	Germany	13.1
Netherlands	11.9	France	10.0
United Kingdom	8.3	United States	7.4
EU28	70.7	EU28	65.0

Balance of payments, reserves and aid, $bn

Visible exports fob	320.2	Overall balance	-1.4
Visible imports fob	-325.2	Change in reserves	-2.6
Trade balance	-5.1	Level of reserves	
Invisibles inflows	191.2	end Dec.	24.4
Invisibles outflows	-178.8	No. months of import cover	0.6
Net transfers	-8.5	Official gold holdings, m oz	7.3
Current account balance	-1.2	Aid given	2.5
– as % of GDP	-0.2	– as % of GDP	0.5
Capital balance	0.3		

Health and education

Health spending, % of GDP	10.6	Education spending, % of GDP	6.4
Doctors per 1,000 pop.	4.9	Enrolment, %: primary	105
Hospital beds per 1,000 pop.	6.5	secondary	163
Improved-water source access,		tertiary	75
% of pop.	100		

Society

No. of households, m	4.8	Cost of living, Dec. 2015	
Av. no. per household	2.3	New York = 100	81
Marriages per 1,000 pop.	3.6	Cars per 1,000 pop.	496
Divorces per 1,000 pop.	2.5	Colour TV households, % with:	
Religion, % of pop.		cable	74.2
Christian	64.2	satellite	5.9
Non-religious	29.0	Telephone lines per 100 pop.	40.7
Muslim	5.9	Mobile telephone subscribers	
Other	0.6	per 100 pop.	114.3
Jewish	0.3	Broadband subs per 100 pop.	36.0
Hindu	<0.1	Internet users, % of pop.	85.0

BRAZIL

Area	8,513,887 sq km	Capital	Brasília
Arable as % of total land	9.1	Currency	Real (R)

People

Population, m	202.0	Life expectancy: men	71.8 yrs
Pop. per sq km	23.7	women	79.1 yrs
Average annual growth		Adult literacy	91.5
in pop. 2015–20, %	0.8	Fertility rate (per woman)	1.7
Pop. aged 0–19, %	31.4	Urban population, %	85.7
Pop. aged 65 and over, %	7.8		per 1,000 pop.
No. of men per 100 women	96.7	Crude birth rate	14.0
Human Development Index	75.5	Crude death rate	6.3

The economy

GDP	R5,687bn	GDP per head	$11,729
GDP	$2,417bn	GDP per head in purchasing	
Av. ann. growth in real		power parity (USA=100)	30.3
GDP 2009–14	3.2%	Economic freedom index	56.5

Origins of GDP		**Components of GDP**	
	% of total		% of total
Agriculture	5	Private consumption	62
Industry, of which:	24	Public consumption	19
manufacturing	12	Investment	21
Services	71	Exports	11
		Imports	-14

Structure of employment

	% of total		% of labour force
Agriculture	14.5	Unemployed 2014	6.8
Industry	22.9	Av. ann. rate 2005–14	7.5
Services	76.6		

Energy

	m TOE		
Total output	252.9	Net energy imports as %	
Total consumption	293.7	of energy use	14
Consumption per head			
kg oil equivalent	1,438		

Inflation and finance

Consumer price		av. ann. increase 2010–15	
inflation 2015	9.0%	Narrow money (M1)	3.4%
Av. ann. inflation 2010–15	6.7%	Broad money	13.2%
Treasury bill rate, Dec. 2015	14.63%		

Exchange rates

	end 2015		December 2015
R per $	3.90	Effective rates	2010 = 100
R per SDR	5.41	– nominal	56.26
R per €	4.27	– real	66.97

Trade

Principal exports		Principal imports	
	$bn fob		$bn cif
Primary products	109.6	Intermediate products & raw	
Manufactured goods	80.2	materials	103.0
Semi-manufactured goods	29.1	Capital gooods	47.8
		Fuels & lubricants	39.5
Total incl. others	**225.1**	Consumer goods	38.8
		Total incl. others	**229.2**

Main export destinations		Main origins of imports	
	% of total		% of total
China	18.0	United States	17.9
United States	12.1	China	16.9
Argentina	6.3	Argentina	6.8
Netherlands	5.8	Netherlands	6.6

Balance of payments, reserves and debt, $bn

Visible exports fob	224.1	Change in reserves	4.4
Visible imports fob	-230.7	Level of reserves	
Trade balance	-6.6	end Dec.	363.3
Invisibles inflows	52.8	No. months of import cover	11.4
Invisibles outflows	-153.1	Official gold holdings, m oz	2.2
Net transfers	2.7	Foreign debt	556.9
Current account balance	-104.2	– as % of GDP	23.0
– as % of GDP	-4.3	– as % of total exports	199.2
Capital balance	111.7	Debt service ratio	21.4
Overall balance	10.8		

Health and education

Health spending, % of GDP	8.3	Education spending, % of GDP	5.8
Doctors per 1,000 pop.	1.9	Enrolment, %: primary	...
Hospital beds per 1,000 pop.	2.3	secondary	...
Improved-water source access,		tertiary	...
% of pop.	98.1		

Society

No. of households, m	61.2	Cost of living, Dec. 2015	
Av. no. per household	3.3	New York = 100	53
Marriages per 1,000 pop.	...	Cars per 1,000 pop.	162
Divorces per 1,000 pop.	...	Colour TV households, % with:	
Religion, % of pop.		cable	11.3
Christian	88.9	satellite	16.9
Non-religious	7.9	Telephone lines per 100 pop.	21.8
Other	3.1	Mobile telephone subscribers	
Hindu	<0.1	per 100 pop.	139.0
Jewish	<0.1	Broadband subs per 100 pop.	11.7
Muslim	<0.1	Internet users, % of pop.	57.6

BULGARIA

Area	111,002 sq km	Capital	Sofia
Arable as % of total land	32.0	Currency	Lev (BGL)

People

Population, m	7.2	Life expectancy: men	71.1 yrs
Pop. per sq km	64.9	women	78.0 yrs
Average annual growth		Adult literacy	98.4
in pop. 2015–20, %	-0.8	Fertility rate (per woman)	1.6
Pop. aged 0–19, %	18.6	Urban population, %	73.9
Pop. aged 65 and over, %	20.0		per 1,000 pop.
No. of men per 100 women	94.5	Crude birth rate	9.5
Human Development Index	78.2	Crude death rate	15.6

The economy

GDP	BGL84bn	GDP per head	$7,876
GDP	$57bn	GDP per head in purchasing	
Av. ann. growth in real		power parity (USA=100)	33.6
GDP 2009–14	1.2%	Economic freedom index	65.9

Origins of GDP		**Components of GDP**	
	% of total		% of total
Agriculture	5	Private consumption	63
Industry, of which:	27	Public consumption	16
manufacturing	...	Investment	21
Services	68	Exports	65
		Imports	-66

Structure of employment

	% of total		% of labour force
Agriculture	6.9	Unemployed 2014	11.6
Industry	30.3	Av. ann. rate 2005–14	9.7
Services	62.8		

Energy

	m TOE		
Total output	10.6	Net energy imports as %	
Total consumption	16.9	of energy use	37
Consumption per head			
kg oil equivalent	2,327		

Inflation and finance

Consumer price		*av. ann. change 2009–14*	
inflation 2015	-1.1%	Narrow money (M1)	14.4%
Av. ann. inflation 2010–15	0.7%	Broad money	7.8%
Money market rate, Dec. 2015	0.01%		

Exchange rates

	end 2015		December 2015
BGL per $	1.79	Effective rates	2010 = 100
BGL per SDR	2.48	– nominal	105.56
BGL per €	1.96	– real	98.26

Trade

Principal exports		Principal imports	
	$bn fob		*$bn cif*
Raw materials	12.1	Raw materials	12.1
Consumer goods	7.6	Capital goods	8.7
Capital goods	5.7	Consumer goods	6.8
Mineral fuels & lubricants	3.9	Mineral fuels & lubricants	5.1
Total incl. others	**29.4**	Total incl. others	**34.7**

Main export destinations		Main origins of imports	
	% of total		*% of total*
Germany	12.0	Russia	16.3
Turkey	9.3	Germany	13.2
Italy	9.0	Italy	7.6
Romania	7.9	Romania	7.3
EU28	62.4	EU28	61.7

Balance of payments, reserves and debt, $bn

Visible exports fob	27.9	Change in reserves	0.1
Visible imports fob	-31.5	Level of reserves	
Trade balance	-3.6	end Dec.	19.9
Invisibles inflows	10.1	No. months of import cover	6.1
Invisibles outflows	-8.0	Official gold holdings, m oz	1.3
Net transfers	2.2	Foreign debt	48.7
Current account balance	0.7	– as % of GDP	85.9
– as % of GDP	1.2	– as % of total exports	122.4
Capital balance	3.3	Debt service ratio	14.5
Overall balance	2.3		

Health and education

Health spending, % of GDP	8.4	Education spending, % of GDP	3.6
Doctors per 1,000 pop.	3.9	Enrolment, %: primary	99
Hospital beds per 1,000 pop.	6.4	secondary	101
Improved-water source access,		tertiary	71
% of pop.	99.4		

Society

No. of households, m	3.0	Cost of living, Dec. 2015	
Av. no. per household	2.4	New York = 100	54
Marriages per 1,000 pop.	3.0	Cars per 1,000 pop.	419
Divorces per 1,000 pop.	1.5	Colour TV households, % with:	
Religion, % of pop.		cable	48.2
Christian	82.1	satellite	28.8
Muslim	13.7	Telephone lines per 100 pop.	21.8
Non-religious	4.2	Mobile telephone subscribers	
Hindu	<0.1	per 100 pop.	137.7
Jewish	<0.1	Broadband subs per 100 pop.	20.7
Other	<0.1	Internet users, % of pop.	55.5

CAMEROON

Area	475,650 sq km	Capital	Yaoundé
Arable as % of total land	13.1	Currency	CFA franc (CFAfr)

People

Population, m	22.8	Life expectancy: men	55.9 yrs
Pop. per sq km	47.9	women	58.2 yrs
Average annual growth		Adult literacy	71.3
in pop. 2015–20, %	2.4	Fertility rate (per woman)	4.5
Pop. aged 0–19, %	53.3	Urban population, %	54.4
Pop. aged 65 and over, %	3.2		per 1,000 pop.
No. of men per 100 women	100.0	Crude birth rate	35.0
Human Development Index	51.2	Crude death rate	10.6

The economy

GDP	CFAfr15,610bn	GDP per head	$1,389
GDP	$32bn	GDP per head in purchasing	
Av. ann. growth in real		power parity (USA=100)	5.5
GDP 2009–14	4.6%	Economic freedom index	54.2

Origins of GDP		**Components of GDP**	
	% of total		% of total
Agriculture	22	Private consumption	77
Industry, of which:	30	Public consumption	12
manufacturing	14	Investment	21
Services	48	Exports	22
		Imports	-31

Structure of employment

	% of total		% of labour force
Agriculture	...	Unemployed 2014	4.3
Industry	...	Av. ann. rate 2005–14	4.2
Services	...		

Energy

	m TOE		
Total output	9.0	Net energy imports as %	
Total consumption	7.3	of energy use	-22
Consumption per head			
kg oil equivalent	331		

Inflation and finance

			av. ann. change 2009–14
Consumer price			
inflation 2015	2.8%	Narrow money (M1)	8.3%
Av. ann. inflation 2010–15	2.4%	Broad money	7.7%
Deposit rate, Dec. 2015	2.45%		

Exchange rates

	end 2015		December 2015
CFAfr per $	602.51	Effective rates	2010 = 100
CFAfr per SDR	834.92	– nominal	100.51
CFAfr per €	658.79	– real	98.18

Trade

Principal exports[a]		**Principal imports**[a]	
	$bn fob		*$bn cif*
Fuels	2.2	Manufactured products	3.2
Timber	0.6	Fuels	1.7
Cocoa beans & products	0.4	Food	1.1
Cotton	0.1		
Total incl. others	**6.1**	**Total incl. others**	**6.2**

Main export destinations		**Main origins of imports**	
	% of total		*% of total*
Spain	13.9	China	26.4
China	11.9	Nigeria	12.1
India	10.1	France	11.9
Netherlands	8.2	Belgium	4.9

Balance of payments[a], reserves[a] and debt, $bn

Visible exports fob	6.1	Change in reserves	0.1
Visible imports fob	-6.2	Level of reserves	
Trade balance	-0.1	end Dec.	3.5
Invisibles inflows	2.1	No. months of import cover	4.3
Invisibles outflows	-3.5	Official gold holdings, m oz	0.0
Net transfers	0.3	Foreign debt	5.3
Current account balance	-1.1	– as % of GDP	16.5
– as % of GDP	-3.8	– as % of total exports	60.7
Capital balance	1.2	Debt service ratio	5.1
Overall balance	-0.1		

Health and education

Health spending, % of GDP	4.1	Education spending, % of GDP	3.0
Doctors per 1,000 pop.	...	Enrolment, %: primary	114
Hospital beds per 1,000 pop.	1.3	secondary	56
Improved-water source access,		tertiary	12
% of pop.	75.6		

Society

No. of households, m	4.4	Cost of living, Dec. 2015	
Av. no. per household	4.8	New York = 100	...
Marriages per 1,000 pop.	...	Cars per 1,000 pop.	11
Divorces per 1,000 pop.	...	Colour TV households, % with:	
Religion, % of pop.		cable	...
Christian	70.3	satellite	2.4
Muslim	18.3	Telephone lines per 100 pop.	4.6
Other	6.0	Mobile telephone subscribers	
Non-religious	5.3	per 100 pop.	75.7
Hindu	<0.1	Broadband subs per 100 pop.	0.1
Jewish	<0.1	Internet users, % of pop.	11.0

a 2013

CANADA

Area[a]	9,984,670 sq km	Capital	Ottawa
Arable as % of total land	5.0	Currency	Canadian dollar (C$)

People

Population, m	35.5	Life expectancy: men	80.8 yrs
Pop. per sq km	3.6	women	84.4 yrs
Average annual growth		Adult literacy	...
in pop. 2015–20, %	0.9	Fertility rate (per woman)	1.6
Pop. aged 0–19, %	21.9	Urban population, %	81.8
Pop. aged 65 and over, %	16.1		per 1,000 pop.
No. of men per 100 women	98.4	Crude birth rate	10.5
Human Development Index	91.3	Crude death rate	7.5

The economy

GDP	C$1,973bn	GDP per head	$50,123
GDP	$1,784bn	GDP per head in purchasing	
Av. ann. growth in real		power parity (USA=100)	82.6
GDP 2009–14	2.5%	Economic freedom index	78.0

Origins of GDP		**Components of GDP**	
	% of total		% of total
Agriculture	2	Private consumption	56
Industry, of which:	29	Public consumption	21
manufacturing	...	Investment	24
Services	69	Exports	32
		Imports	-33

Structure of employment

	% of total		% of labour force
Agriculture	2.1	Unemployed 2014	6.9
Industry	19.8	Av. ann. rate 2005–14	7.0
Services	78.2		

Energy

	m TOE		
Total output	435.1	Net energy imports as %	
Total consumption	253.2	of energy use	-72
Consumption per head			
kg oil equivalent	7,202		

Inflation and finance

			av. ann. increase 2010–15
Consumer price			
inflation 2015	1.1%	Narrow money (M1)	7.7%
Av. ann. inflation 2010–15	1.7%	Broad money	8.0%
Treasury bill rate, Dec. 2015	0.50%		

Exchange rates

	end 2015		December 2015
C$ per $	1.38	Effective rates	2010 = 100
C$ per SDR	1.92	– nominal	79.82
C$ per €	1.51	– real	79.40

Trade

Principal exports	$bn fob	Principal imports	$bn cif
Energy products	116.5	Consumer goods	96.1
Motor vehicles & parts	67.5	Motor vehicles & parts	81.9
Consumer goods	53.2	Electronic & electrical equip.	53.1
Metal & mineral products	52.2	Energy products	39.0
Total incl. others	**478.7**	Total incl. others	**474.4**

Main export destinations	% of total	Main origins of imports	% of total
United States	76.8	United States	54.5
China	3.7	China	11.5
United Kingdom	2.9	Mexico	5.6
Japan	2.0	Germany	3.1
EU28	7.4	EU28	11.3

Balance of payments, reserves and aid, $bn

Visible exports fob	478.3	Overall balance	5.2
Visible imports fob	-473.9	Change in reserves	2.7
Trade balance	4.4	Level of reserves	
Invisibles inflows	164.0	end Dec.	74.7
Invisibles outflows	-206.6	No. months of import cover	1.3
Net transfers	-2.4	Official gold holdings, m oz	0.1
Current account balance	-40.6	Aid given	4.2
– as % of GDP	-2.3	– as % of GDP	0.2
Capital balance	44.6		

Health and education

Health spending, % of GDP	10.4	Education spending, % of GDP	5.3
Doctors per 1,000 pop.	2.1	Enrolment, %: primary	100
Hospital beds per 1,000 pop.	2.7	secondary	110
Improved-water source access,		tertiary	...
% of pop.	99.8		

Society

No. of households, m	13.9	Cost of living, Dec. 2015	
Av. no. per household	2.6	New York = 100	77
Marriages per 1,000 pop.	...	Cars per 1,000 pop.	612
Divorces per 1,000 pop.	2.1	Colour TV households, % with:	
Religion, % of pop.		cable	66.4
Christian	69.0	satellite	22.2
Non-religious	23.7	Telephone lines per 100 pop.	46.2
Other	2.8	Mobile telephone subscribers	
Muslim	2.1	per 100 pop.	81.0
Hindu	1.4	Broadband subs per 100 pop.	35.4
Jewish	1.0	Internet users, % of pop.	87.1

a Including freshwater.

CHILE

Area	756,102 sq km	Capital	Santiago
Arable as % of total land	1.8	Currency	Chilean peso (Ps)

People

Population, m	17.8	Life expectancy: men	79.8 yrs
Pop. per sq km	23.5	women	85.3 yrs
Average annual growth		Adult literacy	96.7
in pop. 2015–20, %	1.0	Fertility rate (per woman)	1.7
Pop. aged 0–19, %	27.5	Urban population, %	89.5
Pop. aged 65 and over, %	11.0		per 1,000 pop.
No. of men per 100 women	97.4	Crude birth rate	12.7
Human Development Index	83.2	Crude death rate	5.2

The economy

GDP	147.5trn pesos	GDP per head	$14,563
GDP	$259bn	GDP per head in purchasing	
Av. ann. growth in real		power parity (USA=100)	42.5
GDP 2009–14	4.6%	Economic freedom index	77.7

Origins of GDP		**Components of GDP**	
	% of total		% of total
Agriculture	3	Private consumption	64
Industry, of which:	35	Public consumption	13
manufacturing	12	Investment	21
Services	62	Exports	34
		Imports	-32

Structure of employment

	% of total		% of labour force
Agriculture	9.2	Unemployed 2014	6.4
Industry	23.7	Av. ann. rate 2005–14	7.4
Services	67.1		

Energy

	m TOE		
Total output	15.0	Net energy imports as %	
Total consumption	38.7	of energy use	61
Consumption per head			
kg oil equivalent	2,201		

Inflation and finance

Consumer price		av. ann. increase 2010–15	
inflation 2015	4.3%	Narrow money (M1)	11.1%
Av. ann. inflation 2010–15	3.4%	Broad money	12.3%
Money market rate, Aug. 2015	3.00%		

Exchange rates

	end 2015		December 2015
Ps per $	707.34	Effective rates	2010 = 100
Ps per SDR	980.18	– nominal	91.40
Ps per €	773.41	– real	93.10

Trade

Principal exports	
	$bn fob
Copper	37.9
Fresh fruit	4.9
Salmon & trout	4.4
Total incl. others	**75.4**

Principal imports	
	$bn cif
Intermediate goods	39.9
Consumer goods	20.0
Capital goods	12.2
Total	**72.2**

Main export destinations	
	% of total
China	24.5
United States	12.4
Japan	10.0
South Korea	6.2

Main origins of imports	
	% of total
China	20.9
United States	19.8
Brazil	7.9
Argentina	4.0

Balance of payments, reserves and debt, $bn

Visible exports fob	74.9	Change in reserves	-0.6
Visible imports fob	-68.6	Level of reserves	
Trade balance	6.3	end Dec.	40.4
Invisibles inflows	19.5	No. months of import cover	4.9
Invisibles outflows	-31.0	Official gold holdings, m oz	0.0
Net transfers	1.8	Foreign debt	149.7
Current account balance	-3.3	– as % of GDP	57.8
– as % of GDP	-1.3	– as % of total exports	161.6
Capital balance	4.9	Debt service ratio	25.0
Overall balance	1.1		

Health and education

Health spending, % of GDP	7.8	Education spending, % of GDP	4.6
Doctors per 1,000 pop.	1.0	Enrolment, %: primary	100
Hospital beds per 1,000 pop.	2.1	secondary	100
Improved-water source access,		tertiary	84
% of pop.	99.0		

Society

No. of households, m	6.0	Cost of living, Dec. 2015	
Av. no. per household	3.0	New York = 100	61
Marriages per 1,000 pop.	3.7	Cars per 1,000 pop.	168
Divorces per 1,000 pop.	0.1	Colour TV households, % with:	
Religion, % of pop.		cable	34.2
Christian	89.4	satellite	5.2
Non-religious	8.6	Telephone lines per 100 pop.	19.2
Other	1.9	Mobile telephone subscribers	
Jewish	0.1	per 100 pop.	133.3
Hindu	<0.1	Broadband subs per 100 pop.	14.1
Muslim	<0.1	Internet users, % of pop.	72.4

CHINA

Area	9,596,961 sq km	Capital	Beijing
Arable as % of total land	11.3	Currency	Yuan

People

Population, m	1,393.8	Life expectancy: men	75.0 yrs
Pop. per sq km	145.2	women	78.1 yrs
Average annual growth		Adult literacy	95.1
in pop. 2015–20, %	0.4	Fertility rate (per woman)	1.6
Pop. aged 0–19, %	23.0	Urban population, %	55.6
Pop. aged 65 and over, %	9.6		per 1,000 pop.
No. of men per 100 women	106.3	Crude birth rate	11.4
Human Development Index	72.7	Crude death rate	7.4

The economy

GDP	Yuan 64,070bn	GDP per head	$7,617
GDP	$10,431bn	GDP per head in purchasing	
Av. ann. growth in real		power parity (USA=100)	24.0
GDP 2009–14	8.6%	Economic freedom index	52.0

Origins of GDP		**Components of GDP**	
	% of total		% of total
Agriculture	9	Private consumption	37
Industry, of which:	43	Public consumption	14
manufacturing	30	Investment	46
Services	48	Exports	23
		Imports	-19

Structure of employment

	% of total		% of labour force
Agriculture	2.5	Unemployed 2014	4.7
Industry	46.9	Av. ann. rate 2005–14	4.3
Services	47.0		

Energy

	m TOE		
Total output	2,613.7	Net energy imports as %	
Total consumption	3,021.9	of energy use	14
Consumption per head			
kg oil equivalent	2,226		

Inflation and finance

		av. ann. increase 2010–15	
Consumer price			
inflation 2015	1.4%	Narrow money (M1)	9.1%
Av. ann. inflation 2010–15	2.8%	Broad money	14.3%
Deposit rate, Dec. 2015	1.50%		

Exchange rates

	end 2015		December 2015
Yuan per $	6.49	Effective rates	2010 = 100
Yuan per SDR	9.00	– nominal	123.52
Yuan per €	7.10	– real	130.71

Trade

Principal exports		Principal imports	
	$bn fob		*$bn cif*
Telecoms equipment	280.4	Electrical machinery	347.1
Electrical goods	279.1	Petroleum products	264.0
Office machinery	221.6	Metal ores & scrap	155.4
Clothing & apparel	186.3	Professional instruments	85.6
Total incl. others	**2,342.3**	Total incl. others	**1,959.5**

Main export destinations		Main origins of imports	
	% of total		*% of total*
Hong Kong	17.0	South Korea	9.7
United States	15.5	Japan	8.3
Japan	6.4	United States	7.9
South Korea	4.3	Taiwan	7.8
EU28	15.8	EU28	12.4

Balance of payments, reserves and debt, $bn

Visible exports fob	2,243.8	Change in reserves	14.7
Visible imports fob	-1,808.7	Level of reserves	
Trade balance	435.0	end Dec.	3,895.1
Invisibles inflows	445.0	No. months of import cover	19.2
Invisibles outflows	-630.1	Official gold holdings, m oz	33.9
Net transfers	-30.2	Foreign debt	959.5
Current account balance	219.7	– as % of GDP	9.2
– as % of GDP	2.1	– as % of total exports	34.9
Capital balance	38.2	Debt service ratio	1.9
Overall balance	117.8		

Health and education

Health spending, % of GDP	5.5	Education spending, % of GDP	...
Doctors per 1,000 pop.	1.9	Enrolment, %: primary	109
Hospital beds per 1,000 pop.	3.8	secondary	96
Improved-water source access,		tertiary	30
% of pop.	95.5		

Society

No. of households, m	445.8	Cost of living, Dec. 2015	
Av. no. per household	3.1	New York = 100	83
Marriages per 1,000 pop.	9.6	Cars per 1,000 pop.	83
Divorces per 1,000 pop.	1.8	Colour TV households, % with:	
Religion, % of pop.		cable	50.0
Non-religious	52.2	satellite	...
Other	22.7	Telephone lines per 100 pop.	17.9
Buddhist	18.2	Mobile telephone subscribers	
Christian	5.1	per 100 pop.	92.3
Muslim	1.8	Broadband subs per 100 pop.	14.4
Jewish	<0.1	Internet users, % of pop.	49.3

Note: Data exclude Special Administrative Regions ie, Hong Kong and Macau.

COLOMBIA

Area	1,141,748 sq km	Capital	Bogotá
Arable as % of total land	1.5	Currency	Colombian peso (peso)

People

Population, m	48.9	Life expectancy: men	71.2 yrs
Pop. per sq km	42.8	women	78.3 yrs
Average annual growth		Adult literacy	93.6
in pop. 2015–20, %	0.8	Fertility rate (per woman)	1.8
Pop. aged 0–19, %	32.7	Urban population, %	76.4
Pop. aged 65 and over, %	7.0		per 1,000 pop.
No. of men per 100 women	97.0	Crude birth rate	14.8
Human Development Index	72.0	Crude death rate	6.1

The economy

GDP	756trn pesos	GDP per head	$7,907
GDP	$378bn	GDP per head in purchasing	
Av. ann. growth in real		power parity (USA=100)	24.4
GDP 2009–14	4.8%	Economic freedom index	70.8

Origins of GDP		**Components of GDP**	
	% of total		% of total
Agriculture	6	Private consumption	61
Industry, of which:	36	Public consumption	18
manufacturing	12	Investment	26
Services	58	Exports	16
		Imports	-21

Structure of employment

	% of total		% of labour force
Agriculture	16.3	Unemployed 2014	10.1
Industry	19.6	Av. ann. rate 2005–14	11.1
Services	64.1		

Energy

	m TOE		
Total output	125.6	Net energy imports as %	
Total consumption	31.6	of energy use	-297
Consumption per head			
kg oil equivalent	669		

Inflation and finance

Consumer price		*av. ann. increase 2010–15*	
inflation 2015	5.0%	Narrow money (M1)	...
Av. ann. inflation 2010–15	3.3%	Broad money	13.10%
Money market rate, Dec. 2015	5.57%		

Exchange rates

	end 2015		December 2015
Peso per $	3,149.50	Effective rates	2010 = 100
Peso per SDR	4,364.30	– nominal	73.44
Peso per €	3,443.60	– real	64.42

Trade

Principal exports		Principal imports	
	$bn fob		*$bn cif*
Petroleum & products	28.9	Intermediate goods & raw	
Coal	6.8	materials	28.0
Coffee	2.5	Capital goods	21.8
Nickel	0.6	Consumer goods	14.3
Total incl. others	**54.8**	**Total incl. others**	**64.0**

Main export destinations		Main origins of imports	
	% of total		*% of total*
United States	26.3	United States	28.5
China	10.5	China	18.4
Panama	6.6	Mexico	8.2
Spain	5.8	Germany	4.0

Balance of payments, reserves and debt, $bn

Visible exports fob	56.9	Change in reserves	3.6
Visible imports fob	-61.6	Level of reserves	
Trade balance	-4.6	end Dec.	46.8
Invisibles inflows	10.9	No. months of import cover	6.1
Invisibles outflows	-30.2	Official gold holdings, m oz	0.3
Net transfers	4.4	Foreign debt	102.3
Current account balance	-19.6	– as % of GDP	27.0
– as % of GDP	-5.2	– as % of total exports	142.2
Capital balance	24.3	Debt service ratio	18.4
Overall balance	4.4		

Health and education

Health spending, % of GDP	7.2	Education spending, % of GDP	4.7
Doctors per 1,000 pop.	1.5	Enrolment, %: primary	...
Hospital beds per 1,000 pop.	1.5	secondary	...
Improved-water source access,		tertiary	51
% of pop.	91.4		

Society

No. of households, m	13.0	Cost of living, Dec. 2015	
Av. no. per household	3.8	New York = 100	55
Marriages per 1,000 pop.	...	Cars per 1,000 pop.	62
Divorces per 1,000 pop.	...	Colour TV households, % with:	
Religion, % of pop.		cable	57.0
Christian	92.5	satellite	7.4
Non-religious	6.6	Telephone lines per 100 pop.	14.7
Other	0.8	Mobile telephone subscribers	
Hindu	<0.1	per 100 pop.	113.1
Jewish	<0.1	Broadband subs per 100 pop.	10.3
Muslim	<0.1	Internet users, % of pop.	52.6

CZECH REPUBLIC

Area	78,867 sq km	Capital	Prague
Arable as % of total land	40.8	Currency	Koruna (Kc)

People

Population, m	10.7	Life expectancy: men	76.3 yrs
Pop. per sq km	135.7	women	81.9 yrs
Average annual growth		Adult literacy	...
in pop. 2015–20, %	0.1	Fertility rate (per woman)	1.5
Pop. aged 0–19, %	19.3	Urban population, %	73.0
Pop. aged 65 and over, %	18.1		per 1,000 pop.
No. of men per 100 women	96.6	Crude birth rate	10.0
Human Development Index	87.0	Crude death rate	10.6

The economy

GDP	Kc4,260bn	GDP per head	$19,470
GDP	$205bn	GDP per head in purchasing	
Av. ann. growth in real		power parity (USA=100)	55.2
GDP 2009–14	1.0%	Economic freedom index	73.2

Origins of GDP		**Components of GDP**	
	% of total		% of total
Agriculture	3	Private consumption	49
Industry, of which:	38	Public consumption	19
manufacturing	27	Investment	25
Services	59	Exports	84
		Imports	-77

Structure of employment

	% of total		% of labour force
Agriculture	2.7	Unemployed 2014	6.2
Industry	38.3	Av. ann. rate 2005–14	6.6
Services	58.9		

Energy

	m TOE		
Total output	30.2	Net energy imports as %	
Total consumption	42.0	of energy use	28
Consumption per head			
kg oil equivalent	3,990		

Inflation and finance

Consumer price		av. ann. increase 2010–15	
inflation 2015	0.3%	Narrow money (M1)	8.90%
Av. ann. inflation 2010–15	1.5%	Broad money	5.40%
Money market rate, Dec. 2015	0.29%		

Exchange rates

	end 2015		December 2015
Kc per $	24.82	Effective rates	2010 = 100
Kc per SDR	34.40	– nominal	92.44
Kc per €	27.14	– real	90.41

Trade

Principal exports	$bn fob	Principal imports	$bn cif
Machinery & transport equip.	96.3	Machinery & transport equip.	66.6
Semi-manufactured goods	28.9	Semi-manufactured goods	27.1
Miscellaneous manuf. goods	20.6	Chemicals	17.9
Chemicals	11.6	Miscellaneous manuf. goods	16.3
Total incl. others	**175.0**	Total incl. others	**154.2**

Main export destinations	% of total	Main origins of imports	% of total
Germany	32.0	Germany	30.1
Slovakia	8.4	Poland	8.5
Poland	6.0	Slovakia	6.8
United Kingdom	5.1	China	6.1
EU28	82.2	EU28	77.4

Balance of payments, reserves and debt, $bn

Visible exports fob	146.6	Change in reserves	-1.8
Visible imports fob	-135.9	Level of reserves	
Trade balance	10.7	end Dec.	54.4
Invisibles inflows	32.5	No. months of import cover	3.7
Invisibles outflows	-42.4	Official gold holdings, m oz	0.3
Net transfers	-0.4	Foreign debt	125.3
Current account balance	0.4	– as % of GDP	61.1
– as % of GDP	0.2	– as % of total exports	6.0
Capital balance	2.0	Debt service ratio	1.1
Overall balance	3.5	Aid given	0.2
		– as % of GDP	0.1

Health and education

Health spending, % of GDP	7.4	Education spending, % of GDP	4.3
Doctors per 1,000 pop.	3.6	Enrolment, %: primary	99
Hospital beds per 1,000 pop.	6.8	secondary	104
Improved-water source access,		tertiary	65
% of pop.	100		

Society

No. of households, m	4.4	Cost of living, Dec. 2015	
Av. no. per household	2.4	New York = 100	62
Marriages per 1,000 pop.	4.1	Cars per 1,000 pop.	461
Divorces per 1,000 pop.	2.7	Colour TV households, % with:	
Religion, % of pop.		cable	24.5
Non-religious	76.4	satellite	27.0
Christian	23.3	Telephone lines per 100 pop.	18.6
Other	0.2	Mobile telephone subscribers	
Hindu	<0.1	per 100 pop.	129.5
Jewish	<0.1	Broadband subs per 100 pop.	27.9
Muslim	<0.1	Internet users, % of pop.	79.7

DENMARK

Area	42,921 sq km	Capital	Copenhagen
Arable as % of total land	56.7	Currency	Danish krone (DKr)

People

Population, m	5.6	Life expectancy: men	78.9 yrs
Pop. per sq km	130.5	women	82.6 yrs
Average annual growth		Adult literacy	...
in pop. 2015–20, %	0.4	Fertility rate (per woman)	1.8
Pop. aged 0–19, %	23.2	Urban population, %	87.7
Pop. aged 65 and over, %	19.0		per 1,000 pop.
No. of men per 100 women	98.6	Crude birth rate	10.7
Human Development Index	92.3	Crude death rate	9.6

The economy

GDP	DKr1,942bn	GDP per head	$61,294
GDP	$346bn	GDP per head in purchasing	
Av. ann. growth in real		power parity (USA=100)	82.6
GDP 2009–14	0.5%	Economic freedom index	75.3

Origins of GDP		**Components of GDP**	
	% of total		% of total
Agriculture	1	Private consumption	49
Industry, of which:	22	Public consumption	27
manufacturing	14	Investment	19
Services	76	Exports	54
		Imports	-48

Structure of employment

	% of total		% of labour force
Agriculture	2.3	Unemployed 2014	6.6
Industry	19.3	Av. ann. rate 2005–14	5.8
Services	78.0		

Energy

	m TOE		
Total output	16.8	Net energy imports as %	
Total consumption	17.4	of energy use	3
Consumption per head			
kg oil equivalent	3,107		

Inflation and finance

Consumer price		*av. ann. increase 2010–15*	
inflation 2015	0.5%	Narrow money (M1)	5.30%
Av. ann. inflation 2010–15	1.4%	Broad money	3.50%
Money market rate, Dec. 2015	-0.46%		

Exchange rates

	end 2015		December 2015
DKr per $	6.83	Effective rates	2010 = 100
DKr per SDR	9.45	– nominal	97.14
DKr per €	7.47	– real	95.36

Trade

Principal exports		Principal imports	
	$bn fob		*$bn cif*
Machinery & transport equip.	29.3	Machinery & transport equip.	31.2
Chemicals & related products	20.6	Food, drink & tobacco	13.4
Food, drink & tobacco	20.3	Chemicals & related products	12.5
Mineral fuels & lubricants	8.2	Mineral fuels & lubricants	8.3
Total incl. others	**110.7**	Total incl. others	**99.5**

Main export destinations		Main origins of imports	
	% of total		*% of total*
Germany	18.1	Germany	20.3
Sweden	11.8	Sweden	12.2
United Kingdom	7.8	Netherlands	7.6
United States	6.8	China	6.9
EU28	63.5	EU28	69.4

Balance of payments, reserves and aid, $bn

Visible exports fob	111.4	Overall balance	-8.0
Visible imports fob	-101.3	Change in reserves	-13.6
Trade balance	10.0	Level of reserves	
Invisibles inflows	103.8	end Dec.	75.1
Invisibles outflows	-85.7	No. months of import cover	4.8
Net transfers	-6.7	Official gold holdings, m oz	2.1
Current account balance	21.4	Aid given	3.0
– as % of GDP	6.3	– as % of GDP	0.9
Capital balance	-35.4		

Health and education

Health spending, % of GDP	10.8	Education spending, % of GDP	8.5
Doctors per 1,000 pop.	3.5	Enrolment, %: primary	102
Hospital beds per 1,000 pop.	3.5	secondary	130
Improved-water source access,		tertiary	81
% of pop.	100		

Society

No. of households, m	2.6	Cost of living, Dec. 2015	
Av. no. per household	2.1	New York = 100	99
Marriages per 1,000 pop.	4.9	Cars per 1,000 pop.	417
Divorces per 1,000 pop.	3.4	Colour TV households, % with:	
Religion, % of pop.		cable	65.3
Christian	83.5	satellite	11.8
Non-religious	11.8	Telephone lines per 100 pop.	33.2
Muslim	4.1	Mobile telephone subscribers	
Hindu	0.4	per 100 pop.	125.9
Other	0.2	Broadband subs per 100 pop.	41.3
Jewish	<0.1	Internet users, % of pop.	96.0

EGYPT

Area	1,002,000 sq km	Capital	Cairo
Arable as % of total land	2.9	Currency	Egyptian pound (£E)

People

Population, m	83.4	Life expectancy: men	69.6 yrs
Pop. per sq km	83.2	women	74.1 yrs
Average annual growth		Adult literacy	75.1
in pop. 2015–20, %	1.9	Fertility rate (per woman)	3.2
Pop. aged 0–19, %	41.8	Urban population, %	43.1
Pop. aged 65 and over, %	5.2		per 1,000 pop.
No. of men per 100 women	102.1	Crude birth rate	25.1
Human Development Index	69.0	Crude death rate	5.9

The economy

GDP	£E2,101bn	GDP per head	$3,365
GDP	$301bn	GDP per head in purchasing	
Av. ann. growth in real		power parity (USA=100)	20.0
GDP 2009–14	2.7%	Economic freedom index	56.0

Origins of GDP		Components of GDP	
	% of total		% of total
Agriculture	11	Private consumption	83
Industry, of which:	39	Public consumption	12
manufacturing	16	Investment	14
Services	50	Exports	14
		Imports	-23

Structure of employment

	% of total		% of labour force
Agriculture	28.0	Unemployed 2014	13.2
Industry	24.1	Av. ann. rate 2005–14	10.9
Services	47.9		

Energy

	m TOE		
Total output	82.8	Net energy imports as %	
Total consumption	77.5	of energy use	-7
Consumption per head			
kg oil equivalent	885		

Inflation and finance

Consumer price		av. ann. increase 2010–15	
inflation 2015	11.0%	Narrow money (M1)	18.4%
Av. ann. inflation 2010–15	9.5%	Broad money	14.4%
Treasury bill rate, Dec. 2015	11.34%		

Exchange rates

	end 2015		December 2015
£E per $	7.81	Effective rates	2010 = 100
£E per SDR	10.82	– nominal	...
£E per €	8.54	– real	...

Trade

Principal exports		Principal imports	
	$bn fob		*$bn cif*
Petroleum & products	11.1	Intermediate goods	18.2
Finished goods incl. textiles	10.1	Consumer goods	14.4
Semi-finished products	2.2	Fuels	11.6
Iron & steel	0.2	Capital goods	9.7
Total incl. others	**25.3**	**Total incl. others**	**64.5**

Main export destinations		Main origins of imports	
	% of total		*% of total*
Italy	9.2	China	11.2
Saudi Arabia	7.4	Germany	7.9
India	7.2	United States	7.4
Turkey	5.4	Kuwait	5.1

Balance of payments, reserves and debt, $bn

Visible exports fob	25.2	Change in reserves	-2.0
Visible imports fob	-56.2	Level of reserves	
Trade balance	-31.0	end Dec.	14.6
Invisibles inflows	22.1	No. months of import cover	2.2
Invisibles outflows	-24.8	Official gold holdings, m oz	2.4
Net transfers	27.7	Foreign debt	39.6
Current account balance	-6.0	– as % of GDP	13.0
– as % of GDP	-2.0	– as % of total exports	59.4
Capital balance	1.0	Debt service ratio	9.0
Overall balance	-3.3		

Health and education

Health spending, % of GDP	5.6	Education spending, % of GDP	...
Doctors per 1,000 pop.	2.8	Enrolment, %: primary	106
Hospital beds per 1,000 pop.	0.5	secondary	86
Improved-water source access,		tertiary	30
% of pop.	99.4		

Society

No. of households, m	22.7	Cost of living, Dec. 2015	
Av. no. per household	3.8	New York = 100	61
Marriages per 1,000 pop.	10.7	Cars per 1,000 pop.	47
Divorces per 1,000 pop.	1.9	Colour TV households, % with:	
Religion, % of pop.		cable	...
Muslim	94.9	satellite	71.6
Christian	5.1	Telephone lines per 100 pop.	7.8
Hindu	<0.1	Mobile telephone subscribers	
Jewish	<0.1	per 100 pop.	114.3
Non-religious	<0.1	Broadband subs per 100 pop.	3.7
Other	<0.1	Internet users, % of pop.	31.7

FINLAND

Area	336,855 sq km	Capital	Helsinki
Arable as % of total land	7.3	Currency	Euro (€)

People

Population, m	5.4	Life expectancy: men	78.8 yrs
Pop. per sq km	16.0	women	84.1 yrs
Average annual growth		Adult literacy	...
in pop. 2015–20, %	0.3	Fertility rate (per woman)	1.8
Pop. aged 0–19, %	21.9	Urban population, %	84.2
Pop. aged 65 and over, %	20.5		per 1,000 pop.
No. of men per 100 women	96.9	Crude birth rate	10.7
Human Development Index	88.3	Crude death rate	9.9

The economy

GDP	€205bn	GDP per head	$49,779
GDP	$273bn	GDP per head in purchasing	
Av. ann. growth in real		power parity (USA=100)	74.5
GDP 2009–14	0.5%	Economic freedom index	72.6

Origins of GDP		**Components of GDP**	
	% of total		% of total
Agriculture	3	Private consumption	55
Industry, of which:	27	Public consumption	25
manufacturing	17	Investment	21
Services	71	Exports	38
		Imports	-39

Structure of employment

	% of total		% of labour force
Agriculture	3.9	Unemployed 2014	8.6
Industry	22.0	Av. ann. rate 2005–14	7.8
Services	73.7		

Energy

	m TOE		
Total output	18.2	Net energy imports as %	
Total consumption	33.0	of energy use	45
Consumption per head			
kg oil equivalent	6,075		

Inflation and finance

Consumer price			av. ann. increase 2010–15
inflation 2015	-0.2%	Euro area:	
Av. ann. inflation 2010–15	1.9%	Narrow money (M1)	6.7%
Money market rate, Dec. 2015	-0.09%	Broad money	3.1%

Exchange rates

	end 2015		December 2015
€ per $	0.92	Effective rates	2010 = 100
€ per SDR	1.27	– nominal	99.57
		– real	97.02

Trade

Principal exports		Principal imports	
	$bn fob		*$bn cif*
Machinery & transport equip.	21.7	Machinery & transport equip.	22.7
Mineral fuels & lubricants	8.4	Mineral fuels & lubricants	15.0
Chemicals & related products	6.1	Chemicals & related products	8.6
Raw materials	6.0	Food, drink & tobacco	5.6
Total incl. others	**75.6**	Total incl. others	**74.4**

Main export destinations		Main origins of imports	
	% of total		*% of total*
Germany	11.8	Sweden	16.2
Sweden	10.8	Germany	15.7
Russia	7.9	Russia	15.1
United States	6.5	Netherlands	9.0
EU28	57.3	EU28	68.1

Balance of payments, reserves and aid, $bn

Visible exports fob	75.6	Overall balance	-2.7
Visible imports fob	-74.4	Change in reserves	-0.8
Trade balance	1.2	Level of reserves	
Invisibles inflows	50.0	end Dec.	10.4
Invisibles outflows	-50.6	No. months of import cover	1.0
Net transfers	-3.2	Official gold holdings, m oz	1.6
Current account balance	-2.7	Aid given	1.6
– as % of GDP	-1.0	– as % of GDP	0.6
Capital balance	10.4		

Health and education

Health spending, % of GDP	9.7	Education spending, % of GDP	7.2
Doctors per 1,000 pop.	2.9	Enrolment, %: primary	101
Hospital beds per 1,000 pop.	5.5	secondary	143
Improved-water source access,		tertiary	91
% of pop.	100		

Society

No. of households, m	2.6	Cost of living, Dec. 2015	
Av. no. per household	2.1	New York = 100	93
Marriages per 1,000 pop.	4.6	Cars per 1,000 pop.	592
Divorces per 1,000 pop.	2.5	Colour TV households, % with:	
Religion, % of pop.		cable	68.5
Christian	81.6	satellite	11.1
Non-religious	17.6	Telephone lines per 100 pop.	11.7
Muslim	0.8	Mobile telephone subscribers	
Hindu	<0.1	per 100 pop.	139.7
Jewish	<0.1	Broadband subs per 100 pop.	32.3
Other	<0.1	Internet users, % of pop.	92.4

FRANCE

Area	551,500 sq km	Capital	Paris
Arable as % of total land	33.4	Currency	Euro (€)

People

Population, m	64.6	Life expectancy: men	80.0 yrs
Pop. per sq km	117.1	women	85.6 yrs
Average annual growth		Adult literacy	...
in pop. 2015–20, %	0.4	Fertility rate (per woman)	2.0
Pop. aged 0–19, %	24.4	Urban population, %	79.5
Pop. aged 65 and over, %	19.1		per 1,000 pop.
No. of men per 100 women	94.8	Crude birth rate	11.9
Human Development Index	88.8	Crude death rate	9.1

The economy

GDP	€2,132bn	GDP per head	$42,719
GDP	$2,834bn	GDP per head in purchasing	
Av. ann. growth in real		power parity (USA=100)	71.9
GDP 2009–14	1.0%	Economic freedom index	62.3

Origins of GDP		**Components of GDP**	
	% of total		% of total
Agriculture	2	Private consumption	55
Industry, of which:	19	Public consumption	24
manufacturing	11	Investment	22
Services	79	Exports	29
		Imports	-31

Structure of employment

	% of total		% of labour force
Agriculture	2.8	Unemployed 2014	9.9
Industry	20.5	Av. ann. rate 2005–14	9.1
Services	75.8		

Energy

	m TOE		
Total output	136.3	Net energy imports as %	
Total consumption	253.3	of energy use	46
Consumption per head			
kg oil equivalent	3,843		

Inflation and finance

Consumer price		av. ann. increase 2010–15	
inflation 2015	0.1%	Euro area:	
Av. ann. inflation 2010–15	1.2%	Narrow money (M1)	6.7%
Deposit rate, h'holds, Dec. 2015	-0.36%	Broad money	3.1%

Exchange rates

	end 2015		December 2015
€ per $	0.92	Effective rates	2010 = 100
€ per SDR	1.27	– nominal	95.29
		– real	92.16

Trade

Principal exports	$bn fob	Principal imports	$bn cif
Machinery & transport equip.	219.7	Machinery & transport equip.	223.1
Chemicals & related products	110.1	Mineral fuels & lubricants	96.2
Food, drink and tobacco	71.6	Chemicals & related products	95.8
Mineral fuels & lubricants	24.2	Food, drink and tobacco	58.9
Total incl. others	**580.3**	Total incl. others	**657.1**

Main export destinations	% of total	Main origins of imports	% of total
Germany	16.5	Germany	19.8
Belgium	7.3	Belgium	11.4
Italy	7.2	Italy	7.8
Spain	7.1	Netherlands	7.7
EU28	60.1	EU28	67.7

Balance of payments, reserves and aid, $bn

Visible exports fob	584.5	Overall balance	1.1
Visible imports fob	-631.1	Change in reserves	-12.7
Trade balance	-46.5	Level of reserves	
Invisibles inflows	484.6	end Dec.	132.5
Invisibles outflows	-402.1	No. months of import cover	1.5
Net transfers	-63.5	Official gold holdings, m oz	78.3
Current account balance	-27.5	Aid given	10.6
– as % of GDP	-1.0	– as % of GDP	0.4
Capital balance	21.1		

Health and education

Health spending, % of GDP	11.5	Education spending, % of GDP	5.5
Doctors per 1,000 pop.	3.2	Enrolment, %: primary	106
Hospital beds per 1,000 pop.	6.4	secondary	111
Improved-water source access,		tertiary	62
% of pop.	100		

Society

No. of households, m	29.1	Cost of living, Dec. 2015	
Av. no. per household	2.2	New York = 100	107
Marriages per 1,000 pop.	3.5	Cars per 1,000 pop.	492
Divorces per 1,000 pop.	1.9	Colour TV households, % with:	
Religion, % of pop.		cable	13.1
Christian	63.0	satellite	34.1
Non-religious	28.0	Telephone lines per 100 pop.	60.0
Muslim	7.5	Mobile telephone subscribers	
Other	1.0	per 100 pop.	101.2
Jewish	0.5	Broadband subs per 100 pop.	32.3
Hindu	<0.1	Internet users, % of pop.	92.4

GERMANY

Area	357,340 sq km	Capital	Berlin
Arable as % of total land	34.1	Currency	Euro (€)

People

Population, m	82.7	Life expectancy: men	79.3 yrs
Pop. per sq km	231.4	women	83.8 yrs
Average annual growth		Adult literacy	...
in pop. 2015–20, %	-0.1	Fertility rate (per woman)	1.4
Pop. aged 0–19, %	17.9	Urban population, %	75.3
Pop. aged 65 and over, %	21.2		per 1,000 pop.
No. of men per 100 women	96.6	Crude birth rate	8.7
Human Development Index	91.6	Crude death rate	11.3

The economy

GDP	€2,915bn	GDP per head	$48,042
GDP	$3,874bn	GDP per head in purchasing	
Av. ann. growth in real		power parity (USA=100)	85.6
GDP 2009–14	2.0%	Economic freedom index	74.4

Origins of GDP		Components of GDP	
	% of total		% of total
Agriculture	1	Private consumption	55
Industry, of which:	30	Public consumption	19
manufacturing	23	Investment	19
Services	69	Exports	46
		Imports	-39

Structure of employment

	% of total		% of labour force
Agriculture	1.3	Unemployed 2014	5.0
Industry	28.3	Av. ann. rate 2005–14	7.4
Services	70.4		

Energy

	m TOE		
Total output	120.4	Net energy imports as %	
Total consumption	317.7	of energy use	62
Consumption per head			
kg oil equivalent	3,868		

Inflation and finance

Consumer price		av. ann. increase 2010–15	
inflation 2015	0.1%	Euro area:	
Av. ann. inflation 2010–15	1.4%	Narrow money (M1)	6.7%
Deposit rate, h'holds, Dec. 2015	0.46%	Broad money	3.1%

Exchange rates

	end 2015		December 2015
€ per $	0.92	Effective rates	2010 = 100
€ per SDR	1.27	– nominal	96.33
		– real	93.40

Trade

Principal exports		Principal imports	
	$bn fob		$bn cif
Machinery & transport equip.	726.7	Machinery & transport equip.	421.6
Chemicals & related products	238.4	Chemicals & related products	161.8
Food, drink and tobacco	83.0	Mineral fuels & lubricants	150.2
Mineral fuels & lubricants	39.7	Food, drink and tobacco	89.3
Total incl. others	**1,498.4**	Total incl. others	**1,212.3**

Main export destinations		Main origins of imports	
	% of total		% of total
France	8.9	Netherlands	13.7
United States	8.5	France	7.8
United Kingdom	7.0	China	6.7
Netherlands	6.4	Belgium	6.2
EU28	57.7	EU28	65.5

Balance of payments, reserves and aid, $bn

Visible exports fob	1,479.2	Overall balance	-3.3
Visible imports fob	-1,179.4	Change in reserves	-21.1
Trade balance	299.9	Level of reserves	
Invisibles inflows	537.0	end Dec.	177.6
Invisibles outflows	-502.6	No. months of import cover	1.3
Net transfers	-54.0	Official gold holdings, m oz	108.8
Current account balance	280.3	Aid given	16.6
– as % of GDP	7.2	– as % of GDP	0.4
Capital balance	-322.7		

Health and education

Health spending, % of GDP	11.3	Education spending, % of GDP	4.9
Doctors per 1,000 pop.	3.9	Enrolment, %: primary	103
Hospital beds per 1,000 pop.	8.2	secondary	102
Improved-water source access,		tertiary	61
% of pop.	100		

Society

No. of households, m	41.3	Cost of living, Dec. 2015	
Av. no. per household	2.0	New York = 100	78
Marriages per 1,000 pop.	4.6	Cars per 1,000 pop.	537
Divorces per 1,000 pop.	2.1	Colour TV households, % with:	
Religion, % of pop.		cable	46.0
Christian	68.7	satellite	45.1
Non-religious	24.7	Telephone lines per 100 pop.	56.9
Muslim	5.8	Mobile telephone subscribers	
Other	0.5	per 100 pop.	120.4
Jewish	0.3	Broadband subs per 100 pop.	35.8
Hindu	<0.1	Internet users, % of pop.	86.2

GREECE

Area	131,957 sq km	Capital	Athens
Arable as % of total land	19.8	Currency	Euro (€)

People

Population, m	11.1	Life expectancy: men	78.8
Pop. per sq km	84.1	women	84.3
Average annual growth		Adult literacy	97.5
in pop. 2015–20, %	-0.2	Fertility rate (per woman)	1.3
Pop. aged 0–19, %	19.3	Urban population, %	78.0
Pop. aged 65 and over, %	21.4		per 1,000 pop.
No. of men per 100 women	95.3	Crude birth rate	8.0
Human Development Index	86.5	Crude death rate	11.3

The economy

GDP	€178bn	GDP per head	$21,448
GDP	$236bn	GDP per head in purchasing	
Av. ann. growth in real		power parity (USA=100)	47.5
GDP 2009–14	-4.9%	Economic freedom index	53.2

Origins of GDP		**Components of GDP**	
	% of total		% of total
Agriculture	4	Private consumption	70
Industry, of which:	16	Public consumption	20
manufacturing	9	Investment	12
Services	80	Exports	33
		Imports	-35

Structure of employment

	% of total		% of labour force
Agriculture	13.0	Unemployed 2014	26.3
Industry	15.1	Av. ann. rate 2005–14	15.2
Services	71.8		

Energy

	m TOE		
Total output	9.3	Net energy imports as %	
Total consumption	23.4	of energy use	60
Consumption per head			
kg oil equivalent	2,134		

Inflation and finance

Consumer price		av. ann. increase 2010–15	
inflation 2015	-1.1%	Euro area:	
Av. ann. inflation 2010–15	0.1%	Narrow money (M1)	6.7%
Treasury bill rate, Dec. 2015	0.06%	Broad money	3.1%

Exchange rates

	end 2015		December 2015
€ per $	0.92	Effective rates	2010 = 100
€ per SDR	1.27	– nominal	97.18
		– real	89.31

Trade

Principal exports		**Principal imports**	
	$bn fob		*$bn cif*
Mineral fuels & lubricants	13.8	Mineral fuels & lubricants	21.3
Food, drink and tobacco	5.8	Machinery & transport equip.	11.4
Chemicals & related products	3.6	Chemicals & related products	8.9
Machinery & transport equip.	3.1	Food, drink and tobacco	7.5
Total incl. others	**36.0**	Total incl. others	**64.2**

Main export destinations		**Main origins of imports**	
	% of total		*% of total*
Turkey	12.0	Germany	10.1
Italy	9.1	Russia	10.1
Germany	6.6	Iraq	8.1
Bulgaria	5.2	Italy	7.9
EU28	48.1	EU28	48.5

Balance of payments, reserves and debt, $bn

Visible exports fob	35.6	Overall balance	5.5
Visible imports fob	-65.1	Change in reserves	-0.1
Trade balance	-29.6	Level of reserves	
Invisibles inflows	50.5	end Dec.	5.7
Invisibles outflows	-25.3	No. months of import cover	0.8
Net transfers	-0.4	Official gold holdings, m oz	3.6
Current account balance	-4.9	Aid given	0.2
– as % of GDP	-2.1	– as % of GDP	0.1
Capital balance	7.7		

Health and education

Health spending, % of GDP	8.1	Education spending, % of GDP	...
Doctors per 1,000 pop.	6.2	Enrolment, %: primary	99
Hospital beds per 1,000 pop.	...	secondary	108
Improved-water source access,		tertiary	110
% of pop.	100		

Society

No. of households, m	4.2	Cost of living, Dec. 2015	
Av. no. per household	2.6	New York = 100	64
Marriages per 1,000 pop.	4.6	Cars per 1,000 pop.	460
Divorces per 1,000 pop.	2.1	Colour TV households, % with:	
Religion, % of pop.		cable	0.9
Christian	88.1	satellite	13.5
Non-religious	6.1	Telephone lines per 100 pop.	46.9
Muslim	5.3	Mobile telephone subscribers	
Other	0.3	per 100 pop.	100.3
Hindu	0.1	Broadband subs per 100 pop.	28.4
Jewish	<0.1	Internet users, % of pop.	63.2

HONG KONG

Area	1,075 sq km	Capital	Victoria
Arable as % of total land	3.0	Currency	Hong Kong dollar (HK$)

People

Population, m	7.3	Life expectancy: men	81.7
Pop. per sq km	6,790.7	women	87.4
Average annual growth		Adult literacy	...
in pop. 2015–20, %	0.7	Fertility rate (per woman)	1.3
Pop. aged 0–19, %	16.9	Urban population, %	100.0
Pop. aged 65 and over, %	15.1		per 1,000 pop.
No. of men per 100 women	88.5	Crude birth rate	9.8
Human Development Index	91.0	Crude death rate	6.6

The economy

GDP	HK$2,258bn	GDP per head	$40,298
GDP	$291bn	GDP per head in purchasing	
Av. ann. growth in real		power parity (USA=100)	102.2
GDP 2009–14	3.8%	Economic freedom index	88.6

Origins of GDP		**Components of GDP**	
	% of total		% of total
Agriculture	0	Private consumption	66
Industry, of which:	7	Public consumption	10
manufacturing	1	Investment	24
Services	93	Exports	220
		Imports	-220

Structure of employment

	% of total		% of labour force
Agriculture	0	Unemployed 2014	3.2
Industry	11.7	Av. ann. rate 2005–14	4.1
Services	79.9		

Energy

	m TOE		
Total output	0.1	Net energy imports as %	
Total consumption	13.9	of energy use	99
Consumption per head			
kg oil equivalent	1,938		

Inflation and finance

			av. ann. increase 2010–15
Consumer price			
inflation 2015	3.0%	Narrow money (M1)	14.1%
Av. ann. inflation 2010–15	4.2%	Broad money	10.2%
Treasury bill rate, Dec. 2015	0.04%		

Exchange rates

	end 2015		December 2015
HK$ per $	7.75	Effective rates	2010 = 100
HK$ per SDR	10.74	– nominal	106.19
HK$ per €	8.47	– real	...

Trade

Principal exports[a]		Principal imports[a]	
	$bn fob		$bn cif
Capital goods	193.0	Raw materials & semi-	
Semi-finished goods	159.4	manufactured goods	192.0
Consumer goods	106.4	Capital goods & raw materials	189.8
Foodstuffs	6.1	Consumer goods	122.1
Total incl. others	**474.0**	Foodstuffs	24.1
		Total incl. others	**544.9**

Main export destinations		Main origins of imports	
	% of total		% of total
China	53.8	China	47.1
United States	9.3	Japan	6.8
Japan	3.6	Singapore	6.2
India	2.6	United States	5.2

Balance of payments, reserves and debt, $bn

Visible exports fob	515.7	Change in reserves	17.3
Visible imports fob	-548.1	Level of reserves	
Trade balance	-32.4	end Dec.	328.5
Invisibles inflows	268.5	No. months of import cover	5.1
Invisibles outflows	-229.8	Official gold holdings, m oz	0.1
Net transfers	-2.6	Foreign debt	229.2
Current account balance	3.8	– as % of GDP	78.7
– as % of GDP	1.3	– as % of total exports	29.2
Capital balance	8.4	Debt service ratio	2.6
Overall balance	17.9		

Health and education

Health spending, % of GDP	...	Education spending, % of GDP	3.6
Doctors per 1,000 pop.	...	Enrolment, %: primary	111
Hospital beds per 1,000 pop.	...	secondary	101
Improved-water source access,		tertiary	69
% of pop.	...		

Society

No. of households, m	2.4	Cost of living, Dec. 2015	
Av. no. per household	3.0	New York = 100	114
Marriages per 1,000 pop.	7.7	Cars per 1,000 pop.	70
Divorces per 1,000 pop.	...	Colour TV households, % with:	
Religion, % of pop.		cable	94.4
Non-religious	56.1	satellite	0.1
Christian	14.3	Telephone lines per 100 pop.	63.1
Other	14.2	Mobile telephone subscribers	
Buddhist	13.2	per 100 pop.	233.6
Muslim	1.8	Broadband subs per 100 pop.	31.4
Hindu	0.4	Internet users, % of pop.	74.6

a Including re-exports.
Note: Hong Kong became a Special Administrative Region of China on July 1 1997.

HUNGARY

Area	93,024 sq km	Capital	Budapest
Arable as % of total land	48.6	Currency	Forint (Ft)

People

Population, m	9.9	Life expectancy: men	71.9 yrs
Pop. per sq km	106.4	women	79.1 yrs
Average annual growth		Adult literacy	99.0
in pop. 2015–20, %	-0.4	Fertility rate (per woman)	1.4
Pop. aged 0–19, %	19.6	Urban population, %	71.2
Pop. aged 65 and over, %	17.8		per 1,000 pop.
No. of men per 100 women	90.8	Crude birth rate	9.4
Human Development Index	82.8	Crude death rate	13.5

The economy

GDP	Ft32,180bn	GDP per head	$13,989
GDP	$138bn	GDP per head in purchasing	
Av. ann. growth in real		power parity (USA=100)	46.3
GDP 2009–14	1.2%	Economic freedom index	66.0

Origins of GDP		**Components of GDP**	
	% of total		% of total
Agriculture	4	Private consumption	50
Industry, of which:	31	Public consumption	20
manufacturing	24	Investment	22
Services	64	Exports	89
		Imports	-82

Structure of employment

	% of total		% of labour force
Agriculture	4.6	Unemployed 2014	7.8
Industry	30.5	Av. ann. rate 2005–14	9.1
Services	64.5		

Energy

	m TOE		
Total output	10.2	Net energy imports as %	
Total consumption	22.6	of energy use	55
Consumption per head			
kg oil equivalent	2,280		

Inflation and finance

		av. ann. increase 2010–15	
Consumer price			
inflation 2015	-0.1%	Narrow money (M1)	14.8%
Av. ann. inflation 2010–15	2.2%	Broad money	3.9%
Treasury bill rate, Dec. 2015	0.84%		

Exchange rates

	end 2015		December 2015
			2010 = 100
Ft per $	286.63	Effective rates	
Ft per SDR	397.19	– nominal	86.63
Ft per €	313.40	– real	88.14

Trade

Principal exports		Principal imports	
	$bn fob		*$bn cif*
Machinery & equipment	61.5	Machinery & equipment	48.3
Manufactured goods	35.6	Manufactured goods	35.8
Food, drink & tobacco	8.6	Fuels & energy	12.5
Raw materials	3.0	Food, drink & tobacco	5.3
Total incl. others	**112.1**	**Total incl. others**	**103.7**

Main export destinations		Main origins of imports	
	% of total		*% of total*
Germany	27.8	Germany	25.6
Austria	5.6	Austria	7.4
Romania	5.5	China	6.2
Slovakia	5.0	Slovakia	5.4
EU28	80.0	EU28	75.2

Balance of payments, reserves and debt, $bn

Visible exports fob	99.2	Change in reserves	-4.5
Visible imports fob	-95.8	Level of reserves	
Trade balance	3.4	end Dec.	42.0
Invisibles inflows	38.7	No. months of import cover	3.8
Invisibles outflows	-38.4	Official gold holdings, m oz	0.1
Net transfers	-1.0	Foreign debt	145.3
Current account balance	2.7	– as % of GDP	105.0
– as % of GDP	2.0	– as % of total exports	104.9
Capital balance	0.0	Debt service ratio	25.9
Overall balance	1.2	Aid given	0.1
		– as % of GDP	0.1

Health and education

Health spending, % of GDP	7.4	Education spending, % of GDP	4.6
Doctors per 1,000 pop.	3.1	Enrolment, %: primary	100
Hospital beds per 1,000 pop.	7.2	secondary	108
Improved-water source access,		tertiary	57
% of pop.	100		

Society

No. of households, m	4.1	Cost of living, Dec. 2015	
Av. no. per household	2.4	New York = 100	55
Marriages per 1,000 pop.	3.7	Cars per 1,000 pop.	314
Divorces per 1,000 pop.	2.0	Colour TV households, % with:	
Religion, % of pop.		cable	56.4
Christian	81.0	satellite	28.5
Non-religious	18.6	Telephone lines per 100 pop.	30.3
Other	0.2	Mobile telephone subscribers	
Jewish	0.1	per 100 pop.	118.1
Hindu	<0.1	Broadband subs per 100 pop.	27.4
Muslim	<0.1	Internet users, % of pop.	76.1

INDIA

Area	3,287,263 sq km	Capital	New Delhi
Arable as % of total land	52.8	Currency	Indian rupee (Rs)

People

Population, m	1,267.4	Life expectancy: men	67.7 yrs
Pop. per sq km	385.5	women	70.6 yrs
Average annual growth		Adult literacy	69.3
in pop. 2015–20, %	1.2	Fertility rate (per woman)	2.3
Pop. aged 0–19, %	38.2	Urban population, %	32.7
Pop. aged 65 and over, %	5.6		per 1,000 pop.
No. of men per 100 women	107.6	Crude birth rate	19.1
Human Development Index	60.9	Crude death rate	7.3

The economy

GDP	Rs124.8trn	GDP per head	$1,577
GDP	$2,043bn	GDP per head in purchasing	
Av. ann. growth in real		power parity (USA=100)	10.4
GDP 2009–14	7.2%	Economic freedom index	56.2

Origins of GDP		Components of GDP	
	% of total		% of total
Agriculture	18	Private consumption	59
Industry, of which:	30	Public consumption	11
manufacturing	17	Investment	32
Services	52	Exports	23
		Imports	-26

Structure of employment

	% of total		% of labour force
Agriculture	49.7	Unemployed 2014	3.6
Industry	21.5	Av. ann. rate 2005–14	3.8
Services	28.7		

Energy

	m TOE		
Total output	523.3	Net energy imports as %	
Total consumption	775.4	of energy use	33
Consumption per head			
kg oil equivalent	606		

Inflation and finance

Consumer price		av. ann. increase 2010–15	
inflation 2015	4.9%	Narrow money (M1)	9.2%
Av. ann. inflation 2010–15	7.9%	Broad money	12.7%
Lending rate, Dec. 2015	9.70%		

Exchange rates

	end 2015		December 2015
Rs per $	66.30	Effective rates	2010 = 100
Rs per SDR	91.91	– nominal	...
Rs per €	72.52	– real	...

Trade

Principal exports		Principal imports	
	$bn fob		*$bn cif*
Engineering products	73.1	Petroleum & products	138.3
Petroleum & products	57.0	Gold & silver	38.9
Gems & jewellery	41.2	Electronic goods	36.9
Agricultural products	31.9	Machinery	28.0
Total incl. others	**310.3**	Total incl. others	**448.0**

Main export destinations		Main origins of imports	
	% of total		*% of total*
United States	13.7	China	13.0
United Arab Emirates	10.7	Saudi Arabia	7.3
Hong Kong	4.4	United Arab Emirates	6.1
China	4.3	United States	4.7

Balance of payments, reserves and debt, $bn

Visible exports fob	329.6	Change in reserves	24.3
Visible imports fob	-415.5	Level of reserves	
Trade balance	-85.9	end Dec.	322.5
Invisibles inflows	167.3	No. months of import cover	6.6
Invisibles outflows	-174.4	Official gold holdings, m oz	17.9
Net transfers	65.6	Foreign debt	463.2
Current account balance	-27.5	– as % of GDP	22.7
– as % of GDP	-1.3	– as % of total exports	81.5
Capital balance	68.1	Debt service ratio	16.3
Overall balance	37.6		

Health and education

Health spending, % of GDP	4.7	Education spending, % of GDP	3.8
Doctors per 1,000 pop.	0.7	Enrolment, %: primary	111
Hospital beds per 1,000 pop.	0.7	secondary	69
Improved-water source access,		tertiary	24
% of pop.	94.1		

Society

No. of households, m	263.3	Cost of living, Dec. 2015	
Av. no. per household	4.8	New York = 100	45
Marriages per 1,000 pop.	...	Cars per 1,000 pop.	17
Divorces per 1,000 pop.	...	Colour TV households, % with:	
Religion, % of pop.		cable	62.5
Hindu	79.5	satellite	17.1
Muslim	14.4	Telephone lines per 100 pop.	2.1
Other	3.6	Mobile telephone subscribers	
Christian	2.5	per 100 pop.	74.5
Jewish	<0.1	Broadband subs per 100 pop.	1.2
Non-religious	<0.1	Internet users, % of pop.	18.0

INDONESIA

Area	1,910,931 sq km	Capital	Jakarta
Arable as % of total land	13.0	Currency	Rupiah (Rp)

People

Population, m	252.8	Life expectancy: men	67.4 yrs
Pop. per sq km	132.3	women	71.7 yrs
Average annual growth		Adult literacy	92.8
in pop. 2015–20, %	1.1	Fertility rate (per woman)	2.4
Pop. aged 0–19, %	36.6	Urban population, %	53.7
Pop. aged 65 and over, %	5.2		per 1,000 pop.
No. of men per 100 women	101.4	Crude birth rate	18.5
Human Development Index	68.4	Crude death rate	7.2

The economy

GDP	Rp10,565trn	GDP per head	$3,500
GDP	$891bn	GDP per head in purchasing	
Av. ann. growth in real		power parity (USA=100)	19.4
GDP 2009–14	5.8%	Economic freedom index	59.4

Origins of GDP		**Components of GDP**	
	% of total		% of total
Agriculture	13	Private consumption	57
Industry, of which:	42	Public consumption	10
manufacturing	21	Investment	35
Services	42	Exports	24
		Imports	-24

Structure of employment

	% of total		% of labour force
Agriculture	34.3	Unemployed 2014	6.2
Industry	21.0	Av. ann. rate 2005–14	7.9
Services	44.8		

Energy

	m TOE		
Total output	460.0	Net energy imports as %	
Total consumption	213.6	of energy use	-115
Consumption per head			
kg oil equivalent	850		

Inflation and finance

Consumer price		av. ann. increase 2010–15	
inflation 2015	6.4%	Narrow money (M1)	16.9%
Av. ann. inflation 2010–15	5.7%	Broad money	13.0%
Money market rate, Dec.2015	6.20%		

Exchange rates

	end 2015		December 2015
Rp per $	13,795	Effective rates	2010 = 100
Rp per SDR	19,116	– nominal	...
Rp per €	15,083	– real	...

Trade

Principal exports	$bn fob	Principal imports	$bn cif
Manufactured goods	118.6	Raw materials & auxiliary	
Mining & other sector products	46.6	materials	121.7
Agricultural goods	5.9	Capital goods	29.4
Unclassified exports	2.6	Consumer goods	25.9
Total incl. others	**176.0**	Total incl. others	**178.2**

Main export destinations	% of total	Main origins of imports	% of total
Japan	13.2	China	17.2
China	10.0	Singapore	14.1
Singapore	9.6	Japan	9.5
United States	9.4	South Korea	6.6

Balance of payments, reserves and debt, $bn

Visible exports fob	175.3	Change in reserves	12.1
Visible imports fob	-168.3	Level of reserves	
Trade balance	7.0	end Dec.	111.5
Invisibles inflows	25.7	No. months of import cover	5.7
Invisibles outflows	-65.4	Official gold holdings, m oz	2.5
Net transfers	5.2	Foreign debt	293.4
Current account balance	-27.5	– as % of GDP	33.0
– as % of GDP	-3.1	– as % of total exports	140.0
Capital balance	45.4	Debt service ratio	22.1
Overall balance	15.2		

Health and education

Health spending, % of GDP	2.8	Education spending, % of GDP	3.4
Doctors per 1,000 pop.	0.2	Enrolment, %: primary	106
Hospital beds per 1,000 pop.	0.9	secondary	82
Improved-water source access,		tertiary	31
% of pop.	87.4		

Society

No. of households, m	64.5	Cost of living, Dec. 2015	
Av. no. per household	3.9	New York = 100	61
Marriages per 1,000 pop.	...	Cars per 1,000 pop.	50
Divorces per 1,000 pop.	...	Colour TV households, % with:	
Religion, % of pop.		cable	6.0
Muslim	87.2	satellite	25.5
Christian	9.9	Telephone lines per 100 pop.	10.4
Hindu	1.7	Mobile telephone subscribers	
Other	1.1	per 100 pop.	128.8
Jewish	<0.1	Broadband subs per 100 pop.	1.2
Non-religious	<0.1	Internet users, % of pop.	17.1

IRAN

Area	1,628,750 sq km	Capital	Tehran
Arable as % of total land	9.1	Currency	Rial (IR)

People

Population, m	78.5	Life expectancy: men	74.7 yrs
Pop. per sq km	48.2	women	77.1 yrs
Average annual growth		Adult literacy	83.6
in pop. 2015–20, %	1.1	Fertility rate (per woman)	1.6
Pop. aged 0–19, %	30.5	Urban population, %	73.4
Pop. aged 65 and over, %	5.1		per 1,000 pop.
No. of men per 100 women	101.4	Crude birth rate	15.6
Human Development Index	76.6	Crude death rate	4.6

The economy

GDP	IR11,033trn	GDP per head	$5,330
GDP	$416bn	GDP per head in purchasing	
Av. ann. growth in real		power parity (USA=100)	32.0
GDP 2009–14	1.1%	Economic freedom index	43.5

Origins of GDP		**Components of GDP**	
	% of total		% of total
Agriculture	9	Private consumption	51
Industry, of which:	38	Public consumption	11
manufacturing	12	Investment	33
Services	52	Exports	24
		Imports	-19

Structure of employment

	% of total		% of labour force
Agriculture	17.9	Unemployed 2014	12.8
Industry	33.8	Av. ann. rate 2005–14	12.2
Services	48.3		

Energy

	m TOE		
Total output	298.9	Net energy imports as %	
Total consumption	228.4	of energy use	-31
Consumption per head			
kg oil equivalent	2,960		

Inflation and finance

Consumer price		av. ann. increase 2010–15	
inflation 2015	12.0%	Narrow money (M1)	12.4%
Av. ann. inflation 2010–15	22.6%	Broad money	27.9%
Treasury bill rate, Dec. 2015	...		

Exchange rates

	end 2015		December 2015
IR per $	30,130	Effective rates	2010 = 100
IR per SDR	41,752	– nominal	40.98
IR per €	32,944	– real	106.15

Trade

Principal exports		Principal imports	
	$bn fob		*$bn cif*
Oil & gas	55.4	Machinery & transport equip.	19.9
Petrochemicals	9.5	Intermediate goods	8.9
Fresh & dry fruits	2.8	Chemicals	7.1
Carpets	0.4		
Total incl. others	**86.5**	Total incl. others	**64.6**

Main export destinations		Main origins of imports	
	% of total		*% of total*
China	29.0	United Arab Emirates	33.3
India	11.9	China	27.7
Turkey	10.4	India	5.0
Japan	6.5	South Korea	4.7

Balance of payments[a], reserves and debt, $bn

Visible exports fob	86.5	Change in reserves	...
Visible imports fob	-65.1	Level of reserves	
Trade balance	21.4	end Dec.	...
Invisibles inflows	11.9	No. months of import cover	...
Invisibles outflows	-17.9	Official gold holdings, m oz	...
Net transfers	0.5	Foreign debt	5.5
Current account balance	15.9	– as % of GDP	1.3
– as % of GDP	3.7	– as % of total exports	5.5
Capital balance	8.7	Debt service ratio	0.5
Overall balance	19.0		

Health and education

Health spending, % of GDP	6.9	Education spending, % of GDP	3.1
Doctors per 1,000 pop.	...	Enrolment, %: primary	109
Hospital beds per 1,000 pop.	0.1	secondary	88
Improved-water source access,		tertiary	66
% of pop.	96.2		

Society

No. of households, m	23.6	Cost of living, Dec. 2015	
Av. no. per household	3.3	New York = 100	48
Marriages per 1,000 pop.	10.1	Cars per 1,000 pop.	153
Divorces per 1,000 pop.	2.0	Colour TV households, % with:	
Religion, % of pop.		cable	...
Muslim	99.5	satellite	37.0
Christian	0.2	Telephone lines per 100 pop.	39.0
Other	0.2	Mobile telephone subscribers	
Non-religious	0.1	per 100 pop.	87.8
Hindu	<0.1	Broadband subs per 100 pop.	9.5
Jewish	<0.1	Internet users, % of pop.	39.4

a Iranian year ending March 20 2015.

IRELAND

Area	69,797 sq km	Capital	Dublin
Arable as % of total land	16.2	Currency	Euro (€)

People

Population, m	4.7	Life expectancy: men	79.5 yrs
Pop. per sq km	67.3	women	83.5 yrs
Average annual growth		Adult literacy	...
in pop. 2015–20, %	0.8	Fertility rate (per woman)	2.0
Pop. aged 0–19, %	27.5	Urban population, %	63.2
Pop. aged 65 and over, %	13.1		per 1,000 pop.
No. of men per 100 women	99.6	Crude birth rate	13.3
Human Development Index	91.6	Crude death rate	6.6

The economy

GDP	€189bn	GDP per head	$53,648
GDP	$251bn	GDP per head in purchasing	
Av. ann. growth in real		power parity (USA=100)	93.1
GDP 2009–14	1.9%	Economic freedom index	77.3

Origins of GDP		**Components of GDP**	
	% of total		% of total
Agriculture	2	Private consumption	44
Industry, of which:	26	Public consumption	17
manufacturing	20	Investment	20
Services	73	Exports	114
		Imports	-95

Structure of employment

	% of total		% of labour force
Agriculture	6.1	Unemployed 2014	11.6
Industry	18.4	Av. ann. rate 2005–14	9.9
Services	75.2		

Energy

	m TOE		
Total output	2.3	Net energy imports as %	
Total consumption	13.1	of energy use	83
Consumption per head			
kg oil equivalent	2,840		

Inflation and finance

Consumer price		av. ann. increase 2010–15	
inflation 2015	0.0%	Euro area:	
Av. ann. inflation 2010–15	0.8%	Narrow money (M1)	6.7%
Deposit rate, h'holds, Dec. 2015	0.93%	Broad money	3.1%

Exchange rates

	end 2015		December 2015
€ per $	0.92	Effective rates	2010 = 100
€ per SDR	1.27	– nominal	92.03
		– real	88.22

Trade

Principal exports		Principal imports	
	$bn fob		*$bn cif*
Chemicals & related products	68.5	Machinery & transport equip.	29.7
Machinery & transport equip.	15.9	Chemicals & related products	15.2
Food, drink and tobacco	13.9	Food, drink and tobacco	9.3
Raw materials	2.5	Mineral fuels & lubricants	8.6
Total incl. others	**122.9**	**Total incl. others**	**80.7**

Main export destinations		Main origins of imports	
	% of total		*% of total*
United States	21.5	United Kingdom	33.9
United Kingdom	14.5	United States	9.8
Belgium	12.7	Germany	7.7
Germany	6.2	Netherlands	5.4
EU28	55.0	EU28	66.5

Balance of payments, reserves and aid, $bn

Visible exports fob	151.8	Overall balance	11.3
Visible imports fob	-94.0	Change in reserves	0.1
Trade balance	57.8	Level of reserves	
Invisibles inflows	216.7	end Dec.	1.7
Invisibles outflows	-261.9	No. months of import cover	0.1
Net transfers	-3.6	Official gold holdings, m oz	0.2
Current account balance	8.9	Aid given	0.8
– as % of GDP	3.6	– as % of GDP	0.4
Capital balance	2.7		

Health and education

Health spending, % of GDP	7.8	Education spending, % of GDP	5.8
Doctors per 1,000 pop.	2.7	Enrolment, %: primary	103
Hospital beds per 1,000 pop.	2.9	secondary	126
Improved-water source access,		tertiary	73
% of pop.	97.9		

Society

No. of households, m	1.7	Cost of living, Dec. 2015	
Av. no. per household	2.7	New York = 100	87
Marriages per 1,000 pop.	4.8	Cars per 1,000 pop.	411
Divorces per 1,000 pop.	0.6	Colour TV households, % with:	
Religion, % of pop.		cable	31.7
Christian	92.0	satellite	47.6
Non-religious	6.2	Telephone lines per 100 pop.	43.2
Muslim	1.1	Mobile telephone subscribers	
Other	0.4	per 100 pop.	105.1
Hindu	0.2	Broadband subs per 100 pop.	26.9
Jewish	<0.1	Internet users, % of pop.	79.7

ISRAEL

Area	22,072 sq km	Capital	Jerusalem[a]
Arable as % of total land	13.2	Currency	New Shekel (NIS)

People

Population, m	7.8	Life expectancy: men	81.3 yrs
Pop. per sq km	353.4	women	84.6 yrs
Average annual growth		Adult literacy	...
in pop. 2015–20, %	1.6	Fertility rate (per woman)	2.9
Pop. aged 0–19, %	35.6	Urban population, %	92.1
Pop. aged 65 and over, %	11.2		per 1,000 pop.
No. of men per 100 women	98.4	Crude birth rate	19.6
Human Development Index	89.4	Crude death rate	5.2

The economy

GDP	NIS1,094bn	GDP per head	$38,500
GDP	$306bn	GDP per head in purchasing	
Av. ann. growth in real		power parity (USA=100)	63.1
GDP 2009–14	3.8%	Economic freedom index	70.7

Origins of GDP		Components of GDP	
	% of total		% of total
Agriculture	2	Private consumption	56
Industry, of which:	27	Public consumption	23
manufacturing	20	Investment	20
Services	69	Exports	32
		Imports	-31

Structure of employment

	% of total		% of labour force
Agriculture	1.1	Unemployed 2014	6.1
Industry	17.6	Av. ann. rate 2005–14	7.0
Services	79.7		

Energy

	m TOE		
Total output	6.4	Net energy imports as %	
Total consumption	23.9	of energy use	73
Consumption per head			
kg oil equivalent	2,971		

Inflation and finance

Consumer price		av. ann. increase 2010–15	
inflation 2015	-0.6%	Narrow money (M1)	17.3%
Av. ann. inflation 2010–15	1.3%	Broad money	9.0%
Treasury Bill rate, Jun. 2015	0.10%		

Exchange rates

	end 2015		December 2015
NIS per $	3.90	Effective rates	2010 = 100
NIS per SDR	5.41	– nominal	110.68
NIS per €	4.27	– real	104.59

Trade

Principal exports		Principal imports	
	$bn fob		$bn cif
Chemicals & chemical products	16.5	Fuel	12.8
Polished diamonds	9.4	Diamonds	8.6
Communications, medical &		Machinery & equipment	5.9
scientific equipment	7.9	Chemicals	4.8
Electronic components &			
computers	5.5		
Total incl. others	**57.7**	Total incl. others	**71.5**

Main export destinations		Main origins of imports	
	% of total		% of total
United States	32.2	United States	12.0
Hong Kong	10.6	China	8.4
United Kingdom	6.9	Switzerland	7.3
Belgium	5.7	Germany	6.5

Balance of payments, reserves and debt, $bn

Visible exports fob	63.3	Change in reserves	4.3
Visible imports fob	-71.2	Level of reserves	
Trade balance	-7.9	end Dec.	86.1
Invisibles inflows	44.4	No. months of import cover	9.9
Invisibles outflows	-33.6	Official gold holdings, m oz	0.0
Net transfers	10.0	Foreign debt	96.2
Current account balance	12.9	– as % of GDP	31.5
– as % of GDP	4.2	– as % of total exports	88.1
Capital balance	-8.4	Debt service ratio	15.4
Overall balance	7.2	Aid given	0.2
		– as % of GDP	0.1

Health and education

Health spending, % of GDP	7.8	Education spending, % of GDP	5.6
Doctors per 1,000 pop.	3.3	Enrolment, %: primary	105
Hospital beds per 1,000 pop.	3.3	secondary	102
Improved-water source access,		tertiary	66
% of pop.	100		

Society

No. of households, m	2.3	Cost of living, Dec. 2015	
Av. no. per household	3.5	New York = 100	95
Marriages per 1,000 pop.	6.4	Cars per 1,000 pop.	317
Divorces per 1,000 pop.	1.7	Colour TV households, % with:	
Religion, % of pop.		cable	77.8
Jewish	75.6	satellite	19.2
Muslim	18.6	Telephone lines per 100 pop.	37.1
Non-religious	3.1	Mobile telephone subscribers	
Christian	2.0	per 100 pop.	121.5
Other	0.6	Broadband subs per 100 pop.	27.2
Hindu	<0.1	Internet users, % of pop.	71.5

a Sovereignty over the city is disputed.

ITALY

Area	302,073 sq km	Capital	Rome
Arable as % of total land	23.3	Currency	Euro (€)

People

Population, m	61.1	Life expectancy: men	81.3 yrs
Pop. per sq km	202.3	women	86.0 yrs
Average annual growth		Adult literacy	99.1
in pop. 2015–20, %	0.0	Fertility rate (per woman)	1.5
Pop. aged 0–19, %	18.4	Urban population, %	69.0
Pop. aged 65 and over, %	22.4		per 1,000 pop.
No. of men per 100 women	94.6	Crude birth rate	8.3
Human Development Index	87.3	Crude death rate	10.2

The economy

GDP	€1,612bn	GDP per head	$35,825
GDP	$2,142bn	GDP per head in purchasing	
Av. ann. growth in real		power parity (USA=100)	65.7
GDP 2009–14	-0.5%	Economic freedom index	61.2

Origins of GDP		Components of GDP	
	% of total		% of total
Agriculture	2	Private consumption	61
Industry, of which:	23	Public consumption	20
manufacturing	15	Investment	16
Services	74	Exports	30
		Imports	-27

Structure of employment

	% of total		% of labour force
Agriculture	3.5	Unemployed 2014	12.5
Industry	27.1	Av. ann. rate 2005–14	8.7
Services	69.5		

Energy

	m TOE		
Total output	36.8	Net energy imports as %	
Total consumption	155.4	of energy use	76
Consumption per head			
kg oil equivalent	2,579		

Inflation and finance

Consumer price		av. ann. increase 2010–15	
inflation 2015	0.1%	Euro area:	
Av. ann. inflation 2010–15	1.6%	Narrow money (M1)	6.7%
Treasury bill rate, Dec. 2015	-0.02%	Broad money	3.1%

Exchange rates

	end 2015		December 2015
€ per $	0.92	Effective rates	2010 = 100
€ per SDR	1.27	– nominal	97.31
		– real	95.11

Trade

Principal exports		Principal imports	
	$bn fob		$bn cif
Machinery & transport equip.	187.5	Machinery & transport equip.	115.8
Chemicals & related products	66.3	Mineral fuels & lubricants	77.5
Food, drink and tobacco	41.2	Chemicals & related products	73.5
Mineral fuels & lubricants	21.1	Food, drink and tobacco	45.7
Total incl. others	**529.8**	Total incl. others	**474.4**

Main export destinations		Main origins of imports	
	% of total		% of total
Germany	12.6	Germany	15.2
France	10.5	France	8.6
United States	7.1	China	7.0
United Kingdom	5.2	Netherlands	5.8
EU28	54.9	EU28	57.1

Balance of payments, reserves and aid, $bn

Visible exports fob	518.3	Overall balance	-1.2
Visible imports fob	-455.2	Change in reserves	-14.6
Trade balance	63.1	Level of reserves	
Invisibles inflows	194.4	end Dec.	131.2
Invisibles outflows	-197.9	No. months of import cover	2.4
Net transfers	-21.1	Official gold holdings, m oz	78.8
Current account balance	38.5	Aid given	4.0
– as % of GDP	1.8	– as % of GDP	0.2
Capital balance	-53.2		

Health and education

Health spending, % of GDP	9.2	Education spending, % of GDP	4.1
Doctors per 1,000 pop.	3.8	Enrolment, %: primary	102
Hospital beds per 1,000 pop.	3.4	secondary	102
Improved-water source access,		tertiary	63
% of pop.	100		

Society

No. of households, m	26.9	Cost of living, Dec. 2015	
Av. no. per household	2.3	New York = 100	82
Marriages per 1,000 pop.	3.2	Cars per 1,000 pop.	607
Divorces per 1,000 pop.	0.9	Colour TV households, % with:	
Religion, % of pop.		cable	1.1
Christian	83.3	satellite	29.0
Non-religious	12.4	Telephone lines per 100 pop.	33.7
Muslim	3.7	Mobile telephone subscribers	
Other	0.4	per 100 pop.	154.2
Hindu	0.1	Broadband subs per 100 pop.	23.5
Jewish	<0.1	Internet users, % of pop.	62.0

IVORY COAST

Area	322,463 sq km	Capital	Yamoussoukro
Arable as % of total land	9.1	Currency	CFA franc (CFAfr)

People

Population, m	20.8	Life expectancy: men	52.0 yrs
Pop. per sq km	64.5	women	53.8 yrs
Average annual growth		Adult literacy	41.0
in pop. 2015–20, %	2.4	Fertility rate (per woman)	4.8
Pop. aged 0–19, %	53.5	Urban population, %	54.2
Pop. aged 65 and over, %	3.0		per 1,000 pop.
No. of men per 100 women	103.5	Crude birth rate	36.2
Human Development Index	46.2	Crude death rate	12.8

The economy

GDP	CFAfr16,665bn	GDP per head	$1,523
GDP	$34bn	GDP per head in purchasing	
Av. ann. growth in real		power parity (USA=100)	6.0
GDP 2009–14	4.8%	Economic freedom index	60.0

Origins of GDP		**Components of GDP**	
	% of total		% of total
Agriculture	22	Private consumption	66
Industry, of which:	21	Public consumption	13
manufacturing	13	Investment	17
Services	57	Exports	43
		Imports	-39

Structure of employment

	% of total		% of labour force
Agriculture	...	Unemployed 2014	4.0
Industry	...	Av. ann. rate 2005–14	4.1
Services	...		

Energy

	m TOE		
Total output	12.6	Net energy imports as %	
Total consumption	13.1	of energy use	4
Consumption per head			
kg oil equivalent	605		

Inflation and finance

Consumer price		av. ann. increase 2010–15	
inflation 2015	0.2%	Narrow money (M1)	13.4%
Av. ann. inflation 2010–15	2.1%	Broad money	12.7%
Deposit rate, Dec. 2015	3.50%		

Exchange rates

	end 2015		December 2015
CFAfr per $	602.51	Effective rates	2010 = 100
CFAfr per SDR	834.92	– nominal	101.59
CFAfr per €	658.79	– real	99.45

Trade

Principal exports[a]		**Principal imports**[a]	
	$bn fob		*$bn cif*
Cocoa beans & butter	4.9	Fuels & lubricants	3.2
Petroleum products	2.9	Capital equip. & raw materials	1.8
Coffee	0.3	Foodstuffs	1.8
Timber	0.3	Consumer goods	0.7
Total incl. others	**13.2**	Total incl. others	**9.6**

Main export destinations		**Main origins of imports**	
	% of total		*% of total*
Netherlands	10.1	Nigeria	22.0
United States	8.5	France	12.3
South Africa	7.2	China	8.8
France	6.3	Bahamas	5.1

Balance of payments[b], reserves[b] and debt, $bn

Visible exports fob	12.0	Change in reserves	0.3
Visible imports fob	-9.1	Level of reserves	
Trade balance	3.0	end Dec.	4.2
Invisibles inflows	1.1	No. months of import cover	3.8
Invisibles outflows	-4.3	Official gold holdings, m oz	0.0
Net transfers	-0.4	Foreign debt	10.9
Current account balance	-0.6	– as % of GDP	31.7
– as % of GDP	-2.0	– as % of total exports	73.3
Capital balance	0.3	Debt service ratio	11.3
Overall balance	0.0		

Health and education

Health spending, % of GDP	5.1	Education spending, % of GDP	4.7
Doctors per 1,000 pop.	0.1	Enrolment, %: primary	90
Hospital beds per 1,000 pop.	...	secondary	40
Improved-water source access,		tertiary	9
% of pop.	81.9		

Society

No. of households, m	3.7	Cost of living, Dec. 2015	
Av. no. per household	5.3	New York = 100	59
Marriages per 1,000 pop.	...	Cars per 1,000 pop.	20
Divorces per 1,000 pop.	...	Colour TV households, % with:	
Religion, % of pop.	...	cable	...
		satellite	...
		Telephone lines per 100 pop.	1.2
		Mobile telephone subscribers	
		per 100 pop.	106.2
		Broadband subs per 100 pop.	0.6
		Internet users, % of pop.	14.6

a Estimate.
b 2013

JAPAN

Area	377,930 sq km	Capital	Tokyo
Arable as % of total land	11.6	Currency	Yen (¥)

People

Population, m	127.0	Life expectancy: men	80.8 yrs
Pop. per sq km	336.0	women	87.3 yrs
Average annual growth		Adult literacy	...
in pop. 2015–20, %	-0.2	Fertility rate (per woman)	1.5
Pop. aged 0–19, %	17.6	Urban population, %	93.5
Pop. aged 65 and over, %	26.3		per 1,000 pop.
No. of men per 100 women	94.7	Crude birth rate	8.1
Human Development Index	89.1	Crude death rate	10.9

The economy

GDP	¥486trn	GDP per head	$36,249
GDP	$4,596bn	GDP per head in purchasing	
Av. ann. growth in real		power parity (USA=100)	69.1
GDP 2009–14	1.5%	Economic freedom index	73.1

Origins of GDP		**Components of GDP**	
	% of total		% of total
Agriculture	1	Private consumption	61
Industry, of which:	26	Public consumption	21
manufacturing	19	Investment	22
Services	73	Exports	18
		Imports	-21

Structure of employment

	% of total		% of labour force
Agriculture	3.7	Unemployed 2014	3.7
Industry	25.8	Av. ann. rate 2005–14	4.3
Services	69.1		

Energy

	m TOE		
Total output	28.0	Net energy imports as %	
Total consumption	454.7	of energy use	94
Consumption per head			
kg oil equivalent	3,570		

Inflation and finance

		av. ann. increase 2010–15	
Consumer price			
inflation 2015	0.8%	Narrow money (M1)	4.3%
Av. ann. inflation 2010–15	0.7%	Broad money	2.9%
Treasury bill rate, Dec. 2015	-0.21%		

Exchange rates

	end 2015		December 2015
¥ per $	120.50	Effective rates	2010 = 100
¥ per SDR	166.98	– nominal	76.72
¥ per €	131.75	– real	70.98

Trade

Principal exports		**Principal imports**	
	$bn fob		*$bn cif*
Capital equipment	351.4	Industrial supplies	430.3
Industrial supplies	178.9	Capital equipment	195.5
Consumer durable goods	108.8	Food & direct consumer goods	63.8
Consumer non-durable goods	4.4	Consumer durable goods	54.4
Total incl. others	**690.8**	**Total incl. others**	**813.0**

Main export destinations		**Main origins of imports**	
	% of total		*% of total*
United States	18.9	China	22.3
China	18.3	United States	9.0
South Korea	7.5	Australia	5.9
Hong Kong	5.5	Saudi Arabia	5.8

Balance of payments, reserves and aid, $bn

Visible exports fob	699.5	Overall balance	8.5
Visible imports fob	-798.7	Change in reserves	-9.8
Trade balance	-99.2	Level of reserves	
Invisibles inflows	397.5	end Dec.	1,257.1
Invisibles outflows	-255.3	No. months of import cover	14.3
Net transfers	-18.9	Official gold holdings, m oz	24.6
Current account balance	24.0	Aid given	9.3
– as % of GDP	0.5	– as % of GDP	0.2
Capital balance	-44.4		

Health and education

Health spending, % of GDP	10.2	Education spending, % of GDP	3.8
Doctors per 1,000 pop.	2.3	Enrolment, %: primary	102
Hospital beds per 1,000 pop.	13.7	secondary	102
Improved-water source access,		tertiary	62
% of pop.	100		

Society

No. of households, m	52.9	Cost of living, Dec. 2015	
Av. no. per household	2.4	New York = 100	97
Marriages per 1,000 pop.	5.2	Cars per 1,000 pop.	478
Divorces per 1,000 pop.	1.8	Colour TV households, % with:	
Religion, % of pop.		cable	52.7
Non-religious	57.0	satellite	42.3
Buddhist	36.2	Telephone lines per 100 pop.	50.1
Other	5.0	Mobile telephone subscribers	
Christian	1.6	per 100 pop.	120.2
Muslim	0.2	Broadband subs per 100 pop.	29.3
Jewish	<0.1	Internet users, % of pop.	90.6

KENYA

Area	591,958 sq km	Capital	Nairobi
Arable as % of total land	10.2	Currency	Kenyan shilling (KSh)

People

Population, m	45.5	Life expectancy: men	61.1 yrs
Pop. per sq km	76.9	women	65.5 yrs
Average annual growth		Adult literacy	...
in pop. 2015–20, %	2.5	Fertility rate (per woman)	4.1
Pop. aged 0–19, %	52.2	Urban population, %	25.6
Pop. aged 65 and over, %	2.8		per 1,000 pop.
No. of men per 100 women	99.9	Crude birth rate	32.8
Human Development Index	54.8	Crude death rate	7.6

The economy

GDP	KSh5,358bn	GDP per head	$1,358
GDP	$61bn	GDP per head in purchasing	
Av. ann. growth in real		power parity (USA=100)	5.5
GDP 2009–14	6.0%	Economic freedom index	57.5

Origins of GDP		Components of GDP	
	% of total		% of total
Agriculture	30	Private consumption	82
Industry, of which:	19	Public consumption	14
manufacturing	11	Investment	21
Services	50	Exports	16
		Imports	-34

Structure of employment

	% of total		% of labour force
Agriculture	...	Unemployed 2012	9.2
Industry	...	Av. ann. rate 2000–12	9.5
Services	...		

Energy

	m TOE		
Total output	17.6	Net energy imports as %	
Total consumption	21.5	of energy use	18
Consumption per head			
kg oil equivalent	492		

Inflation and finance

			av. ann. increase 2010–15
Consumer price			
inflation 2015	6.6%	Narrow money (M1)	12.0%
Av. ann. inflation 2010–15	8.5%	Broad money	15.5%
Treasury bill rate, Aug. 2015	11.54%		

Exchange rates

	end 2015		December 2015
KSh per $	102.31	Effective rates	2010 = 100
KSh per SDR	141.78	– nominal	...
KSh per €	111.87	– real	...

Trade

Principal exports		Principal imports	
	$bn fob		$bn cif
Tea	1.2	Industrial supplies	4.8
Horticultural products	1.2	Machinery & other capital equip.	3.0
Coffee	0.4	Transport equipment	1.9
Fish products	0.1		
Total incl. others	**6.2**	Total incl. others	**17.6**

Main export destinations		Main origins of imports	
	% of total		% of total
Uganda	11.5	China	16.4
Netherlands	8.3	India	15.3
United States	7.9	Japan	10.4
Tanzania	7.4	United Arab Emirates	6.4

Balance of payments, reserves and debt, $bn

Visible exports fob	6.2	Change in reserves	1.3
Visible imports fob	-17.6	Level of reserves	
Trade balance	-11.4	end Dec.	7.9
Invisibles inflows	5.1	No. months of import cover	4.4
Invisibles outflows	-3.8	Official gold holdings, m oz	0.0
Net transfers	3.8	Foreign debt	16.2
Current account balance	-6.3	– as % of GDP	26.6
– as % of GDP	-10.4	– as % of total exports	127.1
Capital balance	6.9	Debt service ratio	9.7
Overall balance	1.4		

Health and education

Health spending, % of GDP	5.7	Education spending, % of GDP	5.5
Doctors per 1,000 pop.	0.2	Enrolment, %: primary	111
Hospital beds per 1,000 pop.	1.4	secondary	68
Improved-water source access,		tertiary	...
% of pop.	63.2		

Society

No. of households, m	10.5	Cost of living, Dec. 2015	
Av. no. per household	4.3	New York = 100	67
Marriages per 1,000 pop.	...	Cars per 1,000 pop.	17
Divorces per 1,000 pop.	...	Colour TV households, % with:	
Religion, % of pop.		cable	2.4
Christian	84.8	satellite	3.4
Muslim	9.7	Telephone lines per 100 pop.	0.4
Other	3.0	Mobile telephone subscribers	
Non-religious	2.5	per 100 pop.	73.8
Hindu	0.1	Broadband subs per 100 pop.	0.2
Jewish	<0.1	Internet users, % of pop.	43.4

MALAYSIA

Area	330,396 sq km	Capital	Kuala Lumpur
Arable as % of total land	2.9	Currency	Malaysian dollar/ringgit (M$)

People

Population, m	30.2	Life expectancy: men	73.0 yrs
Pop. per sq km	91.4	women	77.7 yrs
Average annual growth		Adult literacy	93.1
in pop. 2015–20, %	1.3	Fertility rate (per woman)	1.9
Pop. aged 0–19, %	33.7	Urban population, %	74.7
Pop. aged 65 and over, %	5.9		per 1,000 pop.
No. of men per 100 women	98.2	Crude birth rate	16.6
Human Development Index	77.9	Crude death rate	5.2

The economy

GDP	M$1,107bn	GDP per head	$11,307
GDP	$338bn	GDP per head in purchasing	
Av. ann. growth in real		power parity (USA=100)	47.4
GDP 2009–14	5.8%	Economic freedom index	71.5

Origins of GDP		**Components of GDP**	
	% of total		% of total
Agriculture	9	Private consumption	52
Industry, of which:	40	Public consumption	13
manufacturing	23	Investment	25
Services	51	Exports	74
		Imports	-65

Structure of employment

	% of total		% of labour force
Agriculture	12.2	Unemployed 2014	2.0
Industry	27.4	Av. ann. rate 2005–14	3.2
Services	60.3		

Energy

	m TOE		
Total output	94.6	Net energy imports as %	
Total consumption	89.0	of energy use	-6
Consumption per head			
kg oil equivalent	3,020		

Inflation and finance

Consumer price		av. ann. increase 2010–15	
inflation 2015	2.1%	Narrow money (M1)	9.9%
Av. ann. inflation 2010–15	2.4%	Broad money	8.0%
Treasury bill rate, Sep. 2015	3.02%		

Exchange rates

	end 2015		December 2015
M$ per $	4.29	Effective rates	2010 = 100
M$ per SDR	5.95	– nominal	84.05
M$ per €	4.69	– real	86.37

Trade

Principal exports		Principal imports	
	$bn fob		$bn cif
Machinery & transport equip.	90.7	Machinery & transport equip.	87.2
Mineral fuels	51.5	Mineral fuels	35.1
Manufactured goods	20.7	Manufactured goods	26.7
Chemicals	17.3	Chemicals	20.2
Total incl. others	**234.1**	Total incl. others	**208.9**

Main export destinations		Main origins of imports	
	% of total		% of total
Singapore	14.2	China	16.9
China	12.0	Singapore	12.6
Japan	10.8	Japan	8.0
United States	8.4	United States	7.7

Balance of payments, reserves and debt, $bn

Visible exports fob	207.8	Change in reserves	-19.1
Visible imports fob	-173.2	Level of reserves	
Trade balance	34.6	end Dec.	115.8
Invisibles inflows	58.0	No. months of import cover	5.6
Invisibles outflows	-72.8	Official gold holdings, m oz	1.2
Net transfers	-5.4	Foreign debt	210.8
Current account balance	14.5	– as % of GDP	62.4
– as % of GDP	4.3	– as % of total exports	78.9
Capital balance	-24.6	Debt service ratio	4.8
Overall balance	-11.1		

Health and education

Health spending, % of GDP	4.2	Education spending, % of GDP	6.3
Doctors per 1,000 pop.	1.2	Enrolment, %: primary	106
Hospital beds per 1,000 pop.	1.9	secondary	71
Improved-water source access,		tertiary	39
% of pop.	98.2		

Society

No. of households, m	7.1	Cost of living, Dec. 2015	
Av. no. per household	4.3	New York = 100	57
Marriages per 1,000 pop.	...	Cars per 1,000 pop.	365
Divorces per 1,000 pop.	...	Colour TV households, % with:	
Religion, % of pop.		cable	12.7
Muslim	63.7	satellite	56.2
Buddhist	17.7	Telephone lines per 100 pop.	14.6
Christian	9.4	Mobile telephone subscribers	
Hindu	6.0	per 100 pop.	148.8
Other	2.5	Broadband subs per 100 pop.	10.1
Non-religious	0.7	Internet users, % of pop.	67.5

MEXICO

Area	1,964,375 sq km	Capital	Mexico city
Arable as % of total land	11.8	Currency	Mexican peso (PS)

People

Population, m	123.8	Life expectancy: men	75.2 yrs
Pop. per sq km	63.0	women	79.9 yrs
Average annual growth		Adult literacy	94.0
in pop. 2015–20, %	1.2	Fertility rate (per woman)	2.1
Pop. aged 0–19, %	37.0	Urban population, %	79.2
Pop. aged 65 and over, %	6.5		per 1,000 pop.
No. of men per 100 women	99.0	Crude birth rate	17.7
Human Development Index	75.6	Crude death rate	4.9

The economy

GDP	PS17,252bn	GDP per head	$10,351
GDP	$1,298bn	GDP per head in purchasing	
Av. ann. growth in real		power parity (USA=100)	32.3
GDP 2009–14	3.3%	Economic freedom index	65.2

Origins of GDP

	% of total
Agriculture	3
Industry, of which:	34
manufacturing	18
Services	62

Components of GDP

	% of total
Private consumption	67
Public consumption	12
Investment	22
Exports	32
Imports	-33

Structure of employment

	% of total		% of labour force
Agriculture	13.4	Unemployed 2014	4.9
Industry	23.6	Av. ann. rate 2005–14	4.4
Services	62.4		

Energy

	m TOE		
Total output	216.5	Net energy imports as %	
Total consumption	191.3	of energy use	-13
Consumption per head			
kg oil equivalent	1,546		

Inflation and finance

		av. ann. increase 2010–15	
Consumer price inflation 2015	2.7%	Narrow money (M1)	12.8%
Av. ann. inflation 2010–15	3.6%	Broad money	10.1%
Treasury bill rate, Dec. 2015	3.14%		

Exchange rates

	end 2015		December 2015
PS per $	17.21	Effective rates	2010 = 100
PS per SDR	23.84	– nominal	79.41
PS per €	18.81	– real	87.39

Trade

Principal exports		Principal imports	
	$bn fob		*$bn cif*
Manufactured goods	337.3	Intermediate goods	302.0
Crude oil & products	42.6	Consumer goods	58.3
Agricultural products	12.2	Capital goods	39.6
Mining products	5.1		
Total	**397.1**	Total	**400.0**

Main export destinations		Main origins of imports	
	% of total		*% of total*
United States	80.2	United States	53.7
Canada	2.7	China	18.2
China	1.5	Japan	4.8
Spain	1.5	South Korea	3.8

Balance of payments, reserves and debt, $bn

Visible exports fob	397.9	Change in reserves	14.9
Visible imports fob	-400.4	Level of reserves	
Trade balance	-2.6	end Dec.	195.1
Invisibles inflows	32.1	No. months of import cover	4.9
Invisibles outflows	-77.3	Official gold holdings, m oz	3.9
Net transfers	22.9	Foreign debt	432.6
Current account balance	-24.8	– as % of GDP	33.3
– as % of GDP	-1.9	– as % of total exports	95.4
Capital balance	57.9	Debt service ratio	11.5
Overall balance	16.7		

Health and education

Health spending, % of GDP	6.3	Education spending, % of GDP	5.1
Doctors per 1,000 pop.	2.1	Enrolment, %: primary	104
Hospital beds per 1,000 pop.	1.5	secondary	87
Improved-water source access,		tertiary	29
% of pop.	96.1		

Society

No. of households, m	32.2	Cost of living, Dec. 2015	
Av. no. per household	3.9	New York = 100	69
Marriages per 1,000 pop.	4.9	Cars per 1,000 pop.	206
Divorces per 1,000 pop.	0.9	Colour TV households, % with:	
Religion, % of pop.		cable	21.4
Christian	95.1	satellite	23.5
Non-religious	4.7	Telephone lines per 100 pop.	17.8
Hindu	<0.1	Mobile telephone subscribers	
Jewish	<0.1	per 100 pop.	82.2
Muslim	<0.1	Broadband subs per 100 pop.	10.5
Other	<0.1	Internet users, % of pop.	44.4

MOROCCO

Area	447,400 sq km	Capital	Rabat
Arable as % of total land	18.0	Currency	Dirham (Dh)

People

Population, m	33.5	Life expectancy: men	73.8 yrs
Pop. per sq km	74.9	women	76.0 yrs
Average annual growth		Adult literacy	67.1
in pop. 2015–20, %	1.2	Fertility rate (per woman)	2.4
Pop. aged 0–19, %	35.9	Urban population, %	60.2
Pop. aged 65 and over, %	6.2		per 1,000 pop.
No. of men per 100 women	97.7	Crude birth rate	19.1
Human Development Index	62.8	Crude death rate	5.7

The economy

GDP	Dh925bn	GDP per head	$3,243
GDP	$110bn	GDP per head in purchasing	
Av. ann. growth in real		power parity (USA=100)	14.1
GDP 2009–14	3.8%	Economic freedom index	61.3

Origins of GDP		Components of GDP	
	% of total		% of total
Agriculture	13	Private consumption	60
Industry, of which:	29	Public consumption	20
manufacturing	18	Investment	32
Services	58	Exports	34
		Imports	-47

Structure of employment

	% of total		% of labour force
Agriculture	39.2	Unemployed 2014	10.2
Industry	21.4	Av. ann. rate 2005–14	9.6
Services	39.4		

Energy

	m TOE		
Total output	1.9	Net energy imports as %	
Total consumption	18.9	of energy use	90
Consumption per head			
kg oil equivalent	564		

Inflation and finance

			av. ann. increase 2010–15
Consumer price			
inflation 2015	1.6%	Narrow money (M1)	5.1%
Av. ann. inflation 2010–15	1.2%	Broad money	5.2%
Money market rate, Dec. 2015	2.53%		

Exchange rates

	end 2015		December 2015
Dh per $	9.91	Effective rates	2010 = 100
Dh per SDR	13.73	– nominal	103.91
Dh per €	10.83	– real	98.70

Trade

Principal exports		Principal imports	
	$bn fob		$bn cif
Clothing & textiles	2.4	Fuel & lubricants	11.1
Electric cables & wires	2.2	Semi-finished goods	9.8
Fertilisers & chemicals	2.1	Capital goods	9.8
Phosphoric acid	1.5	Consumer goods	8.2
Total incl. others	**24.0**	Total incl. others	**46.3**

Main export destinations		Main origins of imports	
	% of total		% of total
Spain	22.0	Spain	13.4
France	20.7	France	13.3
Brazil	4.6	China	7.6
Italy	4.3	United States	7.0

Balance of payments[a], reserves[a] and debt, $bn

Visible exports fob	18.3	Change in reserves	2.0
Visible imports fob	-39.9	Level of reserves	
Trade balance	-21.6	end Dec.	19.1
Invisibles inflows	14.8	No. months of import cover	4.6
Invisibles outflows	-9.8	Official gold holdings, m oz	0.7
Net transfers	7.9	Foreign debt	42.8
Current account balance	-8.7	– as % of GDP	38.8
– as % of GDP	-8.1	– as % of total exports	99.5
Capital balance	3.1	Debt service ratio	11.2
Overall balance	-5.3		

Health and education

Health spending, % of GDP	5.9	Education spending, % of GDP	...
Doctors per 1,000 pop.	0.6	Enrolment, %: primary	116
Hospital beds per 1,000 pop.	0.9	secondary	69
Improved-water source access, % of pop.	85.4	tertiary	25

Society

No. of households, m	7.3	Cost of living, Dec. 2015	
Av. no. per household	4.7	New York = 100	57
Marriages per 1,000 pop.	...	Cars per 1,000 pop.	72
Divorces per 1,000 pop.	...	Colour TV households, % with:	
Religion, % of pop.		cable	...
Muslim	99.9	satellite	92.0
Christian	<0.1	Telephone lines per 100 pop.	7.4
Hindu	<0.1	Mobile telephone subscribers	
Jewish	<0.1	per 100 pop.	131.7
Non-religious	<0.1	Broadband subs per 100 pop.	3.0
Other	<0.1	Internet users, % of pop.	56.8

a 2013

NETHERLANDS

Area[a]	37,354 sq km	Capital	Amsterdam
Arable as % of total land	30.8	Currency	Euro (€)

People

Population, m	16.8	Life expectancy: men	80.3 yrs
Pop. per sq km	449.8	women	83.8 yrs
Average annual growth		Adult literacy	...
in pop. 2015–20, %	0.3	Fertility rate (per woman)	1.8
Pop. aged 0–19, %	22.4	Urban population, %	90.5
Pop. aged 65 and over, %	18.2		per 1,000 pop.
No. of men per 100 women	97.7	Crude birth rate	10.5
Human Development Index	92.2	Crude death rate	8.8

The economy

GDP	€663bn	GDP per head	$52,212
GDP	$881bn	GDP per head in purchasing	
Av. ann. growth in real		power parity (USA=100)	88.3
GDP 2009–14	0.5%	Economic freedom index	74.6

Origins of GDP		**Components of GDP**	
	% of total		% of total
Agriculture	2	Private consumption	45
Industry, of which:	21	Public consumption	26
manufacturing	12	Investment	18
Services	77	Exports	83
		Imports	-71

Structure of employment

	% of total		% of labour force
Agriculture	2.5	Unemployed 2014	6.9
Industry	18.4	Av. ann. rate 2005–14	4.6
Services	78.9		

Energy

	m TOE		
Total output	69.4	Net energy imports as %	
Total consumption	77.4	of energy use	10
Consumption per head			
kg oil equivalent	4,605		

Inflation and finance

Consumer price		av. ann. increase 2010–15	
inflation 2015	0.2%	Euro area:	
Av. ann. inflation 2010–15	1.7%	Narrow money (M1)	6.7%
Deposit rate, h'holds, Dec. 2015	1.68%	Broad money	3.1%

Exchange rates

	end 2015		December 2015
€ per $	0.92	Effective rates	2010 = 100
€ per SDR	1.27	– nominal	96.05
		– real	95.88

Trade

Principal exports		Principal imports	
	$bn fob		*$bn cif*
Machinery & transport equip.	197.6	Machinery & transport equip.	172.3
Mineral fuels & lubricants	117.4	Mineral fuels & lubricants	131.3
Chemicals & related products	108.5	Chemicals & related products	74.2
Food, drink & tobacco	86.2	Food, drink & tobacco	55.5
Total incl. others	**575.8**	**Total incl. others**	**508.2**

Main export destinations		Main origins of imports	
	% of total		*% of total*
Germany	28.9	Germany	16.7
Belgium	14.7	China	14.8
United Kingdom	10.2	Belgium	9.8
France	9.8	United States	7.6
EU28	75.9	EU28	45.8

Balance of payments, reserves and aid, $bn

Visible exports fob	574.7	Overall balance	-1.6
Visible imports fob	-469.4	Change in reserves	-6.2
Trade balance	105.2	Level of reserves	
Invisibles inflows	484.7	end Dec.	40.2
Invisibles outflows	-489.0	No. months of import cover	0.5
Net transfers	-17.4	Official gold holdings, m oz	19.7
Current account balance	83.5	Aid given	5.6
– as % of GDP	9.5	– as % of GDP	0.6
Capital balance	-67.2		

Health and education

Health spending, % of GDP	10.9	Education spending, % of GDP	5.5
Doctors per 1,000 pop.	2.9	Enrolment, %: primary	106
Hospital beds per 1,000 pop.	...	secondary	131
Improved-water source access,		tertiary	79
% of pop.	100		

Society

No. of households, m	7.6	Cost of living, Dec. 2015	
Av. no. per household	2.2	New York = 100	74
Marriages per 1,000 pop.	3.8	Cars per 1,000 pop.	488
Divorces per 1,000 pop.	2.0	Colour TV households, % with:	
Religion, % of pop.		cable	69.3
Christian	50.6	satellite	7.2
Non-religious	42.1	Telephone lines per 100 pop.	41.3
Muslim	6.0	Mobile telephone subscribers	
Other	0.6	per 100 pop.	116.4
Hindu	0.5	Broadband subs per 100 pop.	40.8
Jewish	0.2	Internet users, % of pop.	93.2

a Includes water.

NEW ZEALAND

Area	268,107 sq km	Capital	Wellington
Arable as % of total land	2.1	Currency	New Zealand dollar (NZ$)

People

Population, m	4.6	Life expectancy: men	80.8 yrs
Pop. per sq km	17.2	women	84.0 yrs
Average annual growth		Adult literacy	...
in pop. 2015–20, %	0.9	Fertility rate (per woman)	2.0
Pop. aged 0–19, %	27.0	Urban population, %	86.3
Pop. aged 65 and over, %	14.9		per 1,000 pop.
No. of men per 100 women	95.6	Crude birth rate	12.9
Human Development Index	91.3	Crude death rate	6.9

The economy

GDP	NZ$238bn	GDP per head	$44,028
GDP	$198bn	GDP per head in purchasing	
Av. ann. growth in real		power parity (USA=100)	66.0
GDP 2009–14	2.4%	Economic freedom index	81.6

Origins of GDP		**Components of GDP**	
	% of total		% of total
Agriculture	4	Private consumption	56
Industry, of which:	26	Public consumption	19
manufacturing	...	Investment	24
Services	70	Exports	29
		Imports	-27

Structure of employment

	% of total		% of labour force
Agriculture	6.4	Unemployed 2014	5.6
Industry	20.2	Av. ann. rate 2005–14	5.3
Services	73.0		

Energy

	m TOE		
Total output	16.2	Net energy imports as %	
Total consumption	19.5	of energy use	17
Consumption per head			
kg oil equivalent	4,392		

Inflation and finance

Consumer price		av. ann. increase 2010–15	
inflation 2015	0.3%	Narrow money (M1)	7.9%
Av. ann. inflation 2010–15	1.5%	Broad money	6.4%
Treasury bill rate, Dec. 2015	2.55%		

Exchange rates

	end 2015		December 2015
NZ$ per $	1.46	Effective rates	2010 = 100
NZ$ per SDR	2.02	– nominal	110.07
NZ$ per €	1.60	– real	107.48

Trade

Principal exports		Principal imports	
	$bn fob		$bn cif
Dairy produce	12.2	Machinery & electrical equip.	8.2
Meat	4.9	Transport equipment	7.3
Forestry products	3.0	Mineral fuels	6.1
Wool	0.7		
Total incl. others	**41.6**	Total incl. others	**42.5**

Main export destinations		Main origins of imports	
	% of total		% of total
China	19.9	China	16.9
Australia	17.5	Australia	12.2
United States	9.4	United States	11.6
Japan	5.9	Japan	6.7

Balance of payments, reserves and aid, $bn

Visible exports fob	42.0	Overall balance	-0.1
Visible imports fob	-41.0	Change in reserves	-0.5
Trade balance	1.0	Level of reserves	
Invisibles inflows	20.6	end Dec.	15.9
Invisibles outflows	-27.4	No. months of import cover	2.8
Net transfers	-0.3	Official gold holdings, m oz	0.0
Current account balance	-6.1	Aid given	0.5
– as % of GDP	-3.1	– as % of GDP	0.3
Capital balance	3.1		

Health and education

Health spending, % of GDP	11.0	Education spending, % of GDP	7.3
Doctors per 1,000 pop.	...	Enrolment, %: primary	99
Hospital beds per 1,000 pop.	2.3	secondary	117
Improved-water source access,		tertiary	80
% of pop.	100		

Society

No. of households, m	1.5	Cost of living, Dec. 2015	
Av. no. per household	2.9	New York = 100	80
Marriages per 1,000 pop.	4.3	Cars per 1,000 pop.	648
Divorces per 1,000 pop.	1.9	Colour TV households, % with:	
Religion, % of pop.		cable	5.9
Christian	57.0	satellite	40.7
Non-religious	36.6	Telephone lines per 100 pop.	40.6
Other	2.8	Mobile telephone subscribers	
Hindu	2.1	per 100 pop.	112.1
Muslim	1.2	Broadband subs per 100 pop.	31.0
Jewish	0.2	Internet users, % of pop.	85.5

NIGERIA

Area	923,768 sq km	Capital	Abuja
Arable as % of total land	37.3	Currency	Naira (N)

People

Population, m	178.5	Life expectancy: men	53.3 yrs
Pop. per sq km	192.7	women	54.1 yrs
Average annual growth		Adult literacy	...
in pop. 2015–20, %	2.5	Fertility rate (per woman)	5.4
Pop. aged 0–19, %	54.3	Urban population, %	47.8
Pop. aged 65 and over, %	2.7		per 1,000 pop.
No. of men per 100 women	103.8	Crude birth rate	37.9
Human Development Index	51.4	Crude death rate	12.2

The economy

GDP	N90,137bn	GDP per head	$3,234
GDP	$574bn	GDP per head in purchasing	
Av. ann. growth in real		power parity (USA=100)	10.9
GDP 2009–14	6.1%	Economic freedom index	57.5

Origins of GDP		**Components of GDP**	
	% of total		% of total
Agriculture	20	Private consumption	71
Industry, of which:	24	Public consumption	7
manufacturing	10	Investment	16
Services	56	Exports	18
		Imports	-13

Structure of employment

	% of total		% of labour force
Agriculture	...	Unemployed 2014	7.5
Industry	...	Av. ann. rate 2005–14	7.6
Services	...		

Energy

	m TOE		
Total output	255.7	Net energy imports as %	
Total consumption	133.6	of energy use	-91
Consumption per head			
kg oil equivalent	773		

Inflation and finance

Consumer price		av. ann. increase 2010–15	
inflation 2015	9.0%	Narrow money (M1)	3.1%
Av. ann. inflation 2010–15	9.7%	Broad money	8.5%
Deposit rate, Dec. 2015	3.50%		

Exchange rates

	end 2015		December 2015
N per $	197.00	Effective rates	2010 = 100
N per SDR	272.99	– nominal	91.66
N per €	215.40	– real	130.89

Trade

Principal exports		Principal imports[a]	
	$bn fob		$bn cif
Crude oil	66.1	Machinery & transport equip.	14.1
Gas	10.4	Food & live animals	8.2
Cocoa & cocoa butter	0.1	Manufactured goods	7.4
Rubber	0.1	Chemicals	5.9
Total incl. others	**82.6**	Total incl. others	**62.5**

Main export destinations		Main origins of imports	
	% of total		% of total
India	17.3	China	24.1
Brazil	11.5	United States	9.3
Netherlands	9.6	Netherlands	5.5
Spain	9.5	India	4.5

Balance of payments, reserves and debt, $bn

Visible exports fob	81.9	Change in reserves	-8.9
Visible imports fob	-61.1	Level of reserves	
Trade balance	20.8	end Dec.	37.4
Invisibles inflows	3.6	No. months of import cover	4.2
Invisibles outflows	-44.9	Official gold holdings, m oz	0.7
Net transfers	21.7	Foreign debt	26.9
Current account balance	1.3	– as % of GDP	4.7
– as % of GDP	0.2	– as % of total exports	25.2
Capital balance	4.6	Debt service ratio	0.7
Overall balance	-8.4		

Health and education

Health spending, % of GDP	3.7	Education spending, % of GDP	...
Doctors per 1,000 pop.	0.4	Enrolment, %: primary	...
Hospital beds per 1,000 pop.	...	secondary	...
Improved-water source access,		tertiary	...
% of pop.	68.5		

Society

No. of households, m	37.2	Cost of living, Dec. 2015	
Av. no. per household	4.8	New York = 100	50
Marriages per 1,000 pop.	...	Cars per 1,000 pop.	16
Divorces per 1,000 pop.	...	Colour TV households, % with:	
Religion, % of pop.		cable	1.9
Christian	49.3	satellite	...
Muslim	48.8	Telephone lines per 100 pop.	0.1
Other	1.4	Mobile telephone subscribers	
Non-religious	0.4	per 100 pop.	77.8
Hindu	<0.1	Broadband subs per 100 pop.	0.0
Jewish	<0.1	Internet users, % of pop.	42.7

a 2012

NORWAY

Area	323,787 sq km	Capital	Oslo
Arable as % of total land	2.2	Currency	Norwegian krone (Nkr)

People

Population, m	5.1	Life expectancy: men	80.2 yrs
Pop. per sq km	15.8	women	84.0 yrs
Average annual growth		Adult literacy	...
in pop. 2015–20, %	1.1	Fertility rate (per woman)	1.8
Pop. aged 0–19, %	24.2	Urban population, %	80.5
Pop. aged 65 and over, %	16.3		per 1,000 pop.
No. of men per 100 women	101.5	Crude birth rate	11.9
Human Development Index	94.4	Crude death rate	7.9

The economy

GDP	Nkr3,154bn	GDP per head	$97,227
GDP	$501bn	GDP per head in purchasing	
Av. ann. growth in real		power parity (USA=100)	124.2
GDP 2009–14	1.5%	Economic freedom index	70.8

Origins of GDP		**Components of GDP**	
	% of total		% of total
Agriculture	2	Private consumption	41
Industry, of which:	38	Public consumption	22
manufacturing	8	Investment	28
Services	60	Exports	38
		Imports	-30

Structure of employment

	% of total		% of labour force
Agriculture	2.1	Unemployed 2014	3.4
Industry	20.5	Av. ann. rate 2005–14	3.3
Services	77.0		

Energy

	m TOE		
Total output	191.6	Net energy imports as %	
Total consumption	32.7	of energy use	-486
Consumption per head			
kg oil equivalent	6,439		

Inflation and finance

Consumer price		av. ann. increase 2010–15	
inflation 2015	2.2%	Narrow money (M1)	17.5%
Av. ann. inflation 2010–15	1.7%	Broad money	3.7%
Interbank rate, Dec. 2015	1.14%		

Exchange rates

	end 2015		December 2015
Nkr per $	8.81	Effective rates	2010 = 100
Nkr per SDR	12.21	– nominal	81.35
Nkr per €	9.63	– real	82.14

Trade

Principal exports	$bn fob	Principal imports	$bn cif
Mineral fuels & lubricants	93.7	Machinery & transport equip.	35.0
Machinery & transport equip.	13.8	Manufactured goods	13.6
Food & beverages	11.5	Miscellaneous manufactured	
Manufactured goods	11.4	goods	13.6
		Chemicals & mineral products	8.7
Total incl. others	**144.6**	**Total incl. others**	**89.2**

Main export destinations	% of total	Main origins of imports	% of total
United Kingdom	22.2	Sweden	12.3
Germany	16.9	Germany	11.9
Netherlands	13.4	China	9.4
France	6.1	United Kingdom	6.5
EU28	83.0	EU28	64.9

Balance of payments, reserves and aid, $bn

Visible exports fob	143.7	Overall balance	7.2
Visible imports fob	-90.9	Change in reserves	6.5
Trade balance	52.9	Level of reserves	
Invisibles inflows	99.3	end Dec.	64.8
Invisibles outflows	-84.7	No. months of import cover	4.4
Net transfers	-7.6	Official gold holdings, m oz	0.0
Current account balance	59.8	Aid given	5.1
– as % of GDP	12.0	– as % of GDP	1.0
Capital balance	-60.9		

Health and education

Health spending, % of GDP	9.4	Education spending, % of GDP	7.4
Doctors per 1,000 pop.	4.3	Enrolment, %: primary	100
Hospital beds per 1,000 pop.	3.3	secondary	113
Improved-water source access,		tertiary	76
% of pop.	100		

Society

No. of households, m	2.3	Cost of living, Dec. 2015	
Av. no. per household	2.2	New York = 100	96
Marriages per 1,000 pop.	4.7	Cars per 1,000 pop.	498
Divorces per 1,000 pop.	2.0	Colour TV households, % with:	
Religion, % of pop.		cable	44.5
Christian	84.7	satellite	38.5
Non-religious	10.1	Telephone lines per 100 pop.	21.2
Muslim	3.7	Mobile telephone subscribers	
Other	0.9	per 100 pop.	116.1
Hindu	0.5	Broadband subs per 100 pop.	38.8
Jewish	<0.1	Internet users, % of pop.	96.3

PAKISTAN

Area	796,095 sq km	Capital	Islamabad
Arable as % of total land	39.5	Currency	Pakistan rupee (PRs)

People

Population, m	185.1	Life expectancy: men	65.8 yrs
Pop. per sq km	232.5	women	67.8 yrs
Average annual growth		Adult literacy	56.8
in pop. 2015–20, %	2.0	Fertility rate (per woman)	3.4
Pop. aged 0–19, %	45.2	Urban population, %	38.8
Pop. aged 65 and over, %	4.5		per 1,000 pop.
No. of men per 100 women	105.6	Crude birth rate	27.6
Human Development Index	53.8	Crude death rate	7.2

The economy

GDP	PRs25,068bn	GDP per head	$1,315
GDP	$243bn	GDP per head in purchasing	
Av. ann. growth in real		power parity (USA=100)	8.8
GDP 2009–14	3.5%	Economic freedom index	55.9

Origins of GDP		Components of GDP	
	% of total		% of total
Agriculture	25	Private consumption	81
Industry, of which:	21	Public consumption	11
manufacturing	14	Investment	15
Services	54	Exports	12
		Imports	-19

Structure of employment

	% of total		% of labour force
Agriculture	43.5	Unemployed 2014	5.2
Industry	22.5	Av. ann. rate 2005–14	5.4
Services	34.0		

Energy

	m TOE		
Total output	65.2	Net energy imports as %	
Total consumption	86.0	of energy use	24
Consumption per head			
kg oil equivalent	475		

Inflation and finance

Consumer price		av. ann. increase 2010–15	
inflation 2015	4.5%	Narrow money (M1)	15.5%
Av. ann. inflation 2010–15	9.0%	Broad money	13.4%
Treasury bill rate, Dec. 2015	6.36%		

Exchange rates

	end 2015		December 2015
PRs per $	104.87	Effective rates	2010 = 100
PRs per SDR	145.32	– nominal	92.55
PRs per €	114.66	– real	121.79

Trade

Principal exports	$bn fob	Principal imports	$bn cif
Cotton fabrics	2.6	Petroleum products	9.9
Knitwear	2.3	Crude oil	6.4
Rice	2.1	Palm oil	2.1
Cotton yard & thread	1.8	Telecoms equipment	1.3
Total incl. others	**24.8**	Total incl. others	**47.8**

Main export destinations	% of total	Main origins of imports	% of total
United States	13.5	China	30.5
China	10.1	Saudi Arabia	13.7
United Arab Emirates	9.4	United Arab Emirates	13.6
Afghanistan	9.0	Kuwait	7.1

Balance of payments, reserves and debt, $bn

Visible exports fob	24.8	Change in reserves	6.3
Visible imports fob	-42.6	Level of reserves	
Trade balance	-17.8	end Dec.	14.0
Invisibles inflows	6.3	No. months of import cover	3.0
Invisibles outflows	-13.0	Official gold holdings, m oz	2.1
Net transfers	20.9	Foreign debt	62.2
Current account balance	-3.5	– as % of GDP	25.6
– as % of GDP	-1.5	– as % of total exports	129.2
Capital balance	10.6	Debt service ratio	12.2
Overall balance	7.1		

Health and education

Health spending, % of GDP	2.6	Education spending, % of GDP	2.5
Doctors per 1,000 pop.	0.8	Enrolment, %: primary	94
Hospital beds per 1,000 pop.	0.6	secondary	10
Improved-water source access,		tertiary	...
% of pop.	91.4		

Society

No. of households, m	27.5	Cost of living, Dec. 2015	
Av. no. per household	6.7	New York = 100	44
Marriages per 1,000 pop.	...	Cars per 1,000 pop.	13
Divorces per 1,000 pop.	...	Colour TV households, % with:	
Religion, % of pop.		cable	1.3
Muslim	96.4	satellite	15.4
Hindu	1.9	Telephone lines per 100 pop.	2.6
Christian	1.6	Mobile telephone subscribers	
Jewish	<0.1	per 100 pop.	73.3
Non-religious	<0.1	Broadband subs per 100 pop.	1.1
Other	<0.1	Internet users, % of pop.	13.8

PERU

Area	1,285,216 sq km	Capital	Lima
Arable as % of total land	3.2	Currency	Nuevo Sol (new Sol)

People

Population, m	30.8	Life expectancy: men	72.9 yrs
Pop. per sq km	24.0	women	78.1 yrs
Average annual growth		Adult literacy	93.8
in pop. 2015–20, %	1.2	Fertility rate (per woman)	2.4
Pop. aged 0–19, %	36.7	Urban population, %	78.6
Pop. aged 65 and over, %	6.8		per 1,000 pop.
No. of men per 100 women	99.8	Crude birth rate	18.7
Human Development Index	73.4	Crude death rate	5.6

The economy

GDP	New Soles 576bn	GDP per head	$6,551
GDP	$203bn	GDP per head in purchasing	
Av. ann. growth in real		power parity (USA=100)	22.5
GDP 2009–14	5.8%	Economic freedom index	67.4

Origins of GDP		Components of GDP	
	% of total		% of total
Agriculture	7	Private consumption	63
Industry, of which:	37	Public consumption	12
manufacturing	15	Investment	26
Services	56	Exports	22
		Imports	-24

Structure of employment

	% of total		% of labour force
Agriculture	...	Unemployed 2014	4.2
Industry	22.9	Av. ann. rate 2005–14	4.3
Services	75.9		

Energy

	m TOE		
Total output	21.7	Net energy imports as %	
Total consumption	21.7	of energy use	0
Consumption per head			
kg oil equivalent	708		

Inflation and finance

Consumer price		av. ann. increase 2010–15	
inflation 2015	3.5%	Narrow money (M1)	10.9%
Av. ann. inflation 2010–15	3.3%	Broad money	12.0%
Money market rate, Dec. 2015	3.77%		

Exchange rates

	end 2015		December 2015
New Soles per $	3.41	Effective rates	2010 = 100
New Soles per SDR	4.73	– nominal	...
New Soles per €	3.73	– real	...

Trade

Principal exports		Principal imports	
	$bn fob		*$bn cif*
Copper	8.8	Intermediate goods	18.8
Gold	6.7	Capital goods	12.9
Fishmeal	1.7	Consumer goods	8.9
Zinc	1.5	Other goods	0.2
Total incl. others	**39.5**	Total incl. others	**41.0**

Main export destinations		Main origins of imports	
	% of total		*% of total*
China	17.8	China	23.9
United States	15.7	United States	23.8
Switzerland	6.7	Brazil	5.4
Canada	6.4	Mexico	5.2

Balance of payments, reserves and debt, $bn

Visible exports fob	39.5	Change in reserves	-3.4
Visible imports fob	-40.5	Level of reserves	
Trade balance	-0.9	end Dec.	62.4
Invisibles inflows	6.8	No. months of import cover	12.8
Invisibles outflows	-18.2	Official gold holdings, m oz	1.1
Net transfers	4.4	Foreign debt	66.5
Current account balance	-8.0	– as % of GDP	32.8
– as % of GDP	-4.0	– as % of total exports	135.5
Capital balance	5.7	Debt service ratio	10.3
Overall balance	-3.3		

Health and education

Health spending, % of GDP	5.5	Education spending, % of GDP	3.7
Doctors per 1,000 pop.	1.1	Enrolment, %: primary	101
Hospital beds per 1,000 pop.	1.5	secondary	96
Improved-water source access,		tertiary	...
% of pop.	86.7		

Society

No. of households, m	7.7	Cost of living, Dec. 2015	
Av. no. per household	4.0	New York = 100	66
Marriages per 1,000 pop.	2.9	Cars per 1,000 pop.	45
Divorces per 1,000 pop.	0.5	Colour TV households, % with:	
Religion, % of pop.		cable	32.5
Christian	95.5	satellite	0.2
Non-religious	3.0	Telephone lines per 100 pop.	9.9
Other	1.5	Mobile telephone subscribers	
Hindu	<0.1	per 100 pop.	103.6
Jewish	<0.1	Broadband subs per 100 pop.	5.7
Muslim	<0.1	Internet users, % of pop.	40.2

PHILIPPINES

Area	300,000 sq km	Capital	Manila
Arable as % of total land	18.7	Currency	Philippine peso (P)

People

Population, m	100.1	Life expectancy: men	65.4 yrs
Pop. per sq km	333.7	women	72.4 yrs
Average annual growth		Adult literacy	...
in pop. 2015–20, %	1.5	Fertility rate (per woman)	2.9
Pop. aged 0–19, %	42.0	Urban population, %	44.4
Pop. aged 65 and over, %	4.6		per 1,000 pop.
No. of men per 100 women	101.9	Crude birth rate	22.7
Human Development Index	66.8	Crude death rate	6.8

The economy

GDP	P12,634bn	GDP per head	$2,873
GDP	$285bn	GDP per head in purchasing	
Av. ann. growth in real		power parity (USA=100)	12.9
GDP 2009–14	6.2%	Economic freedom index	63.1

Origins of GDP		**Components of GDP**	
	% of total		% of total
Agriculture	11	Private consumption	72
Industry, of which:	31	Public consumption	10
manufacturing	21	Investment	21
Services	57	Exports	29
		Imports	-32

Structure of employment

	% of total		% of labour force
Agriculture	30.4	Unemployed 2014	7.1
Industry	15.9	Av. ann. rate 2005–14	7.3
Services	53.6		

Energy

	m TOE		
Total output	24.5	Net energy imports as %	
Total consumption	44.6	of energy use	45
Consumption per head			
kg oil equivalent	457		

Inflation and finance

			av. ann. increase 2010–15
Consumer price			
inflation 2015	1.4%	Narrow money (M1)	9.0%
Av. ann. inflation 2010–15	3.3%	Broad money	8.1%
Treasury bill rate, Dec. 2015	1.84%		

Exchange rates

	end 2015		December 2015
P per $	47.17	Effective rates	2010 = 100
P per SDR	65.36	– nominal	107.31
P per €	51.57	– real	115.40

Trade

Principal exports		Principal imports	
	$bn fob		*$bn cif*
Electrical & electronic equip.	26.5	Raw materials & intermediate	
Machinery & transport equip.	5.4	goods	26.2
Agricultural products	4.7	Capital goods	16.1
Mineral products	4.0	Mineral fuels & lubricants	13.2
		Consumer goods	9.4
Total incl. others	**62.1**	Total incl. others	**68.7**

Main export destinations		Main origins of imports	
	% of total		*% of total*
Japan	22.4	China	15.5
United States	14.1	United States	9.0
China	12.9	Japan	8.3
Hong Kong	9.0	Singapore	7.2

Balance of payments, reserves and debt, $bn

Visible exports fob	49.8	Change in reserves	-4.5
Visible imports fob	-67.2	Level of reserves	
Trade balance	-17.3	end Dec.	78.7
Invisibles inflows	34.3	No. months of import cover	9.8
Invisibles outflows	-29.0	Official gold holdings, m oz	6.3
Net transfers	22.8	Foreign debt	77.7
Current account balance	10.8	– as % of GDP	27.3
– as % of GDP	3.8	– as % of total exports	68.9
Capital balance	-9.5	Debt service ratio	5.4
Overall balance	-2.9		

Health and education

Health spending, % of GDP	4.7	Education spending, % of GDP	3.4
Doctors per 1,000 pop.	...	Enrolment, %: primary	117
Hospital beds per 1,000 pop.	1.0	secondary	88
Improved-water source access,		tertiary	36
% of pop.	91.8		

Society

No. of households, m	22.3	Cost of living, Dec. 2015	
Av. no. per household	4.5	New York = 100	62
Marriages per 1,000 pop.	...	Cars per 1,000 pop.	31
Divorces per 1,000 pop.	...	Colour TV households, % with:	
Religion, % of pop.		cable	52.5
Christian	92.6	satellite	0.6
Muslim	5.5	Telephone lines per 100 pop.	3.1
Other	1.7	Mobile telephone subscribers	
Non-religious	0.1	per 100 pop.	111.2
Hindu	<0.1	Broadband subs per 100 pop.	23.2
Jewish	<0.1	Internet users, % of pop.	39.7

POLAND

Area	312,888 sq km	Capital	Warsaw
Arable as % of total land	35.2	Currency	Zloty (Zl)

People

Population, m	38.2	Life expectancy: men	74.1 yrs
Pop. per sq km	122.1	women	81.8 yrs
Average annual growth		Adult literacy	99.8
in pop. 2015–20, %	-0.1	Fertility rate (per woman)	1.3
Pop. aged 0–19, %	20.1	Urban population, %	60.5
Pop. aged 65 and over, %	15.5		*per 1,000 pop.*
No. of men per 100 women	93.7	Crude birth rate	9.5
Human Development Index	84.3	Crude death rate	10.4

The economy

GDP	Zl1,613bn	GDP per head	$14,108
GDP	$545bn	GDP per head in purchasing	
Av. ann. growth in real		power parity (USA=100)	45.8
GDP 2009–14	3.1%	Economic freedom index	69.3

Origins of GDP		**Components of GDP**	
	% of total		*% of total*
Agriculture	3	Private consumption	60
Industry, of which:	33	Public consumption	18
manufacturing	18	Investment	20
Services	64	Exports	47
		Imports	-46

Structure of employment

	% of total		*% of labour force*
Agriculture	11.2	Unemployed 2014	9.2
Industry	30.8	Av. ann. rate 2005–14	10.5
Services	57.9		

Energy

	m TOE		
Total output	70.9	Net energy imports as %	
Total consumption	97.6	of energy use	27
Consumption per head			
kg oil equivalent	2,565		

Inflation and finance

Consumer price		*av. ann. increase 2010–15*	
inflation 2015	-0.9%	Narrow money (M1)	9.0%
Av. ann. inflation 2010–15	1.6%	Broad money	8.1%
Money market rate, Dec. 2015	1.50%		

Exchange rates

	end 2015		*December 2015*
Zl per $	3.90	Effective rates	*2010 = 100*
Zl per SDR	5.41	– nominal	94.06
Zl per €	4.27	– real	91.41

Trade

Principal exports	$bn fob	Principal imports	$bn cif
Machinery & transport equip.	83.2	Machinery & transport equip.	75.1
Manufactured goods	43.4	Manufactured goods	38.9
Foodstuffs & live animals	23.5	Chemicals & mineral products	31.9
Total incl. others	**218.9**	Total incl. others	**222.2**

Main export destinations	% of total	Main origins of imports	% of total
Germany	25.8	Germany	27.1
Czech Republic	6.5	Russia	10.2
United Kingdom	6.4	China	6.3
France	5.6	Netherlands	5.7
EU28	77.4	EU28	69.6

Balance of payments, reserves and debt, $bn

Visible exports fob	210.6	Change in reserves	-6.3
Visible imports fob	-214.9	Level of reserves	
Trade balance	-4.3	end Dec.	100.0
Invisibles inflows	63.3	No. months of import cover	4.2
Invisibles outflows	-69.6	Official gold holdings, m oz	3.3
Net transfers	-0.6	Foreign debt	337.8
Current account balance	-11.1	– as % of GDP	62.0
– as % of GDP	-2.0	– as % of total exports	120.2
Capital balance	18.2	Debt service ratio	24.2
Overall balance	0.4	Aid given	0.5
		– as % of GDP	0.1

Health and education

Health spending, % of GDP	6.4	Education spending, % of GDP	4.9
Doctors per 1,000 pop.	2.2	Enrolment, %: primary	101
Hospital beds per 1,000 pop.	6.5	secondary	109
Improved-water source access,		tertiary	71
% of pop.	98.3		

Society

No. of households, m	13.6	Cost of living, Dec. 2015	
Av. no. per household	2.8	New York = 100	59
Marriages per 1,000 pop.	4.7	Cars per 1,000 pop.	523
Divorces per 1,000 pop.	1.7	Colour TV households, % with:	
Religion, % of pop.		cable	33.8
Christian	94.3	satellite	62.8
Non-religious	5.6	Telephone lines per 100 pop.	12.6
Hindu	<0.1	Mobile telephone subscribers	
Jewish	<0.1	per 100 pop.	148.9
Muslim	<0.1	Broadband subs per 100 pop.	18.9
Other	<0.1	Internet users, % of pop.	66.6

PORTUGAL

Area	92,225 sq km	Capital	Lisbon
Arable as % of total land	12.2	Currency	Euro (€)

People

Population, m	10.6	Life expectancy: men	78.8 yrs
Pop. per sq km	114.9	women	84.4 yrs
Average annual growth		Adult literacy	94.5
in pop. 2015–20, %	-0.4	Fertility rate (per woman)	1.2
Pop. aged 0–19, %	19.3	Urban population, %	63.5
Pop. aged 65 and over, %	20.8		per 1,000 pop.
No. of men per 100 women	89.9	Crude birth rate	7.6
Human Development Index	83.0	Crude death rate	10.7

The economy

GDP	€173bn	GDP per head	$22,157
GDP	$230bn	GDP per head in purchasing	
Av. ann. growth in real		power parity (USA=100)	50.1
GDP 2009–14	-1.0%	Economic freedom index	65.1

Origins of GDP		**Components of GDP**	
	% of total		% of total
Agriculture	2	Private consumption	66
Industry, of which:	22	Public consumption	19
manufacturing	13	Investment	15
Services	76	Exports	40
		Imports	-40

Structure of employment

	% of total		% of labour force
Agriculture	5.5	Unemployed 2014	14.2
Industry	24.9	Av. ann. rate 2005–14	11.0
Services	69.5		

Energy

	m TOE		
Total output	5.8	Net energy imports as %	
Total consumption	21.8	of energy use	74
Consumption per head			
kg oil equivalent	2,083		

Inflation and finance

Consumer price		av. ann. increase 2010–15	
inflation 2015	0.5%	Euro area:	
Av. ann. inflation 2010–15	1.4%	Narrow money (M1)	6.7%
Deposit rate, h'holds Dec. 2015	0.75%	Broad money	3.1%

Exchange rates

	end 2015		December 2015
€ per $	0.92	Effective rates	2010 = 100
€ per SDR	1.27	– nominal	96.97
		– real	95.77

Trade

Principal exports		Principal imports	
	$bn fob		$bn cif
Machinery & transport equip.	16.2	Machinery & transport equip.	20.2
Food, drink & tobacco	7.1	Chemicals & related products	13.5
Chemicals & related products	5.7	Mineral fuels & lubricants	10.6
Mineral fuels & lubricants	5.4	Food, drink & tobacco	10.2
Total incl. others	**63.9**	Total incl. others	**78.4**

Main export destinations		Main origins of imports	
	% of total		% of total
Spain	23.5	Spain	32.5
France	11.8	Germany	12.3
Germany	11.7	France	7.1
Angola	6.4	Italy	5.2
EU28	70.9	EU28	74.8

Balance of payments, reserves and debt, $bn

Visible exports fob	62.9	Overall balance	-0.2
Visible imports fob	-75.1	Change in reserves	0.3
Trade balance	-12.3	Level of reserves	
Invisibles inflows	43.7	end Dec.	17.9
Invisibles outflows	-32.0	No. months of import cover	2.0
Net transfers	1.7	Official gold holdings, m oz	12.3
Current account balance	1.2	Aid given	0.4
– as % of GDP	0.5	– as % of GDP	0.2
Capital balance	-1.4		

Health and education

Health spending, % of GDP	9.5	Education spending, % of GDP	5.1
Doctors per 1,000 pop.	4.1	Enrolment, %: primary	110
Hospital beds per 1,000 pop.	3.4	secondary	120
Improved-water source access,		tertiary	66
% of pop.	100		

Society

No. of households, m	4.0	Cost of living, Dec. 2015	
Av. no. per household	2.6	New York = 100	64
Marriages per 1,000 pop.	3.1	Cars per 1,000 pop.	421
Divorces per 1,000 pop.	2.2	Colour TV households, % with:	
Religion, % of pop.		cable	56.1
Christian	93.8	satellite	20.1
Non-religious	4.4	Telephone lines per 100 pop.	43.2
Other	1.0	Mobile telephone subscribers	
Muslim	0.6	per 100 pop.	112.1
Hindu	0.1	Broadband subs per 100 pop.	25.7
Jewish	<0.1	Internet users, % of pop.	64.6

ROMANIA

Area	238,391 sq km	Capital	Bucharest
Arable as % of total land	38.0	Currency	Leu (RON)

People

Population, m	21.6	Life expectancy: men	71.6 yrs
Pop. per sq km	90.6	women	78.7 yrs
Average annual growth		Adult literacy	98.6
in pop. 2015–20, %	-0.7	Fertility rate (per woman)	1.5
Pop. aged 0–19, %	20.9	Urban population, %	54.6
Pop. aged 65 and over, %	17.3		per 1,000 pop.
No. of men per 100 women	93.9	Crude birth rate	9.0
Human Development Index	79.3	Crude death rate	13.7

The economy

GDP	RON668bn	GDP per head	$10,146
GDP	$199bn	GDP per head in purchasing	
Av. ann. growth in real		power parity (USA=100)	37.0
GDP 2009–14	1.4%	Economic freedom index	65.6

Origins of GDP		**Components of GDP**	
	% of total		% of total
Agriculture	5	Private consumption	63
Industry, of which:	27	Public consumption	14
manufacturing	21	Investment	23
Services	67	Exports	41
		Imports	-41

Structure of employment

	% of total		% of labour force
Agriculture	25.4	Unemployed 2014	7.0
Industry	30.1	Av. ann. rate 2005–14	7.0
Services	44.5		

Energy

	m TOE		
Total output	25.9	Net energy imports as %	
Total consumption	31.8	of energy use	19
Consumption per head			
kg oil equivalent	1,592		

Inflation and finance

			av. ann. increase 2010–15
Consumer price			
inflation 2015	-0.6%	Narrow money (M1)	12.9%
Av. ann. inflation 2010–15	2.7%	Broad money	7.1%
Treasury bill rate, Dec. 2015	2.36%		

Exchange rates

	end 2015		December 2015
Lei per $	4.15	Effective rates	2010 = 100
Lei per SDR	5.75	– nominal	93.79
Lei per €	4.54	– real	95.97

Trade

Principal exports		Principal imports	
	$bn fob		*$bn cif*
Machinery & transport equip.	29.6	Machinery & transport equip.	27.9
Basic metals & products	6.3	Chemical products	8.0
Textiles & apparel	5.2	Minerals, fuels & lubricants	7.7
Minerals, fuels & lubricants	4.3	Textiles & products	5.3
Total incl. others	**69.9**	Total incl. others	**77.9**

Main export destinations		Main origins of imports	
	% of total		*% of total*
Germany	19.2	Germany	19.1
Italy	11.9	Italy	10.8
France	6.8	Hungary	7.8
Hungary	5.1	France	5.7
EU28	71.1	EU28	75.4

Balance of payments, reserves and debt, $bn

Visible exports fob	62.2	Change in reserves	-6.1
Visible imports fob	-70.5	Level of reserves	
Trade balance	-8.3	end Dec.	42.7
Invisibles inflows	23.0	No. months of import cover	5.8
Invisibles outflows	-17.8	Official gold holdings, m oz	3.3
Net transfers	2.2	Foreign debt	111.3
Current account balance	-1.0	– as % of GDP	55.8
– as % of GDP	-0.5	– as % of total exports	125.7
Capital balance	5.2	Debt service ratio	27.8
Overall balance	4.0	Aid given	0.2
		– as % of GDP	0.1

Health and education

Health spending, % of GDP	5.6	Education spending, % of GDP	3.0
Doctors per 1,000 pop.	2.4	Enrolment, %: primary	96
Hospital beds per 1,000 pop.	6.1	secondary	98
Improved-water source access,		tertiary	52
% of pop.	100		

Society

No. of households, m	7.0	Cost of living, Dec. 2015	
Av. no. per household	2.8	New York = 100	47
Marriages per 1,000 pop.	5.4	Cars per 1,000 pop.	227
Divorces per 1,000 pop.	1.4	Colour TV households, % with:	
Religion, % of pop.		cable	45.9
Christian	99.5	satellite	37.4
Muslim	0.3	Telephone lines per 100 pop.	21.1
Non-religious	0.1	Mobile telephone subscribers	
Hindu	<0.1	per 100 pop.	105.9
Jewish	<0.1	Broadband subs per 100 pop.	18.5
Other	<0.1	Internet users, % of pop.	54.1

RUSSIA

Area	17,098,246 sq km	Capital	Moscow
Arable as % of total land	7.5	Currency	Rouble (Rb)

People

Population, m	142.5	Life expectancy: men	64.7 yrs
Pop. per sq km	8.3	women	76.1 yrs
Average annual growth		Adult literacy	99.7
in pop. 2015–20, %	-0.1	Fertility rate (per woman)	1.7
Pop. aged 0–19, %	21.2	Urban population, %	74.0
Pop. aged 65 and over, %	13.4		per 1,000 pop.
No. of men per 100 women	86.8	Crude birth rate	12.3
Human Development Index	79.8	Crude death rate	14.3

The economy

GDP	Rb77,893bn	GDP per head	$14,150
GDP	$2,029bn	GDP per head in purchasing	
Av. ann. growth in real		power parity (USA=100)	49.9
GDP 2009–14	2.8%	Economic freedom index	50.6

Origins of GDP		**Components of GDP**	
	% of total		% of total
Agriculture	4	Private consumption	53
Industry, of which:	36	Public consumption	20
manufacturing	16	Investment	20
Services	60	Exports	30
		Imports	-23

Structure of employment

	% of total		% of labour force
Agriculture	6.7	Unemployed 2014	5.1
Industry	27.5	Av. ann. rate 2005–14	6.5
Services	65.8		

Energy

	m TOE		
Total output	1,340.2	Net energy imports as %	
Total consumption	730.9	of energy use	-83
Consumption per head			
kg oil equivalent	5,093		

Inflation and finance

Consumer price		av. ann. increase 2010–15	
inflation 2015	15.5%	Narrow money (M1)	7.4%
Av. ann. inflation 2010–15	8.7%	Broad money	16.7%
Money market rate, Dec. 2015	11.07%		

Exchange rates

	end 2015		December 2015
Rb per $	72.88	Effective rates	2010 = 100
Rb per SDR	101.00	– nominal	58.94
Rb per €	79.69	– real	75.97

Trade

Principal exports[a]		Principal imports[a]	
	$bn fob		$bn cif
Fuels	375.2	Machinery & equipment	157.6
Ores & metals	58.2	Food & agricultural products	47.9
Machinery & equipment	32.0	Chemicals	40.3
Chemicals	26.8	Metals	22.8
Total incl.others	524.7	Total incl.others	317.2

Main export destinations		Main origins of imports	
	% of total		% of total
Netherlands	13.7	China	17.8
China	7.5	Germany	11.5
Germany	7.5	United States	6.5
Italy	7.2	Belarus	4.1

Balance of payments, reserves and debt, $bn

Visible exports fob	497.8	Change in reserves	-129.2
Visible imports fob	-308.0	Level of reserves	
Trade balance	189.7	end Dec.	380.5
Invisibles inflows	112.3	No. months of import cover	8.4
Invisibles outflows	-235.4	Official gold holdings, m oz	38.8
Net transfers	-8.2	Foreign debt	599.1
Current account balance	58.4	– as % of GDP	32.3
– as % of GDP	3.1	– as % of total exports	97.5
Capital balance	-172.2	Debt service ratio	22.4
Overall balance	-107.5	Aid given	0.9
		– as % of GDP	0.05

Health and education

Health spending, % of GDP	7.1	Education spending, % of GDP	4.2
Doctors per 1,000 pop.	4.3	Enrolment, %: primary	100
Hospital beds per 1,000 pop.	...	secondary	99
Improved-water source access,		tertiary	78
% of pop.	96.9		

Society

No. of households, m	56.1	Cost of living, Dec. 2015	
Av. no. per household	2.9	New York = 100	53
Marriages per 1,000 pop.	8.5	Cars per 1,000 pop.	304
Divorces per 1,000 pop.	4.5	Colour TV households, % with:	
Religion, % of pop.		cable	32.9
Christian	73.3	satellite	24.7
Non-religious	16.2	Telephone lines per 100 pop.	26.8
Muslim	10.0	Mobile telephone subscribers	
Jewish	0.2	per 100 pop.	155.1
Hindu	<0.1	Broadband subs per 100 pop.	17.5
Other	<0.1	Internet users, % of pop.	70.5

a 2012

SAUDI ARABIA

Area	2,206,714 sq km	Capital	Riyadh
Arable as % of total land	1.4	Currency	Riyal (SR)

People

Population, m	29.4	Life expectancy: men	73.5 yrs
Pop. per sq km	13.3	women	76.3 yrs
Average annual growth		Adult literacy	94.4
in pop. 2015–20, %	1.7	Fertility rate (per woman)	2.6
Pop. aged 0–19, %	36.6	Urban population, %	83.1
Pop. aged 65 and over, %	2.9		per 1,000 pop.
No. of men per 100 women	130.1	Crude birth rate	18.5
Human Development Index	83.7	Crude death rate	3.5

The economy

GDP	SR2,826bn	GDP per head	$24,407
GDP	$754bn	GDP per head in purchasing	
Av. ann. growth in real		power parity (USA=100)	96.1
GDP 2009–14	5.2%	Economic freedom index	62.1

Origins of GDP		Components of GDP	
	% of total		% of total
Agriculture	2	Private consumption	32
Industry, of which:	56	Public consumption	26
manufacturing	11	Investment	29
Services	41	Exports	47
		Imports	-34

Structure of employment

	% of total		% of labour force
Agriculture	4.9	Unemployed 2014	5.6
Industry	24.2	Av. ann. rate 2005–14	5.7
Services	70.9		

Energy

	m TOE		
Total output	614.5	Net energy imports as %	
Total consumption	192.2	of energy use	-220
Consumption per head			
kg oil equivalent	6,363		

Inflation and finance

		av. ann. increase 2010–15	
Consumer price			
inflation 2015	2.2%	Narrow money (M1)	12.9%
Av. ann. inflation 2010–15	3.0%	Broad money	10.4%
Treasury bill rate, Dec. 2015	0.81%		

Exchange rates

	end 2015		December 2015
SR per $	3.75	Effective rates	2010 = 100
SR per SDR	5.20	– nominal	117.21
SR per €	4.10	– real	121.36

Trade

Principal exports	$bn fob	Principal imports	$bn cif
Crude oil	238.5	Machinery & transport equip.	74.6
Refined petroleum products	43.3	Foodstuffs	24.4
		Chemical & metal products	15.0
Total incl. others	**342.5**	Total incl. others	**173.3**

Main export destinations	% of total	Main origins of imports	% of total
China	13.3	China	13.6
Japan	13.0	United States	12.1
United States	12.9	India	8.3
South Korea	10.0	Germany	6.5

Balance of payments, reserves and aid, $bn

Visible exports fob	342.5	Change in reserves	5.1
Visible imports fob	-158.5	Level of reserves	742.9
Trade balance	184.0	end Dec.	33.1
Invisibles inflows	39.6	No. months of import cover	10.4
Invisibles outflows	-111.1	Official gold holdings, m oz	
Net transfers	-38.7	Foreign debt	166.1
Current account balance	73.8	– as % of GDP	22.0
– as % of GDP	9.8	– as % of total exports	43.5
Capital balance	-57.7	Debt service ratio	3.2
Overall balance	7.5	Aid given	13.6
		– as % of GDP	1.8

Health and education

Health spending, % of GDP	4.7	Education spending, % of GDP	...
Doctors per 1,000 pop.	2.5	Enrolment, %: primary	109
Hospital beds per 1,000 pop.	2.1	secondary	108
Improved-water source access,		tertiary	61
% of pop.	97		

Society

No. of households, m	5.0	Cost of living, Dec. 2015	
Av. no. per household	5.9	New York = 100	55
Marriages per 1,000 pop.	...	Cars per 1,000 pop.	140
Divorces per 1,000 pop.	...	Colour TV households, % with:	
Religion, % of pop.		cable	0.3
Muslim	93.0	satellite	99.5
Christian	4.4	Telephone lines per 100 pop.	12.3
Hindu	1.1	Mobile telephone subscribers	
Other	0.9	per 100 pop.	179.6
Non-religious	0.7	Broadband subs per 100 pop.	23.4
Jewish	<0.1	Internet users, % of pop.	63.7

SINGAPORE

Area	718 sq km	Capital	Singapore
Arable as % of total land	0.8	Currency	Singapore dollar (S$)

People

Population, m	5.5	Life expectancy: men	80.6 yrs
Pop. per sq km	7,660.2	women	86.7 yrs
Average annual growth		Adult literacy	96.5
in pop. 2015–20, %	1.4	Fertility rate (per woman)	1.3
Pop. aged 0–19, %	21.9	Urban population, %	100.0
Pop. aged 65 and over, %	11.7		per 1,000 pop.
No. of men per 100 women	97.4	Crude birth rate	8.7
Human Development Index	91.2	Crude death rate	5.1

The economy

GDP	S$388bn	GDP per head	$55,635
GDP	$306bn	GDP per head in purchasing	
Av. ann. growth in real		power parity (USA=100)	153.2
GDP 2009–14	6.4%	Economic freedom index	87.8

Origins of GDP		Components of GDP	
	% of total		% of total
Agriculture	0	Private consumption	38
Industry, of which:	25	Public consumption	10
manufacturing	18	Investment	28
Services	75	Exports	188
		Imports	-163

Structure of employment

	% of total		% of labour force
Agriculture	1.1	Unemployed 2014	3.0
Industry	28.3	Av. ann. rate 2005–14	3.3
Services	70.6		

Energy

	m TOE		
Total output	0.6	Net energy imports as %	
Total consumption	26.1	of energy use	98
Consumption per head			
kg oil equivalent	4,833		

Inflation and finance

Consumer price		av. ann. increase 2010–15	
inflation 2015	-0.5%	Narrow money (M1)	7.3%
Av. ann. inflation 2010–15	2.5%	Broad money	5.4%
Money market rate, Dec. 2015	0.72%		

Exchange rates

	end 2015		December 2015
S$ per $	1.41	Effective rates	2010 = 100
S$ per SDR	1.96	– nominal	109.97
S$ per €	1.55	– real	109.56

Trade

Principal exports		Principal imports	
	$bn fob		*$bn cif*
Electronic components & parts	100.9	Machinery & transport equip.	151.5
Mineral fuels	97.0	Mineral fuels	113.4
Chemicals & chemical products	53.1	Misc. manufactured articles	27.8
Manufactured products	32.4	Manufactured products	25.1
Total incl.others	**405.4**	Total incl.others	**366.0**

Main export destinations		Main origins of imports	
	% of total		*% of total*
China	12.7	China	12.1
Malaysia	12.1	Malaysia	10.7
Hong Kong	11.1	United States	10.4
Indonesia	9.5	South Korea	5.9

Balance of payments, reserves and debt, $bn

Visible exports fob	437.8	Change in reserves	-16.8
Visible imports fob	-358.2	Level of reserves	
Trade balance	79.6	end Dec.	261.0
Invisibles inflows	214.1	No. months of import cover	5.3
Invisibles outflows	-233.9	Official gold holdings, m oz	4.1
Net transfers	-6.6	Foreign debt	467.6
Current account balance	53.2	– as % of GDP	152.6
– as % of GDP	17.3	– as % of total exports	71.7
Capital balance	-46.2	Debt service ratio	6.2
Overall balance	6.8		

Health and education

Health spending, % of GDP	4.9	Education spending, % of GDP	2.9
Doctors per 1,000 pop.	2.0	Enrolment, %: primary	...
Hospital beds per 1,000 pop.	2.0	secondary	...
Improved-water source access,		tertiary	...
% of pop.	100		

Society

No. of households, m	1.6	Cost of living, Dec. 2015	
Av. no. per household	3.5	New York = 100	116
Marriages per 1,000 pop.	7.3	Cars per 1,000 pop.	118
Divorces per 1,000 pop.	1.6	Colour TV households, % with:	
Religion, % of pop.		cable	55.8
Buddhist	33.9	satellite	...
Christian	18.2	Telephone lines per 100 pop.	36.2
Non-religious	16.4	Mobile telephone subscribers	
Muslim	14.3	per 100 pop.	146.9
Other	12.0	Broadband subs per 100 pop.	26.7
Hindu	5.2	Internet users, % of pop.	82.0

SLOVAKIA

Area	49,035 sq km	Capital	Bratislava
Arable as % of total land	29.0	Currency	Euro (€)

People

Population, m	5.5	Life expectancy: men	73.0 yrs
Pop. per sq km	112.2	women	80.3 yrs
Average annual growth		Adult literacy	...
in pop. 2015–20, %	0.0	Fertility rate (per woman)	1.4
Pop. aged 0–19, %	20.4	Urban population, %	53.6
Pop. aged 65 and over, %	13.8		*per 1,000 pop.*
No. of men per 100 women	94.1	Crude birth rate	10.4
Human Development Index	84.4	Crude death rate	10.2

The economy

GDP	€76bn	GDP per head	$18,501
GDP	$100bn	GDP per head in purchasing	
Av. ann. growth in real		power parity (USA=100)	52.2
GDP 2009–14	2.6%	Economic freedom index	66.6

Origins of GDP		**Components of GDP**	
	% of total		*% of total*
Agriculture	4	Private consumption	57
Industry, of which:	34	Public consumption	19
manufacturing	21	Investment	21
Services	62	Exports	92
		Imports	-88

Structure of employment

	% of total		*% of labour force*
Agriculture	3.5	Unemployed 2014	13.3
Industry	35.5	Av. ann. rate 2005–14	13.2
Services	60.9		

Energy

	m TOE		
Total output	6.7	Net energy imports as %	
Total consumption	17.2	of energy use	61
Consumption per head			
kg oil equivalent	3,178		

Inflation and finance

Consumer price		*av. ann. increase 2010–15*	
inflation 2015	-0.3%	Euro area:	
Av. ann. inflation 2010–15	1.8%	Narrow money (M1)	6.7%
Deposit rate, h'holds Dec. 2015	1.03%	Broad money	3.1%

Exchange rates

	end 2015		*December 2015*
€ per $	0.92	Effective rates	*2010 = 100*
€ per SDR	1.27	– nominal	99.48
		– real	98.42

Trade

Principal exports	$bn fob	Principal imports	$bn cif
Machinery & transport equip.	49.7	Machinery & transport equip.	36.1
Chemicals & related products	4.2	Mineral fuels & lubricants	8.4
Mineral fuels & lubricants	4.1	Chemicals & related products	7.2
Food, drink & tobacco	3.1	Food, drink & tobacco	4.5
Total incl. others	**86.5**	Total incl. others	**83.5**

Main export destinations	% of total	Main origins of imports	% of total
Germany	21.9	Germany	13.8
Czech Republic	12.8	Czech Republic	12.1
Poland	8.5	Austria	6.9
Hungary	6.3	Russia	5.7
EU28	84.4	EU28	76.1

Balance of payments, reserves and debt, $bn

Visible exports fob	83.1	Overall balance	0.6
Visible imports fob	-79.3	Change in reserves	0.3
Trade balance	3.8	Level of reserves	
Invisibles inflows	13.4	end Dec.	2.5
Invisibles outflows	-15.4	No. months of import cover	0.3
Net transfers	-1.6	Official gold holdings, m oz	1.0
Current account balance	0.2	Aid given	0.08
– as % of GDP	0.2	– as % of GDP	0.1
Capital balance	3.6		

Health and education

Health spending, % of GDP	8.1	Education spending, % of GDP	3.9
Doctors per 1,000 pop.	3.3	Enrolment, %: primary	102
Hospital beds per 1,000 pop.	6.0	secondary	92
Improved-water source access,		tertiary	54
% of pop.	100		

Society

No. of households, m	2.3	Cost of living, Dec. 2015	
Av. no. per household	2.4	New York = 100	...
Marriages per 1,000 pop.	4.7	Cars per 1,000 pop.	355
Divorces per 1,000 pop.	2.0	Colour TV households, % with:	
Religion, % of pop.		cable	43.0
Christian	85.3	satellite	49.6
Non-religious	14.3	Telephone lines per 100 pop.	16.8
Muslim	0.2	Mobile telephone subscribers	
Other	0.1	per 100 pop.	116.9
Hindu	<0.1	Broadband subs per 100 pop.	21.8
Jewish	<0.1	Internet users, % of pop.	80.0

SLOVENIA

Area	20,273 sq km	Capital	Ljubljana
Arable as % of total land	8.4	Currency	Euro (€)

People

Population, m	2.1	Life expectancy: men	78.1 yrs
Pop. per sq km	103.6	women	83.9 yrs
Average annual growth		Adult literacy	99.7
in pop. 2015–20, %	0.1	Fertility rate (per woman)	1.7
Pop. aged 0–19, %	19.3	Urban population, %	49.6
Pop. aged 65 and over, %	18.0		per 1,000 pop.
No. of men per 100 women	98.3	Crude birth rate	10.1
Human Development Index	88.0	Crude death rate	10.0

The economy

GDP	€37bn	GDP per head	$23,992
GDP	$50bn	GDP per head in purchasing	
Av. ann. growth in real		power parity (USA=100)	54.9
GDP 2009–14	0.2%	Economic freedom index	60.6

Origins of GDP		Components of GDP	
	% of total		% of total
Agriculture	2	Private consumption	53
Industry, of which:	33	Public consumption	19
manufacturing	23	Investment	20
Services	65	Exports	77
		Imports	-69

Structure of employment

	% of total		% of labour force
Agriculture	7.7	Unemployed 2013	9.5
Industry	31.5	Av. ann. rate 2000–13	7.2
Services	60.2		

Energy

	m TOE		
Total output	3.6	Net energy imports as %	
Total consumption	6.8	of energy use	48
Consumption per person			
kg oil equivalent	3,323		

Inflation and finance

		av. ann. increase 2010–15	
Consumer price			
inflation 2015	-0.5%	Euro area:	
Av. ann. inflation 2010–15	1.2%	Narrow money (M1)	6.7%
Deposit rate, h'holds, Dec. 2015	0.71%	Broad money	3.1%

Exchange rates

	end 2015		December 2015
€ per $	0.82	Effective rates	2010 = 100
€ per SDR	1.19	– nominal	...
		– real	...

Trade

Principal exports		**Principal imports**	
	$bn fob		*$bn cif*
Machinery & transport equip.	13.5	Machinery & transport equip.	11.0
Manufactured goods	11.2	Manufactured goods	9.5
Chemicals	5.9	Chemicals	4.7
Miscellaneous manufactures	5.3	Mineral fuels & lubricants	4.0
Total incl. others	**36.0**	Total incl. others	**34.0**

Main export destinations		**Main origins of imports**	
	% of total		*% of total*
Germany	18.9	Germany	16.2
Italy	11.2	Italy	14.4
Austria	8.6	Austria	10.3
Croatia	6.7	South Korea	4.6
EU28	75.3	EU28	69.1

Balance of payments, reserves and debt, $bn

Visible exports fob	30.5	Overall balance	0.1
Visible imports fob	-28.9	Change in reserves	0.1
Trade balance	1.6	Level of reserves	
Invisibles inflows	9.2	end Dec.	1.0
Invisibles outflows	-7.0	No. months of import cover	0.3
Net transfers	-0.3	Official gold holdings, m oz	0.1
Current account balance	3.5	Aid given	0.06
– as % of GDP	7.0	– as % of GDP	0.1
Capital balance	-3.2		

Health and education

Health spending, % of GDP	9.2	Education spending, % of GDP	5.7
Doctors per 1,000 pop.	2.5	Enrolment, %: primary	99
Hospital beds per 1,000 pop.	4.6	secondary	111
Improved-water source access,		tertiary	85
% of pop.	99.5		

Society

No. of households, m	0.8	Cost of living, Dec. 2015	
Av. no. per household	2.4	New York = 100	...
Marriages per 1,000 pop.	3.0	Cars per 1,000 pop.	513
Divorces per 1,000 pop.	1.1	Colour TV households, % with:	
Religion, % of pop.		cable	70.7
Christian	78.4	satellite	9.1
Non-religious	18.0	Telephone lines per 100 pop.	37.1
Muslim	3.6	Mobile telephone subscribers	
Hindu	<0.1	per 100 pop.	112.1
Jewish	<0.1	Broadband subs per 100 pop.	26.6
Other	<0.1	Internet users, % of pop.	71.6

SOUTH AFRICA

Area	1,215,037 sq km	Capital	Pretoria
Arable as % of total land	10.3	Currency	Rand (R)

People

Population, m	53.1	Life expectancy: men	55.7 yrs
Pop. per sq km	43.7	women	59.3 yrs
Average annual growth		Adult literacy	93.7
in pop. 2015–20, %	0.8	Fertility rate (per woman)	2.3
Pop. aged 0–19, %	38.9	Urban population, %	64.8
Pop. aged 65 and over, %	5.0		per 1,000 pop.
No. of men per 100 women	96.8	Crude birth rate	19.8
Human Development Index	66.6	Crude death rate	12.6

The economy

GDP	R3,797bn	GDP per head	$6,488
GDP	$350bn	GDP per head in purchasing	
Av. ann. growth in real		power parity (USA=100)	24.8
GDP 2009–14	2.4%	Economic freedom index	61.9

Origins of GDP		Components of GDP	
	% of total		% of total
Agriculture	2	Private consumption	61
Industry, of which:	29	Public consumption	20
manufacturing	13	Investment	20
Services	68	Exports	31
		Imports	-33

Structure of employment

	% of total		% of labour force
Agriculture	4.6	Unemployed 2014	25.1
Industry	23.5	Av. ann. rate 2005–14	23.9
Services	71.9		

Energy

	m TOE		
Total output	165.7	Net energy imports as %	
Total consumption	141.3	of energy use	-17
Consumption per head			
kg oil equivalent	2,658		

Inflation and finance

Consumer price		av. ann. increase 2010–15	
inflation 2015	4.6%	Narrow money (M1)	10.7%
Av. ann. inflation 2010–15	5.4%	Broad money	7.4%
Money market rate, Dec. 2015	6.20%		

Exchange rates

	end 2015		December 2015
		Effective rates	2010 = 100
R per $	15.55		
R per SDR	21.54	– nominal	57.13
R per €	17.00	– real	68.53

Trade

Principal exports		Principal imports	
	$bn fob		*$bn cif*
Gold	7.7	Petrochemicals	16.0
Platinum	5.9	Petroleum oils & other	5.0
Coal	5.9	Equipment components for cars	4.6
Car & other components	2.6	Car & other components	4.5
Total incl. others	**91.1**	Total incl. others	**100.0**

Main export destinations		Main origins of imports	
	% of total		*% of total*
China	9.6	China	17.0
United States	7.1	Germany	11.0
Japan	5.4	Saudi Arabia	7.9
Botswana	5.2	United States	7.3

Balance of payments, reserves and debt, $bn

Visible exports fob	92.5	Change in reserves	-1.2
Visible imports fob	-98.8	Level of reserves	
Trade balance	-6.4	end Dec.	48.5
Invisibles inflows	24.4	No. months of import cover	4.4
Invisibles outflows	-34.0	Official gold holdings, m oz	4.0
Net transfers	-3.2	Foreign debt	144.0
Current account balance	-19.1	– as % of GDP	41.1
– as % of GDP	-5.5	– as % of total exports	122.1
Capital balance	15.4	Debt service ratio	8.5
Overall balance	1.4		

Health and education

Health spending, % of GDP	8.8	Education spending, % of GDP	6.1
Doctors per 1,000 pop.	0.8	Enrolment, %: primary	100
Hospital beds per 1,000 pop.	...	secondary	98
Improved-water source access,		tertiary	20
% of pop.	93.2		

Society

No. of households, m	15.1	Cost of living, Dec. 2015	
Av. no. per household	3.5	New York = 100	50
Marriages per 1,000 pop.	...	Cars per 1,000 pop.	120
Divorces per 1,000 pop.	...	Colour TV households, % with:	
Religion, % of pop.		cable	...
Christian	81.2	satellite	8.9
Non-religious	14.9	Telephone lines per 100 pop.	6.9
Muslim	1.7	Mobile telephone subscribers	
Hindu	1.1	per 100 pop.	149.2
Other	0.9	Broadband subs per 100 pop.	3.2
Jewish	0.1	Internet users, % of pop.	49.0

SOUTH KOREA

Area	100,266 sq km	Capital	Seoul
Arable as % of total land	15.3	Currency	Won (W)

People

Population, m	49.5	Life expectancy: men	79.5 yrs
Pop. per sq km	493.7	women	85.7 yrs
Average annual growth		Adult literacy	...
in pop. 2015–20, %	0.4	Fertility rate (per woman)	1.3
Pop. aged 0–19, %	20.5	Urban population, %	82.5
Pop. aged 65 and over, %	13.1		per 1,000 pop.
No. of men per 100 women	98.8	Crude birth rate	9.1
Human Development Index	89.8	Crude death rate	6.1

The economy

GDP	W1,485trn	GDP per head	$28,166
GDP	$1,410bn	GDP per head in purchasing	
Av. ann. growth in real		power parity (USA=100)	65.6
GDP 2009–14	3.7%	Economic freedom index	71.7

Origins of GDP		Components of GDP	
	% of total		% of total
Agriculture	2	Private consumption	50
Industry, of which:	38	Public consumption	15
manufacturing	30	Investment	29
Services	59	Exports	51
		Imports	-45

Structure of employment

	% of total		% of labour force
Agriculture	6.1	Unemployed 2014	3.5
Industry	24.4	Av. ann. rate 2005–14	3.4
Services	69.5		

Energy

	m TOE		
Total output	43.6	Net energy imports as %	
Total consumption	263.8	of energy use	83
Consumption per head			
kg oil equivalent	5,253		

Inflation and finance

Consumer price		av. ann. increase 2010–15	
inflation 2015	0.7%	Narrow money (M1)	10.6%
Av. ann. inflation 2010–15	1.9%	Broad money	6.2%
Money market rate, Dec. 2015	1.48%		

Exchange rates

	end 2015		December 2015
W per $	1,172.50	Effective rates	2010 = 100
W per SDR	1,624.80	– nominal	...
W per €	1,282.00	– real	...

Trade

Principal exports		Principal imports	
	$bn fob		*$bn cif*
Machinery & transport equip.	315.1	Mineral fuels & lubricants	175.6
Manufactured goods	75.6	Machinery & transport equip.	141.6
Chemicals & related products	67.7	Manufactured goods	58.0
Miscellaneous manufact. articles	47.9	Chemicals & related products	47.5
Total incl. others	**572.7**	Total incl. others	**525.5**

Main export destinations		Main origins of imports	
	% of total		*% of total*
China	25.4	China	17.1
United States	12.3	Japan	10.2
Japan	5.6	United States	8.7
Hong Kong	4.8	Germany	7.0

Balance of payments, reserves and debt, $bn

Visible exports fob	613.0	Change in reserves	16.6
Visible imports fob	-524.1	Level of reserves	
Trade balance	88.9	end Dec.	362.3
Invisibles inflows	138.9	No. months of import cover	6.6
Invisibles outflows	-138.5	Official gold holdings, m oz	3.4
Net transfers	-5.0	Foreign debt	370.4
Current account balance	84.4	– as % of GDP	26.2
– as % of GDP	6.0	– as % of total exports	49.3
Capital balance	-71.5	Debt service ratio	3.5
Overall balance	17.4	Aid given	1.9
		– as % of GDP	0.1

Health and education

Health spending, % of GDP	7.4	Education spending, % of GDP	4.6
Doctors per 1,000 pop.	2.1	Enrolment, %: primary	99
Hospital beds per 1,000 pop.	...	secondary	98
Improved-water source access,		tertiary	95
% of pop.	97.6		

Society

No. of households, m	18.5	Cost of living, Dec. 2015	
Av. no. per household	2.7	New York = 100	99
Marriages per 1,000 pop.	6.4	Cars per 1,000 pop.	318
Divorces per 1,000 pop.	2.3	Colour TV households, % with:	
Religion, % of pop.		cable	81.8
Non-religious	46.4	satellite	13.5
Christian	29.4	Telephone lines per 100 pop.	59.5
Buddhist	22.9	Mobile telephone subscribers	
Other	1.0	per 100 pop.	115.7
Muslim	0.2	Broadband subs per 100 pop.	38.8
Jewish	<0.1	Internet users, % of pop.	84.3

SPAIN

Area	505,992 sq km	Capital	Madrid
Arable as % of total land	25.1	Currency	Euro (€)

People

Population, m	47.1	Life expectancy: men	80.5 yrs
Pop. per sq km	93.1	women	85.8 yrs
Average annual growth		Adult literacy	98.1
in pop. 2015–20, %	0.0	Fertility rate (per woman)	1.4
Pop. aged 0–19, %	19.4	Urban population, %	79.6
Pop. aged 65 and over, %	18.8		per 1,000 pop.
No. of men per 100 women	96.3	Crude birth rate	8.6
Human Development Index	87.6	Crude death rate	9.1

The economy

GDP	€1,041bn	GDP per head	$29,908
GDP	$1,384bn	GDP per head in purchasing	
Av. ann. growth in real		power parity (USA=100)	61.7
GDP 2009–14	-0.5%	Economic freedom index	68.5

Origins of GDP		**Components of GDP**	
	% of total		% of total
Agriculture	3	Private consumption	58
Industry, of which:	22	Public consumption	19
manufacturing	13	Investment	20
Services	75	Exports	33
		Imports	-30

Structure of employment

	% of total		% of labour force
Agriculture	4.2	Unemployed 2014	24.7
Industry	19.5	Av. ann. rate 2005–14	17.4
Services	76.3		

Energy

	m TOE		
Total output	34.5	Net energy imports as %	
Total consumption	116.7	of energy use	70
Consumption per head			
kg oil equivalent	2,504		

Inflation and finance

Consumer price		av. ann. increase 2010–15	
inflation 2015	-0.5%	Euro area:	
Av. ann. inflation 2010–15	1.3%	Narrow money (M1)	6.7%
Money market rate, Dec. 2015	-0.30%	Broad money	3.1%

Exchange rates

	end 2015		December 2015
€ per $	0.92	Effective rates	2010 = 100
€ per SDR	1.27	– nominal	96.30
		– real	93.73

Trade

Principal exports		Principal imports	
	$bn fob		*$bn cif*
Machinery & transport equip.	103.4	Machinery & transport equip.	99.4
Food, drink & tobacco	45.7	Mineral fuels & lubricants	72.5
Chemicals & related products	43.6	Chemicals & related products	51.8
Mineral fuels & lubricants	32.5	Food, drink & tobacco	33.9
Total incl. others	**318.9**	**Total incl. others**	**351.4**

Main export destinations		Main origins of imports	
	% of total		*% of total*
France	16.1	Germany	13.5
Germany	10.6	France	12.1
Portugal	7.4	Italy	6.3
Italy	7.3	China	6.2
EU28	63.8	EU28	57.3

Balance of payments, reserves and aid, $bn

Visible exports fob	317.1	Overall balance	4.9
Visible imports fob	-347.0	Change in reserves	2.7
Trade balance	-29.9	Level of reserves	
Invisibles inflows	199.5	end Dec.	49.1
Invisibles outflows	-141.3	No. months of import cover	1.2
Net transfers	-15.4	Official gold holdings, m oz	9.1
Current account balance	12.8	Aid given	1.9
– as % of GDP	0.9	– as % of GDP	0.1
Capital balance	-17.5		

Health and education

Health spending, % of GDP	9.0	Education spending, % of GDP	4.4
Doctors per 1,000 pop.	4.9	Enrolment, %: primary	106
Hospital beds per 1,000 pop.	3.1	secondary	131
Improved-water source access,		tertiary	87
% of pop.	100		

Society

No. of households, m	18.6	Cost of living, Dec. 2015	
Av. no. per household	2.5	New York = 100	81
Marriages per 1,000 pop.	3.3	Cars per 1,000 pop.	468
Divorces per 1,000 pop.	2.0	Colour TV households, % with:	
Religion, % of pop.		cable	13.9
Christian	78.6	satellite	12.7
Non-religious	19.0	Telephone lines per 100 pop.	40.6
Muslim	2.1	Mobile telephone subscribers	
Jewish	0.1	per 100 pop.	107.8
Other	0.1	Broadband subs per 100 pop.	27.3
Hindu	<0.1	Internet users, % of pop.	76.2

SWEDEN

Area	450,295 sq km	Capital	Stockholm
Arable as % of total land	6.4	Currency	Swedish krona (Skr)

People

Population, m	9.6	Life expectancy: men	81.1 yrs
Pop. per sq km	21.3	women	84.4 yrs
Average annual growth		Adult literacy	...
in pop. 2015–20, %	0.7	Fertility rate (per woman)	1.9
Pop. aged 0–19, %	22.5	Urban population, %	85.8
Pop. aged 65 and over, %	19.9		per 1,000 pop.
No. of men per 100 women	99.9	Crude birth rate	12.2
Human Development Index	90.7	Crude death rate	9.0

The economy

GDP	Skr3,918bn	GDP per head	$58,857
GDP	$571bn	GDP per head in purchasing	
Av. ann. growth in real		power parity (USA=100)	85.5
GDP 2009–14	2.4%	Economic freedom index	72.0

Origins of GDP		Components of GDP	
	% of total		% of total
Agriculture	1	Private consumption	46
Industry, of which:	26	Public consumption	26
manufacturing	16	Investment	24
Services	73	Exports	45
		Imports	-41

Structure of employment

	% of total		% of labour force
Agriculture	1.7	Unemployed 2014	8.0
Industry	18.7	Av. ann. rate 2005–14	7.7
Services	79.0		

Energy

	m TOE		
Total output	35.1	Net energy imports as %	
Total consumption	49.3	of energy use	29
Consumption per head			
kg oil equivalent	5,132		

Inflation and finance

Consumer price		av. ann. increase 2010–15	
inflation 2015	0.7%	Narrow money (M1)	7.6%
Av. ann. inflation 2010–15	0.7%	Broad money	4.5%
Treasury bill rate, Dec. 2015	-0.38%		

Exchange rates

	end 2015		December 2015
Skr per $	8.44	Effective rates	2010 = 100
Skr per SDR	11.70	– nominal	101.14
Skr per €	9.23	– real	95.35

Trade

Principal exports		Principal imports	
	$bn fob		*$bn cif*
Machinery & transport equip.	62.1	Machinery & transport equip.	59.2
Chemicals & related products	19.7	Mineral fuels & lubricants	22.0
Mineral fuels & lubricants	14.4	Chemicals & related products	19.4
Raw materials	11.6	Food, drink & tobacco	16.3
Total incl. others	**164.6**	Total incl. others	**162.2**

Main export destinations		Main origins of imports	
	% of total		*% of total*
Norway	10.5	Germany	17.4
Germany	10.0	Norway	7.9
United Kingdom	7.2	Netherlands	7.7
Finland	7.0	Denmark	7.3
EU28	58.5	EU28	68.8

Balance of payments, reserves and aid, $bn

Visible exports fob	179.6	Overall balance	0.5
Visible imports fob	-160.6	Change in reserves	-3.4
Trade balance	19.0	Level of reserves	
Invisibles inflows	136.6	end Dec.	62.0
Invisibles outflows	-115.4	No. months of import cover	2.7
Net transfers	-9.6	Official gold holdings, m oz	4.0
Current account balance	30.6	Aid given	6.2
– as % of GDP	5.4	– as % of GDP	1.1
Capital balance	-17.4		

Health and education

Health spending, % of GDP	11.9	Education spending, % of GDP	7.7
Doctors per 1,000 pop.	3.9	Enrolment, %: primary	120
Hospital beds per 1,000 pop.	2.7	secondary	128
Improved-water source access,		tertiary	63
% of pop.	100		

Society

No. of households, m	4.2	Cost of living, Dec. 2015	
Av. no. per household	2.3	New York = 100	80
Marriages per 1,000 pop.	5.4	Cars per 1,000 pop.	478
Divorces per 1,000 pop.	2.8	Colour TV households, % with:	
Religion, % of pop.		cable	57.5
Christian	67.2	satellite	20.1
Non-religious	27.0	Telephone lines per 100 pop.	39.2
Muslim	4.6	Mobile telephone subscribers	
Other	0.8	per 100 pop.	127.8
Hindu	0.2	Broadband subs per 100 pop.	34.1
Jewish	0.1	Internet users, % of pop.	92.5

SWITZERLAND

Area	41,285 sq km	Capital	Berne
Arable as % of total land	10.2	Currency	Swiss franc (SFr)

People

Population, m	8.2	Life expectancy: men	81.6 yrs
Pop. per sq km	198.6	women	85.5 yrs
Average annual growth		Adult literacy	...
in pop. 2015–20, %	0.8	Fertility rate (per woman)	1.6
Pop. aged 0–19, %	20.0	Urban population, %	73.9
Pop. aged 65 and over, %	18.0		per 1,000 pop.
No. of men per 100 women	98.1	Crude birth rate	10.5
Human Development Index	93.0	Crude death rate	8.0

The economy

GDP	SFr642bn	GDP per head	$85,397
GDP	$701bn	GDP per head in purchasing	
Av. ann. growth in real		power parity (USA=100)	106.2
GDP 2009–14	1.9%	Economic freedom index	81.0

Origins of GDP		**Components of GDP**	
	% of total		% of total
Agriculture	1	Private consumption	54
Industry, of which:	26	Public consumption	11
manufacturing	19	Investment	23
Services	73	Exports	64
		Imports	-53

Structure of employment

	% of total		% of labour force
Agriculture	3.2	Unemployed 2014	4.5
Industry	20.1	Av. ann. rate 2005–14	4.1
Services	73.9		

Energy

	m TOE		
Total output	13.0	Net energy imports as %	
Total consumption	26.7	of energy use	52
Consumption per head			
kg oil equivalent	3,304		

Inflation and finance

		av. ann. increase 2010–15	
Consumer price			
inflation 2015	-1.1%	Narrow money (M1)	5.6%
Av. ann. inflation 2010–15	-0.4%	Broad money	6.5%
Treasury bill rate, Dec. 2015	-0.92%		

Exchange rates

	end 2015		December 2015
SFr per $	0.99	Effective rates	2010 = 100
SFr per SDR	1.37	– nominal	123.23
SFr per €	1.08	– real	110.79

Trade

Principal exports		Principal imports	
	$bn fob		*$bn cif*
Chemicals	93.2	Chemicals	46.9
Precision instruments, watches		Machinery, equipment &	
& jewellery	51.4	electronics	33.1
Machinery, equipment &		Precision instruments, watches	
electronics	36.4	& jewellery	21.9
Metals & metal manufactures	13.6	Motor vehicles	17.6
Total incl. others	**227.9**	**Total incl. others**	**195.4**

Main export destinations		Main origins of imports	
	% of total		*% of total*
Germany	19.2	Germany	29.1
United States	13.6	Italy	10.1
France	7.6	France	8.5
Italy	6.9	United States	6.8
EU28	54.7	EU28	72.2

Balance of payments, reserves and aid, $bn

Visible exports fob	327.7	Overall balance	35.9
Visible imports fob	-273.7	Change in reserves	4.6
Trade balance	53.9	Level of reserves	
Invisibles inflows	270.6	end Dec.	540.9
Invisibles outflows	-244.4	No. months of import cover	12.5
Net transfers	-18.6	Official gold holdings, m oz	33.4
Current account balance	61.5	Aid given	3.5
– as % of GDP	8.8	– as % of GDP	0.5
Capital balance	-29.3		

Health and education

Health spending, % of GDP	11.7	Education spending, % of GDP	5.0
Doctors per 1,000 pop.	4.0	Enrolment, %: primary	103
Hospital beds per 1,000 pop.	5.0	secondary	96
Improved-water source access,		tertiary	56
% of pop.	100		

Society

No. of households, m	3.7	Cost of living, Dec. 2014	
Av. no. per household	2.2	New York = 100	108
Marriages per 1,000 pop.	4.9	Cars per 1,000 pop.	535
Divorces per 1,000 pop.	2.1	Colour TV households, % with:	
Religion, % of pop.		cable	82.4
Christian	81.3	satellite	16.0
Non-religious	11.9	Telephone lines per 100 pop.	53.6
Muslim	5.5	Mobile telephone subscribers	
Other	0.6	per 100 pop.	136.7
Hindu	0.4	Broadband subs per 100 pop.	42.5
Jewish	0.3	Internet users, % of pop.	87.0

TAIWAN

Area	36,179 sq km	Capital	Taipei
Arable as % of total land	...	Currency	Taiwan dollar (T$)

People

Population, m	23.4	Life expectancy: men	76.9 yrs
Pop. per sq km	646.8	women	83.3 yrs
Average annual growth		Adult literacy	...
in pop. 2015–20, %	0.2	Fertility rate (per woman)	1.1
Pop. aged 0–19, %	20.0	Urban population, %	78.0
Pop. aged 65 and over, %	12.5		per 1,000 pop.
No. of men per 100 women	99.0	Crude birth rate	8.0
Human Development Index	...	Crude death rate	7.1

The economy

GDP	T$16,097bn	GDP per head	$22,574
GDP	$530bn	GDP per head in purchasing	
Av. ann. growth in real		power parity (USA=100)	84.7
GDP 2009–14	4.5%	Economic freedom index	74.7

Origins of GDP		**Components of GDP**	
	% of total		% of total
Agriculture	2	Private consumption	53
Industry, of which:	36	Public consumption	15
manufacturing	...	Investment	22
Services	70	Exports	70
		Imports	-60

Structure of employment

	% of total		% of labour force
Agriculture	...	Unemployed 2014	...
Industry	...	Av. ann. rate 2005–14	...
Services	...		

Energy

	m TOE		
Total output	...	Net energy imports as %	
Total consumption	...	of energy use	...
Consumption per person			
kg oil equivalent	...		

Inflation and finance

Consumer price		av. ann. increase 2010–15	
inflation 2015	-0.3%	Narrow money (M1)	5.9%
Av. ann. inflation 2010–15	1.0%	Broad money	5.2%
Treasury bill rate, Dec. 2015	...		

Exchange rates

	end 2015		December 2015
T$ per $	31.99	Effective rates	2010 = 100
T$ per SDR	...	– nominal	...
T$ per €	34.98	– real	...

Trade

Principal exports		Principal imports	
	$bn fob		$bn cif
Machinery & electrical equip.	158.1	Machinery & electrical equip.	88.6
Basic metals & articles	29.1	Minerals	70.1
Plastic & rubber articles	24.4	Chemicals & related products	30.3
Chemicals	22.2	Basic metals & articles	23.4
Total incl. others	**296.1**	Total incl. others	**281.0**

Main export destinations		Main origins of imports	
	% of total		% of total
China	28.6	China	17.5
Hong Kong	14.8	Japan	14.9
United States	11.9	United States	10.7
Singapore	7.0	South Korea	5.4

Balance of payments, reserves and debt, $bn

Visible exports fob	311.6	Change in reserves	0.2
Visible imports fob	-270.1	Level of reserves	
Trade balance	41.5	end Dec.	433.4
Invisibles inflows	87.8	No. months of import cover	15.7
Invisibles outflows	-61.1	Official gold holdings, m oz	13.6
Net transfers	-2.8	Foreign debt	177.9
Current account balance	65.3	– as % of GDP	33.6
– as % of GDP	12.3	– as % of total exports	43.9
Capital balance	53.0	Debt service ratio	2.6
Overall balance	119.1	Aid given	0.3
		– as % of GDP	0.05

Health and education

Health spending, % of GDP	...	Education spending, % of GDP	...
Doctors per 1,000 pop.	...	Enrolment, %: primary	...
Hospital beds per 1,000 pop.	...	secondary	...
Improved-water source access,		tertiary	...
% of pop.	...		

Society

No. of households, m	7.7	Cost of living, Dec. 2015	
Av. no. per household	3.0	New York = 100	72
Marriages per 1,000 pop.	...	Cars per 1,000 pop.	274
Divorces per 1,000 pop.	...	Colour TV households, % with:	
Religion, % of pop.		cable	84.6
Other	60.5	satellite	0.4
Buddhist	21.3	Telephone lines per 100 pop.	60.2
Non-religious	12.7	Mobile telephone subscribers	
Christian	5.5	per 100 pop.	130.2
Hindu	<0.1	Broadband subs per 100 pop.	31.9
Jewish	<0.1	Internet users, % of pop.	84.0

THAILAND

Area	513,120 sq km	Capital	Bangkok
Arable as % of total land	32.9	Currency	Baht (Bt)

People

Population, m	67.2	Life expectancy: men	71.8 yrs
Pop. per sq km	131.0	women	78.5 yrs
Average annual growth		Adult literacy	96.4
in pop. 2015–20, %	0.2	Fertility rate (per woman)	1.5
Pop. aged 0–19, %	24.2	Urban population, %	50.4
Pop. aged 65 and over, %	10.5		per 1,000 pop.
No. of men per 100 women	97.2	Crude birth rate	9.9
Human Development Index	72.6	Crude death rate	8.4

The economy

GDP	Bt13,132bn	GDP per head	$5,970
GDP	$404bn	GDP per head in purchasing	
Av. ann. growth in real		power parity (USA=100)	29.5
GDP 2009–14	3.8%	Economic freedom index	63.9

Origins of GDP		**Components of GDP**	
	% of total		% of total
Agriculture	10	Private consumption	52
Industry, of which:	37	Public consumption	17
manufacturing	28	Investment	24
Services	53	Exports	69
		Imports	-63

Structure of employment

	% of total		% of labour force
Agriculture	41.9	Unemployed 2014	0.9
Industry	20.3	Av. ann. rate 2005–14	1.0
Services	37.5		

Energy

	m TOE		
Total output	78.1	Net energy imports as %	
Total consumption	134.1	of energy use	42
Consumption per head			
kg oil equivalent	1,988		

Inflation and finance

Consumer price		av. ann. increase 2010–15	
inflation 2015	-0.9%	Narrow money (M1)	6.4%
Av. ann. inflation 2010–15	2.0%	Broad money	8.3%
Money market rate, Dec. 2015	1.46%		

Exchange rates

	end 2015		December 2015
			2010 = 100
Bt per $	36.09	Effective rates	
Bt per SDR	50.01	– nominal	...
Bt per €	39.46	– real	...

Trade

Principal exports[a]	$bn fob	Principal imports[a]	$bn cif
Machinery, equip. & supplies	93.7	Machinery, equip. & supplies	86.2
Manufactured goods	29.1	Fuel & lubricants	52.0
Food	26.8	Manufactured goods	40.6
Chemicals	24.0	Chemicals	23.6
Total incl. others	**225.9**	Total incl. others	**249.7**

Main export destinations	% of total	Main origins of imports	% of total
China	11.0	Japan	16.9
United States	10.5	China	15.6
Japan	9.6	United States	6.4
Malaysia	5.6	Malaysia	5.6

Balance of payments, reserves and debt, $bn

Visible exports fob	224.8	Change in reserves	-10.8
Visible imports fob	-200.2	Level of reserves	
Trade balance	24.6	end Dec.	156.4
Invisibles inflows	62.4	No. months of import cover	6.7
Invisibles outflows	-80.4	Official gold holdings, m oz	4.9
Net transfers	8.8	Foreign debt	135.8
Current account balance	15.4	– as % of GDP	33.6
– as % of GDP	3.8	– as % of total exports	46.4
Capital balance	-16.4	Debt service ratio	5.1
Overall balance	-1.2	Aid given	0.07
		– as % of GDP[a]	0.02

Health and education

Health spending, % of GDP	6.5	Education spending, % of GDP	4.9
Doctors per 1,000 pop.	0.4	Enrolment, %: primary	98
Hospital beds per 1,000 pop.	2.1	secondary	86
Improved-water source access,		tertiary	51
% of pop.	97.8		

Society

No. of households, m	22.1	Cost of living, Dec. 2015	
Av. no. per household	3.1	New York = 100	73
Marriages per 1,000 pop.	...	Cars per 1,000 pop.	125
Divorces per 1,000 pop.	...	Colour TV households, % with:	
Religion, % of pop.		cable	9.9
Buddhist	93.2	satellite	4.9
Muslim	5.5	Telephone lines per 100 pop.	8.5
Christian	0.9	Mobile telephone subscribers	
Non-religious	0.3	per 100 pop.	144.4
Hindu	0.1	Broadband subs per 100 pop.	8.5
Jewish	<0.1	Internet users, % of pop.	34.9

a 2013

TURKEY

Area	783,562 sq km	Capital	Ankara
Arable as % of total land	26.7	Currency	Turkish Lira (YTL)

People

Population, m	75.8	Life expectancy: men	73.0 yrs
Pop. per sq km	96.7	women	79.3 yrs
Average annual growth		Adult literacy	95.3
in pop. 2015–20, %	0.9	Fertility rate (per woman)	2.0
Pop. aged 0–19, %	34.2	Urban population, %	73.4
Pop. aged 65 and over, %	7.5		per 1,000 pop.
No. of men per 100 women	96.7	Crude birth rate	15.7
Human Development Index	76.1	Crude death rate	5.8

The economy

GDP	YTL1,747bn	GDP per head	$10,298
GDP	$798bn	GDP per head in purchasing	
Av. ann. growth in real		power parity (USA=100)	36.0
GDP 2009–14	5.4%	Economic freedom index	62.1

Origins of GDP		**Components of GDP**	
	% of total		% of total
Agriculture	8	Private consumption	69
Industry, of which:	27	Public consumption	15
manufacturing	18	Investment	20
Services	65	Exports	28
		Imports	-32

Structure of employment

	% of total		% of labour force
Agriculture	19.7	Unemployed 2014	9.2
Industry	28.4	Av. ann. rate 2005–14	10.5
Services	51.9		

Energy

	m TOE		
Total output	32.3	Net energy imports as %	
Total consumption	116.5	of energy use	72
Consumption per head			
kg oil equivalent	1,553		

Inflation and finance

		av. ann. increase 2010–15	
Consumer price			
inflation 2015	7.7%	Narrow money (M1)	18.2%
Av. ann. inflation 2010–15	7.9%	Broad money	14.9%
Deposit rate, Dec. 2015	16.00%		

Exchange rates

	end 2015		December 2015
YTL per $	2.91	Effective rates	2010 = 100
YTL per SDR	4.03	– nominal	...
YTL per €	3.18	– real	...

Trade

Principal exports		Principal imports	
	$bn fob		*$bn cif*
Agricultural products	29.3	Fuels	55.0
Transport equipment	19.4	Chemicals	33.2
Iron & steel	17.5	Mechanical equipment	21.8
Textiles & clothing	16.5	Transport equipment	19.4
Total incl. others	**157.6**	Total incl. others	**242.2**

Main export destinations		Main origins of imports	
	% of total		*% of total*
Germany	9.6	Russia	10.4
Iraq	6.9	China	10.3
United Kingdom	6.3	Germany	9.2
Italy	4.5	United States	5.3
EU28	43.5	EU28	36.7

Balance of payments, reserves and debt, $bn

Visible exports fob	168.9	Change in reserves	-6.1
Visible imports fob	-232.5	Level of reserves	
Trade balance	-63.6	end Dec.	124.9
Invisibles inflows	56.7	No. months of import cover	5.5
Invisibles outflows	-38.1	Official gold holdings, m oz	17.0
Net transfers	1.4	Foreign debt	408.2
Current account balance	-43.6	– as % of GDP	51.1
– as % of GDP	-5.5	– as % of total exports	181.5
Capital balance	41.5	Debt service ratio	24.9
Overall balance	-0.5	Aid given	3.6
		– as % of GDP	0.4

Health and education

Health spending, % of GDP	5.4	Education spending, % of GDP	...
Doctors per 1,000 pop.	1.7	Enrolment, %: primary	107
Hospital beds per 1,000 pop.	2.5	secondary	115
Improved-water source access,		tertiary	79
% of pop.	100		

Society

No. of households, m	20.8	Cost of living, Dec. 2015	
Av. no. per household	3.7	New York = 100	67
Marriages per 1,000 pop.	7.9	Cars per 1,000 pop.	130
Divorces per 1,000 pop.	1.6	Colour TV households, % with:	
Religion, % of pop.		cable	7.0
Muslim	98.0	satellite	51.0
Non-religious	1.2	Telephone lines per 100 pop.	16.5
Christian	0.4	Mobile telephone subscribers	
Other	0.3	per 100 pop.	94.8
Hindu	<0.1	Broadband subs per 100 pop.	11.7
Jewish	<0.1	Internet users, % of pop.	51.0

UKRAINE

Area	603,500 sq km	Capital	Kiev
Arable as % of total land	56.1	Currency	Hryvnya (UAH)

People

Population, m	44.9	Life expectancy: men	66.2 yrs
Pop. per sq km	74.4	women	76.1 yrs
Average annual growth		Adult literacy	99.7
in pop. 2015–20, %	-0.5	Fertility rate (per woman)	1.6
Pop. aged 0–19, %	19.7	Urban population, %	69.7
Pop. aged 65 and over, %	15.3		per 1,000 pop.
No. of men per 100 women	86.3	Crude birth rate	10.7
Human Development Index	74.7	Crude death rate	15.7

The economy

GDP	UAH1,587bn	GDP per head	$2,941
GDP	$132bn	GDP per head in purchasing	
Av. ann. growth in real		power parity (USA=100)	15.3
GDP 2009–14	-0.3%	Economic freedom index	46.8

Origins of GDP		**Components of GDP**	
	% of total		% of total
Agriculture	12	Private consumption	71
Industry, of which:	25	Public consumption	19
manufacturing	13	Investment	14
Services	63	Exports	49
		Imports	-53

Structure of employment

	% of total		% of labour force
Agriculture	14.8	Unemployed 2014	7.7
Industry	26.1	Av. ann. rate 2005–14	7.4
Services	59.1		

Energy

	m TOE		
Total output	85.9	Net energy imports as %	
Total consumption	116.1	of energy use	26
Consumption per head			
kg oil equivalent	2,553		

Inflation and finance

			av. ann. increase 2010–15
Consumer price			
inflation 2015	48.7%	Narrow money (M1)	10.3%
Av. ann. inflation 2010–15	12.5%	Broad money	10.7%
Money market rate, Dec. 2015	19.32%		

Exchange rates

	end 2015		December 2015
UAH per $	24.00	Effective rates	2010 = 100
UAH per SDR	33.26	– nominal	49.40
UAH per €	26.24	– real	76.60

Trade

Principal exports		Principal imports	
	$bn fob		$bn cif
Food & beverages	16.7	Fuels	16.1
Non-precious metals	15.2	Machinery & equipment	11.4
Machinery & equipment	7.1	Chemicals	6.8
Fuels	6.1	Food & beverages	6.1
Total incl. others	**54.2**	Total incl. others	**54.3**

Main export destinations		Main origins of imports	
	% of total		% of total
Russia	18.1	Russia	21.8
Turkey	6.6	China	9.3
Egypt	5.3	Germany	9.2
China	4.9	Belarus	6.8
EU28	31.6	EU28	38.7

Balance of payments, reserves and debt, $bn

Visible exports fob	50.6	Change in reserves	-13.0
Visible imports fob	-57.7	Level of reserves	
Trade balance	-7.1	end Dec.	7.4
Invisibles inflows	20.4	No. months of import cover	1.2
Invisibles outflows	-19.4	Official gold holdings, m oz	0.8
Net transfers	1.5	Foreign debt	130.7
Current account balance	-4.6	– as % of GDP	99.2
– as % of GDP	-3.5	– as % of total exports	166.1
Capital balance	-9.2	Debt service ratio	32.4
Overall balance	-13.3		

Health and education

Health spending, % of GDP	7.1	Education spending, % of GDP	6.7
Doctors per 1,000 pop.	3.5	Enrolment, %: primary	104
Hospital beds per 1,000 pop.	9.0	secondary	99
Improved-water source access,		tertiary	82
% of pop.	96.2		

Society

No. of households, m	17.7	Cost of living, Dec. 2015	
Av. no. per household	2.6	New York = 100	48
Marriages per 1,000 pop.	6.7	Cars per 1,000 pop.	163
Divorces per 1,000 pop.	3.6	Colour TV households, % with:	
Religion, % of pop.		cable	23.2
Christian	83.8	satellite	15.5
Non-religious	14.7	Telephone lines per 100 pop.	24.6
Muslim	1.2	Mobile telephone subscribers	
Jewish	0.1	per 100 pop.	144.1
Other	0.1	Broadband subs per 100 pop.	9.3
Hindu	<0.1	Internet users, % of pop.	43.4

UNITED ARAB EMIRATES

Area	83,600 sq km	Capital	Abu Dhabi
Arable as % of total land	0.4	Currency	Dirham (AED)

People

Population, m	9.4	Life expectancy: men	76.9 yrs
Pop. per sq km	112.4	women	79.1 yrs
Average annual growth		Adult literacy	...
in pop. 2015–20, %	1.4	Fertility rate (per woman)	1.7
Pop. aged 0–19, %	18.6	Urban population, %	85.5
Pop. aged 65 and over, %	1.1		per 1,000 pop.
No. of men per 100 women	274.0	Crude birth rate	10.0
Human Development Index	83.5	Crude death rate	1.8

The economy

GDP	AED1,467bn	GDP per head	$43,963
GDP	$399bn	GDP per head in purchasing	
Av. ann. growth in real		power parity (USA=100)	125.1
GDP 2009–14	4.5%	Economic freedom index	72.6

Origins of GDP		Components of GDP	
	% of total		% of total
Agriculture	1	Private consumption	48
Industry, of which:	55	Public consumption	8
manufacturing	...	Investment	24
Services	44	Exports	98
		Imports	-78

Structure of employment

	% of total		% of labour force
Agriculture	...	Unemployed 2014	3.6
Industry	...	Av. ann. rate 2005–14	3.8
Services	...		

Energy

	m TOE		
Total output	201.7	Net energy imports as %	
Total consumption	69.5	of energy use	-190
Consumption per head			
kg oil equivalent	7,691		

Inflation and finance

		av. ann. increase 2010–15	
Consumer price inflation 2015	4.1%	Narrow money (M1)	14.4%
Av. ann. inflation 2010–15	1.8%	Broad money	8.9%
Treasury bill rate, Dec. 2015	...		

Exchange rates

	end 2015		December 2015
			2010 = 100
AED per $	3.67	Effective rates	
AED per SDR	5.09	– nominal	125.42
AED per €	4.02	– real	...

Trade

Principal exports	$bn fob	Principal imports	$bn cif
Re-exports	143.6	Precious stones & metals	49.5
Crude oil	90.1	Machinery & electrical equip.	37.6
Gas	12.7	Vehicles & other transport equipment	28.3
		Base metals & related products	14.7
Total incl. others	**367.5**	**Total incl. others**	**282.1**

Main export destinations	% of total	Main origins of imports	% of total
Japan	14.7	China	15.7
Iran	11.3	India	13.3
India	9.6	United States	8.9
China	5.5	Germany	6.0

Balance of payments, reserves and debt, $bn

Visible exports fob	367.5	Change in reserves	10.2
Visible imports fob	-239.8	Level of reserves	
Trade balance	127.7	end Dec.	78.4
Invisibles inflows	45.4	No. months of import cover	2.9
Invisibles outflows	-85.7	Official gold holdings, m oz	0.0
Net transfers	-28.6	Foreign debt	192.5
Current account balance	58.7	– as % of GDP	48.2
– as % of GDP	14.7	– as % of total exports	46.7
Capital balance	-11.3	Debt service ratio	4.4
Overall balance	-0.4	Aid given	5.1
		– as % of GDP	1.3

Health and education

Health spending, % of GDP	3.6	Education spending, % of GDP	...
Doctors per 1,000 pop.	2.5	Enrolment, %: primary	107
Hospital beds per 1,000 pop.	1.1	secondary	...
Improved-water source access, % of pop.	99.6	tertiary	22

Society

No. of households, m	1.7	Cost of living, Dec. 2015	
Av. no. per household	5.0	New York = 100	74
Marriages per 1,000 pop.	...	Cars per 1,000 pop.	195
Divorces per 1,000 pop.	...	Colour TV households, % with:	
Religion, % of pop.		cable	1.0
Muslim	76.9	satellite	98.4
Christian	12.6	Telephone lines per 100 pop.	22.3
Hindu	6.6	Mobile telephone subscribers	
Other	2.8	per 100 pop.	178.1
Non-religious	1.1	Broadband subs per 100 pop.	11.6
Jewish	<0.1	Internet users, % of pop.	90.4

UNITED KINGDOM

Area	242,495 sq km	Capital	London
Arable as % of total land	25.9	Currency	Pound (£)

People

Population, m	63.5	Life expectancy: men	79.4 yrs
Pop. per sq km	261.9	women	83.1 yrs
Average annual growth		Adult literacy	...
in pop. 2015–20, %	0.6	Fertility rate (per woman)	1.9
Pop. aged 0–19, %	23.6	Urban population, %	82.6
Pop. aged 65 and over, %	17.8		per 1,000 pop.
No. of men per 100 women	97.2	Crude birth rate	12.4
Human Development Index	90.7	Crude death rate	9.1

The economy

GDP	£1,817bn	GDP per head	$46,504
GDP	$2,992bn	GDP per head in purchasing	
Av. ann. growth in real		power parity (USA=100)	74.3
GDP 2009–14	1.8%	Economic freedom index	76.4

Origins of GDP		**Components of GDP**	
	% of total		% of total
Agriculture	1	Private consumption	65
Industry, of which:	21	Public consumption	20
manufacturing	11	Investment	17
Services	78	Exports	28
		Imports	-30

Structure of employment

	% of total		% of labour force
Agriculture	1.1	Unemployed 2014	6.3
Industry	18.9	Av. ann. rate 2005–14	6.6
Services	79.1		

Energy

	m TOE		
Total output	110.1	Net energy imports as %	
Total consumption	191.0	of energy use	42
Consumption per head			
kg oil equivalent	2,978		

Inflation and finance

Consumer price			av. ann. increase 2010–15
inflation 2015	0.1%	Narrow money (M1)	...
Av. ann. inflation 2010–15	2.3%	Broad money	...
Money market rate, Dec. 2015	0.46%		

Exchange rates

	end 2015		December 2015
£ per $	0.67	Effective rates	2010 = 100
£ per SDR	0.94	– nominal	114.43
£ per €	0.74	– real	122.28

Trade

Principal exports		Principal imports	
	$bn fob		*$bn cif*
Machinery & transport equip.	176.1	Machinery & transport equip.	244.4
Chemicals & related products	79.7	Chemicals & related products	83.4
Mineral fuels & lubricants	55.6	Mineral fuels & lubricants	80.5
Food, drink & tobacco	31.2	Food, drink & tobacco	63.9
Total incl. others	**483.3**	Total incl. others	**686.0**

Main export destinations		Main origins of imports	
	% of total		*% of total*
United States	12.5	Germany	14.3
Germany	10.3	China	8.8
Netherlands	7.6	United States	7.8
Switzerland	6.9	Netherlands	7.7
EU28	47.9	EU28	53.0

Balance of payments, reserves and aid, $bn

Visible exports fob	483.4	Overall balance	10.1
Visible imports fob	-685.9	Change in reserves	1.8
Trade balance	-202.5	Level of reserves	
Invisibles inflows	598.7	end Dec.	106.3
Invisibles outflows	-506.8	No. months of import cover	1.1
Net transfers	-41.3	Official gold holdings, m oz	10.0
Current account balance	-151.9	Aid given	19.3
– as % of GDP	-5.1	– as % of GDP	0.7
Capital balance	175.5		

Health and education

Health spending, % of GDP	9.1	Education spending, % of GDP	5.7
Doctors per 1,000 pop.	2.8	Enrolment, %: primary	...
Hospital beds per 1,000 pop.	2.9	secondary	...
Improved-water source access,		tertiary	...
% of pop.	100		

Society

No. of households, m	27.0	Cost of living, Dec. 2015	
Av. no. per household	2.4	New York = 100	101
Marriages per 1,000 pop.	4.5	Cars per 1,000 pop.	514
Divorces per 1,000 pop.	2.0	Colour TV households, % with:	
Religion, % of pop.		cable	14.4
Christian	71.1	satellite	41.7
Non-religious	21.3	Telephone lines per 100 pop.	52.4
Muslim	4.4	Mobile telephone subscribers	
Other	1.4	per 100 pop.	123.6
Hindu	1.3	Broadband subs per 100 pop.	37.4
Jewish	0.5	Internet users, % of pop.	91.6

UNITED STATES

Area	9,833,517 sq km	Capital	Washington DC
Arable as % of total land	16.6	Currency	US dollar ($)

People

Population, m	322.6	Life expectancy: men	77.3 yrs
Pop. per sq km	32.8	women	81.9 yrs
Average annual growth		Adult literacy	...
in pop. 2015–20, %	0.7	Fertility rate (per woman)	1.9
Pop. aged 0–19, %	25.4	Urban population, %	81.6
Pop. aged 65 and over, %	14.8		per 1,000 pop.
No. of men per 100 women	98.3	Crude birth rate	12.6
Human Development Index	91.5	Crude death rate	8.4

The economy

GDP	$17,348bn	GDP per head	$54,306
Av. ann. growth in real		GDP per head in purchasing	
GDP 2009–14	2.1%	power parity (USA=100)	100.0
		Economic freedom index	75.4

Origins of GDP		Components of GDP	
	% of total		% of total
Agriculture	1	Private consumption	69
Industry, of which:	21	Public consumption	15
manufacturing	12	Investment	20
Services	78	Exports	13
		Imports	-16

Structure of employment

	% of total		% of labour force
Agriculture	1.6	Unemployed 2014	6.2
Industry	17.2	Av. ann. rate 2005–14	7.0
Services	81.2		

Energy

	m TOE		
Total output	1,881.0	Net energy imports as %	
Total consumption	2,188.4	of energy use	14
Consumption per head			
kg oil equivalent	6,914		

Inflation and finance

			av. ann. increase 2010–15
Consumer price			
inflation 2015	0.1%	Narrow money (M1)	11.4%
Av. ann. inflation 2010–15	1.7%	Broad money	4.6%
Treasury bill rate, Dec. 2015	0.26%		

Exchange rates

	end 2015		December 2015
$ per SDR	1.39	Effective rates	2010 = 100
$ per €	1.09	– nominal	121.16
		– real	118.49

Trade

Principal exports		Principal imports	
	$bn fob		$bn fob
Capital goods, excl. vehicles	551.1	Industrial supplies	666.8
Industrial supplies	505.1	Capital goods, excl. vehicles	591.1
Consumer goods, excl. vehicles	198.9	Consumer goods, excl. vehicles	557.8
Vehicles & products	159.7	Vehicles & products	327.7
Total incl. others	**1,620.5**	Total incl. others	**2,347.7**

Main export destinations		Main origins of imports	
	% of total		% of total
Canada	19.3	China	19.9
Mexico	14.8	Canada	14.8
China	7.6	Mexico	12.5
Japan	4.1	Japan	5.7
EU28	17.0	EU28	17.8

Balance of payments, reserves and aid, $bn

Visible exports fob	1,632.6	Overall balance	-3.6
Visible imports fob	-2,374.1	Change in reserves	-52.7
Trade balance	-741.5	Level of reserves	
Invisibles inflows	1,533.9	end Dec.	396.2
Invisibles outflows	-1,062.8	No. months of import cover	1.4
Net transfers	-119.2	Official gold holdings, m oz	261.5
Current account balance	-389.5	Aid given	33.1
– as % of GDP	-2.2	– as % of GDP	0.2
Capital balance	236.0		

Health and education

Health spending, % of GDP	17.1	Education spending, % of GDP	5.2
Doctors per 1,000 pop.	2.5	Enrolment, %: primary	99
Hospital beds per 1,000 pop.	2.9	secondary	96
Improved-water source access,		tertiary	89
% of pop.	99.2		

Society

No. of households, m	123.0	Cost of living, Dec. 2015	
Av. no. per household	2.6	New York = 100	100
Marriages per 1,000 pop.	6.8	Cars per 1,000 pop.	375
Divorces per 1,000 pop.	2.8	Colour TV households, % with:	
Religion, % of pop.		cable	56.6
Christian	78.3	satellite	29.5
Non-religious	16.4	Telephone lines per 100 pop.	39.8
Other	2.0	Mobile telephone subscribers	
Jewish	1.8	per 100 pop.	110.2
Muslim	0.9	Broadband subs per 100 pop.	31.1
Hindu	0.6	Internet users, % of pop.[a]	87.4

a Includes all hosts ending ".com", ".net" and ".org" which exaggerates the numbers.

VENEZUELA

Area	912,050 sq km	Capital	Caracas
Arable as % of total land	3.1	Currency	Bolivar (Bs)

People

Population, m	30.9	Life expectancy: men	70.9 yrs
Pop. per sq km	33.9	women	79.0 yrs
Average annual growth		Adult literacy	94.8
in pop. 2015–20, %	1.3	Fertility rate (per woman)	2.3
Pop. aged 0–19, %	37.0	Urban population, %	89.0
Pop. aged 65 and over, %	6.3		per 1,000 pop.
No. of men per 100 women	99.1	Crude birth rate	18.5
Human Development Index	76.2	Crude death rate	5.7

The economy

GDP	Bs3,521bn	GDP per head	$8,154
GDP	$250bn	GDP per head in purchasing	
Av. ann. growth in real		power parity (USA=100)	32.5
GDP 2009–14	1.1%	Economic freedom index	33.7

Origins of GDP		Components of GDP	
	% of total		% of total
Agriculture	5	Private consumption	65
Industry, of which:	49	Public consumption	12
manufacturing	14	Investment	27
Services	66	Exports	25
		Imports	-30

Structure of employment

	% of total		% of labour force
Agriculture	7.4	Unemployed 2014	8.6
Industry	21.3	Av. ann. rate 2005–14	8.4
Services	71.1		

Energy

	m TOE		
Total output	129.1	Net energy imports as %	
Total consumption	68.8	of energy use	-179
Consumption per head			
kg oil equivalent	2,271		

Inflation and finance

Consumer price		av. ann. increase 2010–15	
inflation 2015	121.7%	Narrow money (M1)	70.6%
Av. ann. inflation 2010–15	50.5%	Broad money	68.4%
Money market rate, Dec. 2015	6.00%		

Exchange rates

	end 2015		December 2015
Bs per $	6.28	Effective rates	2010 = 100
Bs per SDR	8.71	– nominal	50.91
Bs per €	6.87	– real	481.54

Trade

Principal exports[a]		Principal imports[a]	
	$bn fob		*$bn cif*
Oil	85.6	Intermediate goods	25.9
non-oil	3.2	Capital goods	11.1
		Consumer goods	8.7
Total	**88.8**	**Total incl. others**	**49.4**

Main export destinations		Main origins of imports	
	% of total		*% of total*
United States	35.3	United States	22.4
India	16.8	Colombia	16.8
China	13.1	Brazil	12.9
Singapore	7.0	Argentina	6.2

Balance of payments, reserves and debt, $bn

Visible exports fob	74.7	Change in reserves	-0.5
Visible imports fob	-47.5	Level of reserves	
Trade balance	27.2	end Dec.	19.8
Invisibles inflows	3.7	No. months of import cover	3.2
Invisibles outflows	-27.1	Official gold holdings, m oz	11.6
Net transfers	-0.2	Foreign debt	107.3
Current account balance	3.6	– as % of GDP	24.0
– as % of GDP	1.4	– as % of total exports	136.2
Capital balance	-0.6	Debt service ratio	19.1
Overall balance	-0.6		

Health and education

Health spending, % of GDP	5.3	Education spending, % of GDP	...
Doctors per 1,000 pop.	...	Enrolment, %: primary	101
Hospital beds per 1,000 pop.	0.9	secondary	92
Improved-water source access,		tertiary	...
% of pop.	93.1		

Society

No. of households, m	7.7	Cost of living, Dec. 2015	
Av. no. per household	4.0	New York = 100	46
Marriages per 1,000 pop.	3.3	Cars per 1,000 pop.	114
Divorces per 1,000 pop.	...	Colour TV households, % with:	
Religion, % of pop.		cable	29.3
Christian	89.3	satellite	5.7
Non-religious	10.0	Telephone lines per 100 pop.	25.3
Muslim	0.3	Mobile telephone subscribers	
Other	0.3	per 100 pop.	99.0
Hindu	<0.1	Broadband subs per 100 pop.	7.8
Jewish	<0.1	Internet users, % of pop.	57.0

a 2013

VIETNAM

Area	330,967 sq km	Capital	Hanoi
Arable as % of total land	20.7	Currency	Dong (D)

People

Population, m	92.5	Life expectancy: men	71.7 yrs
Pop. per sq km	279.5	women	80.8 yrs
Average annual growth		Adult literacy	...
in pop. 2015–20, %	1.0	Fertility rate (per woman)	2.0
Pop. aged 0–19, %	30.6	Urban population, %	33.6
Pop. aged 65 and over, %	6.7		per 1,000 pop.
No. of men per 100 women	97.9	Crude birth rate	16.2
Human Development Index	66.6	Crude death rate	5.9

The economy

GDP	D3,937bn	GDP per head	$2,011
GDP	$186bn	GDP per head in purchasing	
Av. ann. growth in real		power parity (USA=100)	10.2
GDP 2009–14	5.9%	Economic freedom index	54.0

Origins of GDP		**Components of GDP**	
	% of total		% of total
Agriculture	18	Private consumption	64
Industry, of which:	39	Public consumption	6
manufacturing	17	Investment	27
Services	43	Exports	86
		Imports	-83

Structure of employment

	% of total		% of labour force
Agriculture	46.8	Unemployed 2014	2.3
Industry	21.2	Av. ann. rate 2005–14	2.3
Services	32.0		

Energy

	m TOE		
Total output	69.3	Net energy imports as %	
Total consumption	59.9	of energy use	-16
Consumption per head			
kg oil equivalent	668		

Inflation and finance

		av. ann. increase 2010–15	
Consumer price			
inflation 2015	0.6%	Narrow money (M1)	15.8%
Av. ann. inflation 2010–15	7.6%	Broad money	17.6%
Treasury bill rate, Jul. 2015	4.00%		

Exchange rates

	end 2015		December 2015
D per $	21,890.00	Effective rates	2010 = 100
D per SDR	30,334.00	– nominal	...
D per €	23,935.00	– real	...

Trade

Principal exports		Principal imports	
	$bn fob		$bn cif
Telephones & mobile phones	23.6	Machinery & equipment	22.4
Textiles & garments	20.9	Electronics, computers & parts	18.7
Computers & electronic products	11.4	Telephones & mobile phones	9.4
Footwear	10.3	Textiles	8.5
Total incl. others	**150.1**	Total incl. others	**149.3**

Main export destinations		Main origins of imports	
	% of total		% of total
United States	20.0	China	30.3
China	10.4	South Korea	15.0
Japan	10.3	Japan	8.9
South Korea	5.0	Thailand	4.9

Balance of payments, reserves and debt, $bn

Visible exports fob	150.2	Change in reserves	8.3
Visible imports fob	-138.1	Level of reserves	
Trade balance	12.1	end Dec.	34.2
Invisibles inflows	11.3	No. months of import cover	2.5
Invisibles outflows	-23.7	Official gold holdings, m oz	0.0
Net transfers	9.6	Foreign debt	71.9
Current account balance	9.4	– as % of GDP	38.7
– as % of GDP	5.0	– as % of total exports	41.4
Capital balance	5.6	Debt service ratio	3.9
Overall balance	8.4		

Health and education

Health spending, % of GDP	7.1	Education spending, % of GDP	6.3
Doctors per 1,000 pop.	1.2	Enrolment, %: primary	109
Hospital beds per 1,000 pop.	2.0	secondary	...
Improved-water source access,		tertiary	30
% of pop.	97.6		

Society

No. of households, m	26.4	Cost of living, Dec. 2015	
Av. no. per household	3.5	New York = 100	73
Marriages per 1,000 pop.	...	Cars per 1,000 pop.	21
Divorces per 1,000 pop.	...	Colour TV households, % with:	
Religion, % of pop.		cable	17.8
Other	45.6	satellite	19.5
Non-religious	29.6	Telephone lines per 100 pop.	6.0
Buddhist	16.4	Mobile telephone subscribers	
Christian	8.2	per 100 pop.	147.1
Muslim	0.2	Broadband subs per 100 pop.	6.5
Jewish	<0.1	Internet users, % of pop.	48.3

ZIMBABWE

Area	390,757 sq km	Capital	Harare
Arable as % of total land	10.3	Currency	Zimbabwe dollar (Z$)[a]

People

Population, m	14.6	Life expectancy: men	60.8 yrs
Pop. per sq km	37.4	women	64.0 yrs
Average annual growth		Adult literacy	83.6
in pop. 2015–20, %	2.3	Fertility rate (per woman)	3.7
Pop. aged 0–19, %	52.3	Urban population, %	32.4
Pop. aged 65 and over, %	3.0		per 1,000 pop.
No. of men per 100 women	97.1	Crude birth rate	32.4
Human Development Index	50.9	Crude death rate	7.8

The economy

GDP	$14bn	GDP per head	$931
Av. ann. growth in real		GDP per head in purchasing	
GDP 2009–14	8.3%	power parity (USA=100)	3.3
		Economic freedom index	38.2

Origins of GDP		**Components of GDP**	
	% of total		% of total
Agriculture	14	Private consumption	88
Industry, of which:	29	Public consumption	24
manufacturing	12	Investment	13
Services	57	Exports	27
		Imports	-52

Structure of employment

	% of total		% of labour force
Agriculture	65.8	Unemployed 2014	5.4
Industry	9.1	Av. ann. rate 2005–14	5.4
Services	25.0		

Energy

	m TOE		
Total output	9.9	Net energy imports as %	
Total consumption	11.3	of energy use	12
Consumption per head			
kg oil equivalent	758		

Inflation and finance

Consumer price			av. ann. increase 2010–15
inflation 2015	-2.4%	Narrow money (M1)	...
Av. ann. inflation 2010–15	1.2%	Broad money	...
Treasury bill rate, Dec. 2015	...		

Exchange rates

	end 2015		December 2015
Z$ per $	...	Effective rates	2010 = 100
Z$ per SDR	...	– nominal	...
Z$ per €	...	– real	...

Trade

Principal exports		Principal imports	
	$bn fob		$bn cif
Gold	0.8	Machinery & transport equip.	0.5
Platinum	0.8	Fuels & lubricants	0.4
Tobacco	0.5	Manufactured goods	0.3
Ferro-alloys	0.4	Chemicals	0.2
Total incl. others	**3.5**	Total incl. others	**4.5**

Main export destinations		Main origins of imports	
	% of total		% of total
China	22.1	South Africa	56.3
Congo-Kinshasa	9.8	China	10.0
Botswana	8.7	India	4.9
South Africa	5.4	Zambia	4.8

Balance of payments, reserves and debt, $bn

Visible exports fob	3.5	Change in reserves	-0.1
Visible imports fob	-6.3	Level of reserves	
Trade balance	-2.8	end Dec.	0.4
Invisibles inflows	0.2	No. months of import cover	0.6
Invisibles outflows	-1.3	Official gold holdings, m oz	0.0
Net transfers	2.0	Foreign debt	10.6
Current account balance	-2.3	– as % of GDP	74.5
– as % of GDP	-15.9	– as % of total exports	232.4
Capital balance	0.0	Debt service ratio	72.7
Overall balance	-2.3		

Health and education

Health spending, % of GDP	6.4	Education spending, % of GDP	2.0
Doctors per 1,000 pop.	0.1	Enrolment, %: primary	102
Hospital beds per 1,000 pop.	1.7	secondary	47
Improved-water source access,		tertiary	6
% of pop.	76.9		

Society

No. of households, m	3.1	Cost of living, Dec. 2015	
Av. no. per household	4.5	New York = 100	...
Marriages per 1,000 pop.	...	Cars per 1,000 pop.	54
Divorces per 1,000 pop.	...	Colour TV households, % with:	
Religion, % of pop.		cable	...
Christian	87.0	satellite	...
Non-religious	7.9	Telephone lines per 100 pop.	2.3
Other	4.2	Mobile telephone subscribers	
Muslim	0.9	per 100 pop.	80.8
Hindu	<0.1	Broadband subs per 100 pop.	1.0
Jewish	<0.1	Internet users, % of pop.	19.9

a Zimbabwe adopted a multi-currency system in 2009. Its dollar was decommissioned in mid-2015.

EURO AREA[a]

Area	2,578,704 sq km	Capital	–
Arable as % of total land	24.5	Currency	Euro (€)

People

Population, m	336.7	Life expectancy: men	79.8 yrs
Pop. per sq km	130.6	women	84.8 yrs
Average annual growth		Adult literacy	98.9
in pop. 2015–20, %	0.1	Fertility rate (per woman)	1.6
Pop. aged 0–19, %	20.2	Urban population, %	75.9
Pop. aged 65 and over, %	20.0		per 1,000 pop.
No. of men per 100 women	95.6	Crude birth rate	9.5
Human Development Index	88.8	Crude death rate	10.0

The economy

GDP	€10,070bn	GDP per head	$39,732
GDP	$13,374bn	GDP per head in purchasing	
Av. ann. growth in real		power parity (USA=100)	71.9
GDP 2009–14	0.7%	Economic freedom index	67.4

Origins of GDP		**Components of GDP**	
	% of total		% of total
Agriculture	2	Private consumption	56
Industry, of which:	25	Public consumption	21
manufacturing	16	Investment	20
Services	74	Exports	45
		Imports	-41

Structure of employment

	% of total		% of labour force
Agriculture	3.1	Unemployed 2014	11.5
Industry	23.9	Av. ann. rate 2005–14	9.7
Services	72.4		

Energy

	m TOE		
Total output	478.3	Net energy imports as %	
Total consumption	1,077.4	of energy use	58
Consumption per person			
kg oil equivalent	3,276		

Inflation and finance

Consumer price		*av. ann. increase 2010–15*	
inflation 2015	0.3%	Narrow money (M1)	6.7%
Av. ann. inflation 2010–15	1.4%	Broad money	3.1%
Interbank rate, Dec. 2015	-0.20%		

Exchange rates

	end 2015		December 2015
€ per $	0.92	Effective rates	2010 = 100
€ per SDR	1.27	– nominal	96.07
		– real	90.36

Trade[b]

Principal exports		Principal imports	
	$bn fob		$bn cif
Machinery & transport equip.	942.5	Machinery & transport equip.	610.4
Other manufactured goods	513.6	Mineral fuels & lubricants	590.3
Chemicals & related products	370.3	Other manufactured goods	542.4
Mineral fuels & lubricants	145.5	Chemicals & related products	219.7
Food, drink & tobacco	142.9	Food, drink & tobacco	130.7
Total incl. others	**2,262.5**	Total incl. others	**2,247.7**

Main export destinations		Main origins of imports	
	% of total		% of total
United States	18.3	China	17.9
China	9.7	United States	12.4
Switzerland	8.2	Russia	10.8
Russia	6.1	Switzerland	5.7

Balance of payments, reserves and aid, $bn

Visible exports fob	2,611.7	Overall balance	19.2
Visible imports fob	-2,281.2	Change in reserves	-53.8
Trade balance	330.5	Level of reserves	
Invisibles inflows	1,779.4	end Dec.	695.1
Invisibles outflows	-1,607.8	No. months of import cover	2.1
Net transfers	-187.1	Official gold holdings, m oz	346.7
Current account balance	315.0	Aid given	46.0
– as % of GDP	2.3	– as % of GDP	0.4
Capital balance	-358.1		

Health and education

Health spending, % of GDP	10.4	Education spending, % of GDP	...
Doctors per 1,000 pop.	3.9	Enrolment, %: primary	103
Hospital beds per 1,000 pop.	5.6	secondary	110
Improved-water source access,		tertiary	68
% of pop.	99.9		

Society

No. of households, m, m	149.7	Colour TV households, % with:	
Av. no. per household	2.2	cable	41.0
Marriages per 1,000 pop.	3.8	satellite	25.4
Divorces per 1,000 pop.	1.8	Telephone lines per 100 pop.	46.1
Cost of living, Dec. 2014		Mobile telephone subscribers	
New York = 100	...	per 100 pop.	122.3
Cars per 1,000 pop.	516	Broadband subs per 100 pop.	...
		Internet users, % of pop.	78.3

a Data generally refer to the 18 EU members that had adopted the euro as at December 31 2014: Austria, Belgium, Cyprus, Estonia, Finland, France, Germany, Greece, Ireland, Italy, Latvia, Luxembourg, Malta, Netherlands, Portugal, Slovakia, Slovenia and Spain.
b EU28, excluding intra-trade.

WORLD

Area	148,698,382 sq km	Capital	...
Arable as % of total land	10.8	Currency	...

People

Population, m	7,244.0	Life expectancy: men	69.5 yrs
Pop. per sq km	48.7	women	73.9 yrs
Average annual growth		Adult literacy	84.3
in pop. 2015–20	1.1	Fertility rate (per woman)	2.5
Pop. aged 0–19, %	34.1	Urban population, %	54.0
Pop. aged 65 and over, %	8.3		per 1,000 pop.
No. of men per 100 women	101.8	Crude birth rate	18.6
Human Development Index	71.1	Crude death rate	7.8

The economy

GDP	$77.8trn	GDP per head	$10,100
Av. ann. growth in real		GDP per head in purchasing	
GDP 2009–14	4.0%	power parity (USA=100)	29.3
		Economic freedom index	57.8

Origins of GDP		**Components of GDP**	
	% of total		% of total
Agriculture	3	Private consumption	60
Industry, of which:	26	Public consumption	17
manufacturing	16	Investment	22
Services	71	Exports	30
		Imports	-29

Structure of employment

	% of total		% of labour force
Agriculture	19.8	Unemployed 2014	5.9
Industry	28.8	Av. ann. rate 2005–14	5.9
Services	51.4		

Energy

	m TOE		
Total output	13,604.8	Net energy imports as %	
Total consumption	13,166.7	of energy use	-3
Consumption per person			
kg oil equivalent	1,894		

Inflation and finance

		av. ann. increase 2010–15	
Consumer price			
inflation 2015	2.8%	Narrow money (M1)[a]	9.1%
Av. ann. inflation 2010–15	3.8%	Broad money[a]	5.5%
LIBOR $ rate, 3-month, Nov. 2015	0.37%		

Trade

World exports

	$bn fob		$bn fob
Manufactured goods	13,200	Ores & minerals	765
Fuels	2,487	Agricultural raw materials	306
Food	1,722		
		Total incl. others	**19,131**

Main export destinations		**Main origins of imports**	
	% of total		% of total
United States	12.6	China	12.8
China	10.5	United States	8.8
Germany	6.5	Germany	8.1
Japan	4.3	Japan	3.8
United Kingdom	3.7	Netherlands	3.7

Balance of payments, reserves and aid, $bn

Visible exports fob	18,433	Overall balance	...
Visible imports fob	-17,820	Change in reserves	-288
Trade balance	613	Level of reserves	
Invisibles inflows	8,900	end Dec.	13,074
Invisibles outflows	-8,859	No. months of import cover	5.9
Net transfers	-258	Official gold holdings, m oz	1,030
Current account balance	397	Aid given	...
– as % of GDP	0.5	– as % of GDP	...
Capital balance	...		

Health and education

Health spending, % of GDP	10	Education spending, % of GDP	4.8
Doctors per 1,000 pop.	1.5	Enrolment, %: primary	108
Hospital beds per 1,000 pop.	...	secondary	73
Improved-water source access,		tertiary	32
% of pop.	89.3		

Society

No. of households, m, m	2,012.2	Cost of living, Dec. 2014	
Av. no. per household	3.6	New York = 100	...
Marriages per 1,000 pop.	...	Cars per 1,000 pop.	132
Divorces per 1,000 pop.	...	Colour TV households, % with:	
Religion, % of pop.		cable	...
Christian	31.5	satellite	...
Muslim	23.2	Telephone lines per 100 pop.	20
Non-religious	16.3	Mobile telephone subscribers	
Hindu	15.0	per 100 pop.	101
Other	13.8	Broadband subs per 100 pop.	19.8
Jewish	0.2	Internet users, % of pop.	132.9

a OECD countries.

WORLD RANKINGS QUIZ

Test your knowledge with our new world rankings quiz.
Answers can be found on the pages indicated.

Geography and demographics

1 Which country is largest (in terms of sq km)?
a United States b China c Canada d India   *page 12*

2 Which desert is largest (in terms of sq km)?
a Gobi b Great Victoria c Arabian d Sahara   *page 13*

3 The Caspian Sea is the world's largest lake.
a True b False   *page 13*

4 Japan has more people than Russia.
a True b False   *page 14*

5 Which country has the fastest-growing population?
a India b Niger c Nigeria d Afghanistan   *page 15*

6 More teenage women give birth in Ethiopia than in
the United States.
a True b False   *page 16*

7 In which of these countries are there more men
than women?
a Portugal b Latvia c Bulgaria d Saudi Arabia   *page 17*

8 Which country has the highest share of its population
aged 65 or over?
a France b Italy c Germany d Greece   *page 18*

9 What is the most populous city in the world?
a Tokyo b Shanghai c Delhi d New York   *page 19*

10 Iran has a bigger urban population than the United Kingdom.
a True b False   *page 20*

11 The tallest building in the world is in New York.
a True b False   *page 21*

12 Which of these countries has the biggest migrant
population?
a Italy b Thailand c France d Australia   *page 22*

13 Which country has the biggest refugee population?
a Jordan b Iran c Lebanon d Turkey   *page 23*

Economics

1 Which country has the biggest economy?
   a Mexico b Indonesia c Nigeria d Turkey   *page 24*

2 On average, countries of which region have grown
   fastest in the past ten years?
   a Africa b Asia c Europe d The Americas   *page 30*

3 Which country has a larger current-account surplus?
   a Saudi Arabia b United Arab Emirates
   c Kuwait d Iran   *page 34*

4 Which country has the highest consumer
   price inflation?
   a Ukraine b Australia c Venezuela d Canada   *page 38*

5 Brazil has more foreign debt than Russia.
   a True b False   *page 40*

6 Which country in Europe donates the most foreign aid?
   a France b Germany c United Kingdom
   d Switzerland   *page 43*

7 India's fisheries and aquaculture production is
   bigger than Vietnam's.
   a True b False   *page 47*

8 China is the world's biggest producer and
   consumer of rice.
   a True b False   *page 48*

9 Which country produces the most silver?
   a Chile b Mexico c Peru d Bolivia   *page 51*

10 Russia produces more energy than the United States.
   a True b False   *page 54*

11 Which country relies most on coal for its electricity?
   a United Kingdom b China c Kosovo
   d South Africa   *page 55*

12 Which country has the most male-dominated workforce?
   a Oman b Syria c Qatar d Saudi Arabia   *page 56*

13 Which country has the highest youth unemployment rate?
   a Greece b South Africa c Macedonia d Spain   *page 57*

Business

1 London has the world's most expensive office rents.
   a True b False   *page 59*

2 The United States has the biggest inflows and
   outflows of foreign-direct investment.
   a True b False   *page 59*

3 Which country attracts the most foreign-direct
   investment?
   a Singapore b Malaysia c Hong Kong
   d Indonesia   *page 59*

4 Which country has the largest share of entrepreneurs?
   a Malawi b Uganda c Angola d Zambia   *page 60*

5 Switzerland has the world's lowest brain drain.
   a True b False   *page 60*

6 Germany spends more on R&D than France.
   a True b False   *page 61*

7 Which company is largest in terms of market
   capitalisation?
   a Facebook b Amazon c Exxon Mobil
   d Microsoft   *page 62*

8 Which company had the largest net profit in 2015?
   a Novartis b Samsung Electronics c Exxon Mobil
   d Toyota Motor   *page 62*

9 Industrial & Commercial Bank of China has a bigger
   market capitalisation than JPMorgan Chase.
   a True b False   *page 63*

10 The four biggest banks in the world by assets are all
   Chinese.
   a True b False   *page 63*

11 Which country's stockmarket performed worst in 2015?
   a Canada b France c Japan d Egypt   *page 64*

12 Which stock exchange has the most listed companies?
   a NYSE b Nasdaq c London Stock Exchange
   d Euronext   *page 65*

Politics and society

1 Japanese government debt to GDP is over 200%.
   a True b False   *page 66*

2 Rwanda has the highest proportion of women in
   parliament.
   a True b False   *page 67*

3 Haiti has the highest primary enrolment rate.
   a True b False   *page 68*

4 Which country's secondary enrolment rate is lowest?
   a Belgium b Canada c Turkey d Estonia   *page 68*

5 Which country has the highest tertiary enrolment rate?
   a United States b Greece c Canada d India   *page 68*

6 Afghanistan has the lowest adult literacy rate.
   a True b False   *page 69*

7 Which country spends the least on education as
   % of national GDP?
   a Congo-Kinshasa b Bangladesh c Sri Lanka
   d South Sudan   *page 69*

8 Which country has the highest marriage rate?
   a Bulgaria b China c Egypt d Tajikistan   *page 70*

9 In Bangladesh, the average age of brides at
   first marriage is 16.
   a True b False   *page 71*

10 The first non-American and non-Soviet astronaut
   was from which country?
   a United Kingdom b Afghanistan
   c Czechoslovakia d Canada   *page 84*

11 The United States emits more carbon per person than
   Luxembourg.
   a True b False   *page 85*

12 Which is the world's most polluted capital city?
   a Beijing b Delhi c Mexico City d Warsaw   *page 86*

13 Which country has the largest forested area?
   a Brazil b Canada c Russia d United States   *page 87*

Health and welfare

1 Which country has the highest life expectancy in Asia?
a Hong Kong b Japan c Singapore
d South Korea   *page 90*

2 What is the average life expectancy in Monaco (in years)?
a 79 b 85 c 89 d 95   *page 90*

3 Which country has the lowest life expectancy?
a Afghanistan b Chad c Sierra Leone
d Swaziland   *page 91*

4 Lesotho is the only country where men have a
longer life expectancy than women.
a True b False   *page 91*

5 The countries with the five lowest death rates
are all in the Middle East.
a True b False   *page 93*

6 Which country has the world's highest infant
mortality rate?
a Angola b Benin c Chad d Guinea-Bissau   *page 93*

7 Which country has the highest prevalence of
adult diabetes?
a Fiji b Mauritius c Mexico d Saudi Arabia   *page 94*

8 Where is tuberculosis most prevalent?
a Cambodia b Gabon c North Korea
d Timor-Leste   *page 94*

9 Which country has the lowest share of one-year-olds
immunised against measles?
a Afghanistan b Haiti c South Sudan
d South Africa   *page 95*

10 Which country spends most on health as a share of its GDP?
a Sweden b Switzerland c France d Austria   *page 96*

11 Which country has the highest obesity rate?
a Kuwait b Saudi Arabia c United Arab Emirates
d Qatar   *page 97*

12 A third of Americans are obese.
a True b False   *page 97*

Culture and entertainment

1 Which country has most mobile phone subscriptions
   per population?
   a Singapore b Macau c Hong Kong
   d Cambodia   *page 98*

2 Which country has most internet users?
   a Iceland b Sweden c Finland d Norway   *page 99*

3 Japan has more broadband users per population
   than South Korea.
   a True b False   *page 99*

4 Which Latin American country has most cinema visits?
   a Colombia b Brazil c Argentina d Mexico   *page 101*

5 *Slumdog Millionaire* won more Oscars than
   West Side Story.
   a True b False   *page 101*

6 Which of these countries scores worst on press freedom?
   a Libya b Russia c Turkey d Saudi Arabia   *page 102*

7 In what year was the first Nobel prize in economics
   awarded?
   a 1956 b 1969 c 1976 d 1979   *page 103*

8 Which country has won the men's football
   world cup most times?
   a Germany b Italy c Argentina d Brazil   *page 104*

9 Norway has more Winter Olympic games medals
   than any other country.
   a True b False   *page 105*

10 Belgium consumes more beer per person than Australia.
    a True b False   *page 106*

11 Ukrainians smoke more cigarettes per person than Greeks.
    a True b False   *page 106*

12 Which country is the most popular tourist destination?
    a Spain b China c France d Mexico   *page 107*

13 Which country earns most from tourism?
    a Australia b Thailand c Italy d Macau   *page 107*

Glossary

Balance of payments The record of a country's transactions with the rest of the world. The **current account** of the balance of payments consists of: visible trade (goods); "invisible" trade (services and income); private transfer payments (eg, remittances from those working abroad); official transfers (eg, payments to international organisations, famine relief). Visible imports and exports are normally compiled on rather different definitions to those used in the trade statistics (shown in principal imports and exports) and therefore the statistics do not match. The **capital account** consists of long- and short-term transactions relating to a country's assets and liabilities (eg, loans and borrowings). The **current and capital accounts**, plus an errors and omissions item, make up the **overall balance. Changes in reserves** include gold at market prices and are shown without the practice often followed in balance of payments presentations of reversing the sign.

Big Mac index A light-hearted way of looking at exchange rates. If the dollar price of a burger at McDonald's in any country is higher than the price in the United States, converting at market exchange rates, then that country's currency could be thought to be over-valued against the dollar and vice versa.

Body-mass index A measure for assessing obesity – weight in kilograms divided by height in metres squared. An index of 30 or more is regarded as an indicator of obesity; 25 to 29.9 as over-weight. Guidelines vary for men and for women and may be adjusted for age.

CFA Communauté Financière Africaine. Its members, most of the francophone African nations, share a common currency, the CFA franc, pegged to the euro.

Cif/fob Measures of the value of merchandise trade. Imports include the cost of "carriage, insurance and freight" (cif) from the exporting country to the importing country. The value of exports does not include these elements and is recorded "free on board" (fob). Balance of payments statistics are generally adjusted so that both exports and imports are shown fob; the cif elements are included in invisibles.

CIS is the Commonwealth of Independent States, including Georgia, Turkmenistan and Ukraine.

Crude birth rate The number of live births in a year per 1,000 population. The crude rate will automatically be relatively high if a large proportion of the population is of childbearing age.

Crude death rate The number of deaths in a year per 1,000 population. Also affected by the population's age structure.

Debt, foreign Financial obligations owed by a country to the rest of the world and repayable in foreign currency. The **debt service ratio** is debt service (principal repayments plus interest payments) expressed as a percentage of the country's earnings from exports of goods and services.

Debt, household All liabilities that require payment of interest or principal in the future.

Economic Freedom Index The ranking includes data on labour and business freedom as well as trade policy, taxation, monetary policy, the banking system, foreign-investment rules, property rights, government spending, regulation policy, the level of corruption and the extent of wage and price controls.

Effective exchange rate The nominal index measures a currency's depreciation (figures below 100) or appreciation (figures over 100) from a base date against a trade-weighted basket of the currencies of the country's main trading partners. The real effective exchange rate reflects adjustments for relative movements in prices or costs.

EU European Union. Members are: Austria, Belgium, Bulgaria, Croatia, Cyprus, Czech Republic, Denmark, Estonia, Finland, France, Germany, Greece, Hungary, Ireland, Italy, Latvia,

Lithuania, Luxembourg, Malta, Netherlands, Poland, Portugal, Romania, Slovakia, Slovenia, Spain, Sweden and the United Kingdom.

Euro area The 19 euro area members of the EU are Austria, Belgium, Cyprus, Estonia, Finland, France, Germany, Greece, Ireland, Italy, Latvia, Lithuania, Luxembourg, Malta, Netherlands, Portugal, Slovakia, Slovenia and Spain. Their common currency is the euro.

Fertility rate The average number of children born to a woman who completes her childbearing years.

G7 Group of seven countries: United States, Japan, Germany, United Kingdom, France, Italy and Canada.

GDP Gross domestic product. The sum of all output produced by economic activity within a country. GNP (gross national product) and GNI (gross national income) include net income from abroad, eg, rent, profits.

Import cover The number of months of imports covered by reserves, ie, reserves ÷ $\frac{1}{12}$ annual imports (visibles and invisibles).

Inflation The annual rate at which prices are increasing. The most common measure and the one shown here is the increase in the consumer price index.

Life expectancy The average length of time a baby born today can expect to live.

Literacy is defined by UNESCO as the ability to read and write a simple sentence, but definitions can vary from country to country.

Median age Divides the age distribution into two halves. Half of the population is above and half below the median age.

Money supply A measure of the "money" available to buy goods and services. Various definitions exist. The measures shown here are based on definitions used by the IMF and may differ from measures used nationally. Narrow money (M1) consists of cash in circulation and demand deposits (bank deposits that can be withdrawn on demand). "Quasi-money" (time, savings and foreign currency deposits) is added to this to create broad money.

OECD Organisation for Economic Co-operation and Development. The "rich countries" club was established in 1961 to promote economic growth and the expansion of world trade. It is based in Paris and now has 34 members.

Official reserves The stock of gold and foreign currency held by a country to finance any calls that may be made for the settlement of foreign debt.

Opec Organisation of Petroleum Exporting Countries. Set up in 1960 and based in Vienna, Opec is mainly concerned with oil pricing and production issues. Members are: Algeria, Angola, Ecuador, Iran, Iraq, Kuwait, Libya, Nigeria, Qatar, Saudi Arabia, United Arab Emirates and Venezuela. Indonesia rejoined on January 1 2016.

PPP Purchasing power parity. PPP statistics adjust for cost of living differences by replacing normal exchange rates with rates designed to equalise the prices of a standard "basket"of goods and services. These are used to obtain PPP estimates of GDP per head. PPP estimates are shown on an index, taking the United States as 100.

Real terms Figures adjusted to exclude the effect of inflation.

SDR Special drawing right. The reserve currency, introduced by the IMF in 1970, was intended to replace gold and national currencies in settling international transactions. The IMF uses SDRs for book-keeping purposes and issues them to member countries. Their value is based on a basket of the US dollar (with a weight of 41.9%), the euro (37.4%), the Japanese yen (9.4%) and the pound sterling (11.3%).

List of countries

	Population	GDP	GDP per head	Area '000 sq	Median age
	m, 2014	$bn, 2014	$PPP, 2014	km	yrs, 2015
Afghanistan	31.3	20.4	1,943	653	17.5
Albania	3.2	13.3	10,873	29	34.3
Algeria	39.9	213.5	13,841	2,382	27.6
Andorra	0.1	3.3ª	44,882	1	41.6
Angola	22.1	126.8	8,022	1,247	16.1
Argentina	41.8	544.7	22,749	2,780	30.8
Armenia	3.0	11.6	8,066	30	34.6
Australia	23.6	1,442.0	46,591	7,692	37.5
Austria	8.5	437.6	46,439	84	43.2
Azerbaijan	9.5	75.3	17,012	87	30.9
Bahamas	0.4	8.5	23,275	14	32.4
Bahrain	1.3	33.8	45,159	1	30.3
Bangladesh	158.5	183.8	3,385	148	25.6
Barbados	0.3	4.4ª	16,076	0	38.5
Belarus	9.3	76.1	18,193	208	39.6
Belgium	11.1	532.4	43,478	31	41.5
Benin	10.6	9.6	1,985	115	18.6
Bermuda	0.1	5.6	54,878	0.1	39.0
Bolivia	10.8	33.2	6,553	1,099	24.1
Bosnia & Herz.	3.8	18.5	10,245	51	41.5
Botswana	2.0	15.9	15,300	582	24.2
Brazil	202.0	2,417.2	16,273	8,516	31.3
Brunei	0.4	17.1	77,880	6	30.6
Bulgaria	7.2	56.7	18,405	111	43.5
Burkina Faso	17.4	12.5	1,689	274	17.0
Burundi	10.5	2.9	712	28	17.6
Cambodia	15.4	16.8	3,259	181	23.9
Cameroon	22.8	31.6	2,980	475	18.5
Canada	35.5	1,783.8	44,986	9,985	40.6
Central African Rep.	4.7	1.7	585	623	20.0
Chad	13.2	13.9	2,246	1,284	16.0
Channel Islands	0.2	9.2	56,610	0	42.6
Chile	17.8	258.7	23,020	756	34.4
China	1,393.8	10,430.7	12,886	9,597	37.0
Colombia	48.9	377.9	13,110	1,142	30.0
Congo-Brazzaville	4.6	13.6	6,138	342	18.7
Congo-Kinshasa	69.4	35.9	832	2,345	16.9
Costa Rica	4.9	49.6	14,875	51	31.4
Croatia	4.3	57.2	20,926	57	42.8
Cuba	11.3	82.8	20,725	110	41.2
Cyprus	1.2	23.1	23,466	9	35.9
Czech Republic	10.7	205.3	29,959	79	41.5
Denmark	5.6	346.1	44,663	43	41.6
Dominican Rep.	10.5	64.1	12,190	49	26.1
Ecuador	16.0	100.9	11,344	257	26.6
Egypt	83.4	301.4	11,939	1,002	24.7
El Salvador	6.4	25.2	8,356	21	26.7

	Population	GDP	GDP per head	Area '000 sq	Median age
	m, 2014	$bn, 2014	$PPP, 2014	km	yrs, 2015
Equatorial Guinea	0.8	15.5	33,873	28	20.5
Eritrea	6.5	4.1	1,575	118	18.6
Estonia	1.3	26.5	28,025	45	41.7
Ethiopia	96.5	55.5	1,505	1,104	18.6
Fiji	0.9	4.5	8,564	18	27.6
Finland	5.4	272.8	40,304	337	42.5
France	64.6	2833.6c	40,111	552	41.2
French Guiana	0.3	5.0	18,390	549	24.5
French Polynesia	0.3	5.6	25,286	4	31.5
Gabon	1.7	18.2	19,076	268	21.4
Gambia, The	1.9	0.8	1,554	11	16.8
Georgia	4.3	16.5	8,577	70	37.5
Germany	82.7	3,874.4	45,322	357	46.2
Ghana	26.4	38.6	4,157	239	20.6
Greece	11.1	235.9	25,567	132	43.6
Guadeloupe	0.5	12.0ab	26,750	2	39.4
Guam	0.2	4.6ab	28,737	1	30.1
Guatemala	15.9	58.8	7,536	109	21.2
Guinea	12.0	6.7	1,234	246	18.5
Guinea-Bissau	1.7	1.1	1,373	36	19.4
Guyana	0.8	3.1	7,216	215	24.7
Haiti	10.5	8.7	1,716	28	23.0
Honduras	8.3	19.5	4,857	112	23.4
Hong Kong	7.3	291.2	55,020	1	43.2
Hungary	9.9	138.3	25,223	93	41.3
Iceland	0.3	17.2	43,813	103	36.0
India	1,267.4	2,042.6	5,797	3,287	26.6
Indonesia	252.8	890.6	10,622	1,911	28.4
Iran	78.5	416.5	17,287	1,629	29.5
Iraq	34.8	223.5	15,118	435	19.3
Ireland	4.7	250.8	50,421	70	36.9
Israel	7.8	305.7	33,744	22	30.3
Italy	61.1	2,141.9	34,913	302	45.9
Ivory Coast	20.8	33.7	3,446	322	18.4
Jamaica	2.8	13.9	8,641	11	29.1
Japan	127.0	4,596.2	37,477	378	46.5
Jordan	7.5	35.9	10,522	89	22.5
Kazakhstan	16.6	217.9	25,302	2,725	29.3
Kenya	45.5	60.9	2,923	592	18.9
Kosovo	1.9	7.4	8,880	11	24.0
Kuwait	3.5	172.0	72,704	18	31.0
Kyrgyzstan	5.6	7.5	3,237	200	25.1
Laos	6.9	11.7	4,820	237	21.9
Latvia	2.0	31.3	24,004	64	42.9
Lebanon	5.0	49.9	13,916	10	28.5
Lesotho	2.1	2.2	2,611	30	21.0
Liberia	4.4	2.0	824	111	18.6

	Population	GDP	GDP per head	Area '000 sq	Median age
	m, 2014	$bn, 2014	$PPP, 2014	km	yrs, 2015
Libya	6.3	44.4	15,599	1,760	27.5
Liechtenstein	0.0	5.9	85,263	0.2	42.0
Lithuania	3.0	48.5	27,883	65	43.1
Luxembourg	0.5	65.0	93,086	3	39.2
Macau	0.6	55.5	138,310	0	37.9
Macedonia	2.1	11.3	13,343	26	37.5
Madagascar	23.6	10.7	1,443	587	18.7
Malawi	16.8	6.1	1,165	118	17.2
Malaysia	30.2	338.1	25,478	331	28.5
Mali	15.8	14.4	2,116	1,240	16.2
Malta	0.4	10.8	34,516	0	41.5
Martinique	0.4	12.0[ab]	26,750	1	46.1
Mauritania	4.0	5.3	3,891	1,031	19.8
Mauritius	1.2	12.6	18,479	2	35.2
Mexico	123.8	1,297.9	17,369	1,964	27.4
Moldova	3.5	8.0	4,378	34	35.6
Monaco	5.4	7.1	179,958	0	56.0
Mongolia	2.9	12.2	11,797	1,564	27.3
Montenegro	0.6	4.6	15,256	14	37.6
Morocco	33.5	110.0	7,739	447	28.0
Mozambique	26.5	16.9	1,166	799	17.1
Myanmar	53.7	65.8	4,884	677	27.9
Namibia	2.3	13.2	9,764	824	21.2
Nepal	28.1	19.8	2,389	147	23.1
Netherlands	16.8	880.7	48,143	37	42.7
New Caledonia	0.3	10.2	42,186	19	33.1
New Zealand	4.6	197.9	35,563	268	38.0
Nicaragua	6.2	11.8	4,881	130	25.2
Niger	18.5	8.3	980	1,267	14.8
Nigeria	178.5	574.0	5,899	924	17.9
North Korea	25.0	17.4	1,600	121	33.9
Norway	5.1	500.5	66,636	324	39.1
Oman	3.9	77.8	36,291	310	29.0
Pakistan	185.1	243.4	4,777	796	22.5
Panama	3.9	49.2	20,772	75	28.7
Papua New Guinea	7.5	16.7	2,441	463	21.2
Paraguay	6.9	30.9	8,827	407	24.9
Peru	30.8	202.9	12,115	1,285	27.5
Philippines	100.1	284.8	6,927	300	24.2
Poland	38.2	544.9	25,145	312	39.6
Portugal	10.6	230.5	27,320	92	44.0
Puerto Rico	3.7	103.7	35,906	9	36.3
Qatar	2.3	210.1	137,167	12	30.7
Réunion	0.9	22.0[ab]	23,960	3	34.3
Romania	21.6	199.4	18,286	238	42.1
Russia	142.5	2,029.6	26,835	17,098	38.7
Rwanda	12.1	7.9	1,562	26	19.2

	Population	GDP	GDP per head	Area '000 sq	Median age
	m, 2014	$bn, 2014	$PPP, 2014	km	yrs, 2015
Saudi Arabia	29.4	753.8	54,840	2,150	28.3
Senegal	14.5	15.4	2,352	197	18.0
Serbia	9.5	44.2	10,826	88	40.6
Sierra Leone	6.2	4.7	1,947	72	18.5
Singapore	5.5	306.4	81,731	1	40.0
Slovakia	5.5	100.3	28,356	49	39.1
Slovenia	2.1	49.6	29,773	20	43.1
Somalia	10.8	5.7	411	638	16.5
South Africa	53.1	350.1	13,319	1,221	25.7
South Korea	49.5	1,410.4	36,039	100	40.6
South Sudan	11.7	13.9	2,008	659	18.6
Spain	47.1	1,383.5	32,893	506	43.2
Sri Lanka	21.4	75.0	9,810	66	32.3
Sudan	38.8	74.4	4,116	1,879	19.4
Suriname	0.5	5.2	16,551	164	29.0
Swaziland	1.3	4.4	8,207	17	20.5
Sweden	9.6	571.1	46,044	447	41.0
Switzerland	8.2	701.2	57,059	41	42.3
Syria	22.0	34.0	2,536	185	20.8
Taiwan	23.4	530.0	46,157	36	37.5
Tajikistan	8.4	9.2	2,641	143	22.5
Tanzania	50.8	48.1	2,523	947	17.3
Thailand	67.2	404.3	15,878	513	38.0
Timor-Leste	1.2	4.4[a]	5,521	15	18.5
Togo	7.0	4.6	1,397	57	18.7
Trinidad & Tobago	1.3	27.3	32,830	5	33.8
Tunisia	11.1	47.6	11,235	164	31.2
Turkey	75.8	798.3	19,985	784	29.8
Turkmenistan	5.3	46.2	15,328	488	26.4
Uganda	38.8	27.5	1,941	242	15.9
Ukraine	44.9	132.3	8,306	604	40.3
United Arab Emirates	9.4	399.5	67,395	84	33.3
United Kingdom	63.5	2,991.7	40,857	242	40.0
United States	322.6	17,348.1	53,776	9,834	38.0
Uruguay	3.4	57.5	20,887	174	34.9
Uzbekistan	29.3	63.1	5,880	447	26.3
Venezuela	30.9	250.3	17,524	912	27.4
Vietnam	92.5	185.9	5,541	331	30.4
Virgin Islands (US)	0.1	5.1[ab]	14,500	0.4	41.0
West Bank & Gaza	4.7	11.3[a]	4,920	6	19.3
Yemen	25.0	43.2	4,160	528	19.3
Zambia	15.0	27.1	3,994	753	16.9
Zimbabwe	14.6	14.2	1,878	391	18.9
Euro area (18)	336.7	13,374.4	38,992	2,694	43.8
World	7,244.0	77,825.3	15,730	134,323	29.6

a Latest available year. b Estimate.
c Including French Guiana, Guadeloupe, Martinique and Réunion.

Sources

Academy of Motion Pictures
AFM Research
Airports Council International,
    Worldwide Airport Traffic Report

Bloomberg
BP, *Statistical Review of World
    Energy*

CAF, *The World Giving Index*
Canadean
CBRE, *Global Prime Office
    Occupancy Costs*
Central banks
Central Intelligence Agency, *The
    World Factbook*
Centres for Disease Control and
    Prevention
Clarkson Research, *World Fleet
    Register*
Company reports
The Conference Board
Cornell University
Council of Tall Buildings and
    Urban Habitat

The Economist,
    www.economist.com
Economist Intelligence Unit, *Cost
    of Living Survey; Country
    Forecasts; Country Reports*
Encyclopaedia Britannica
Euromonitor International
Eurostat, *Statistics in Focus*

FIFA
Finance ministries
Food and Agriculture
    Organisation

Global Democracy Ranking
Global Entrepreneurship Monitor
Government statistics

H2 Gambling Capital
The Heritage Foundation, *Index
    of Economic Freedom*
Holman Fenwick Willan

IFPI
IMD, *World Competitiveness
    Yearbook*
IMF, *International Financial
    Statistics; World Economic
    Outlook*
INSEAD
Institute for Criminal Policy
    Research
International Agency for
    Research on Cancer
International Civil Aviation
    Organisation
International Cocoa
    Organisation, *Quarterly
    Bulletin of Cocoa Statistics*
International Coffee
    Organisation
International Cotton Advisory
    Committee, *March Bulletin*
International Cricket Council
International Diabetes
    Federation, *Diabetes Atlas*
International Grains Council
International Institute for
    Strategic Studies, *Military
    Balance*
International Labour
    Organisation
International Olympic Committee
International Organisation of
    Motor Vehicle Manufacturers
International Publishers
    Association
International Rubber Study
    Group, *Rubber Statistical
    Bulletin*
International Sugar
    Organisation, *Statistical
    Bulletin*
International
    Telecommunication Union,
    ITU Indicators
International Union of Railways
Inter-Parliamentary Union

Johnson Matthey